Canadian-American Economic Relations

CANADIAN-AMERICAN ECONOMIC RELATIONS

Conflict and Cooperation on a Continental Scale

EDITED BY David L. McKee

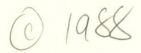

© 1988

PRAEGER

New York
Westport, Connecticut
London

Library of Congress Cataloging-in-Publication Data

Canadian-American economic relations : conflict and cooperation on a
    continental scale / edited by David L. McKee.
        p.   cm.
    Papers based on a conference "Canada-USA: the Economic
Relationship" sponsored by the Graduate School of Management and the
Dept. of Economics of Kent State University on Oct, 5, 1987.
    Bibliography: p.
    Includes index.
    ISBN 0–275–92836–5 (alk. paper)
        1. United States—Foreign economic relations—Canada—Congresses.
2. Canada—Foreign economic relations—United States—Congresses.
I. McKee, David L.   II. Kent State University. Graduate School of
Management.   III. Kent State Unviersity. Dept. of Economics.
HF1456.5.C2C36   1988
337.73071—dc19

Library of Congress Catalog Card Number: 88–6610

ISBN: 0–275–92836–5

First published in 1988

Praeger Publishers, One Madison Avenue, New York, NY   10010
A division of Greenwood Press, Inc.

Printed in the United States of America

The paper used in this book complies with the
Permanent Paper Standard issued by the National
Information Standards Organization (Z39.48–1984).

10   9   8   7   6   5   4   3   2   1

Contents

Tables and Figures

TABLES

FIGURES

Preface

The articles contained in this volume are the result of a conference, "Canada-USA: The Economic Relationship," that was sponsored by the Graduate School of Management and the Department of Economics of Kent State University on October 5, 1987. Although the conference was the catalyst that generated the research for the present volume, every effort has been made to make the volume more than just a report of conference proceedings.

The timing of the conference, following as it did by less than one day the successful conclusion of negotiations aimed at a comprehensive trade agreement between Canada and the United States, necessitated the re-working of many of the conference papers. Thus, the present volume reflects perceptions concerning relationships between the two nations in the time frame immediately following the conclusion of the trade negotiations.

The conference received generous financial assistance from the Canadian Department of External Affairs through its Canadian Studies Conference Grant Program. Lawrence D. Lederman, head of the Consular Post and Canadian Consul in Cleveland, Ohio, has been especially supportive of the project as has Dorothy Peters, Public Affairs Officer of the Canadian Consulate.

The project could not have been successfully concluded without the strong support of Dean Robert Trumble and Associate Dean Michael Sesnowitz of the Graduate School of Management at Kent State University. The same level of support was provided by Richard E. Bennett, Chairman of the Department of Economics at Kent State. Special thanks are also extended to Carol Sesnowitz of the College of Continuing Studies.

Various colleagues were helpful in special ways in the successful completion of the project. Prominent among those were Edward R. Bruning, Lorraine Eden, Richard J. Kent, Frank Millerd, R. D. Norton, John K. Ryans, Jr., Max D. Stewart, and John A. Weir. The preparation of the manuscript was simplified substantially through the able editorial assistance of Linda Poje and Diane Williams here at Kent State.

PART I
INTRODUCTION

1
A Preliminary Overview
David L. McKee

When Canada gained practical control of its affairs in 1867 the United States was enmeshed in post–Civil War adjustments. Given the history of the relationship between the United States and Great Britain prior to that time, it is hardly surprising that some in Canada cast uneasy eyes upon their more powerful neighbor to the south. Those fears notwithstanding, the two North American nations went on to forge a relationship that has been unparalleled in international affairs.

The fact that there have never been hostilities between the two countries (the War of 1812 predates the emergence of Canada as a nation) and that the border between them is undefended is not to suggest that the relationship between them has always been problem-free. What has made the relationship unique is that the parties to it have generally been able to talk out their difficulties.

In recent years however the discussions have become more strident, particularly where economic considerations have been concerned. From an economic climate where agreements relating to the automobile industry seemed to be pushing the two nations toward a more open trading agenda, the two neighbors have slipped into a behavioral mode that may well lead them to protectionist tactics that will undoubtedly harm the economies of both nations.

Whether or not the negotiations that were concluded on October 4, 1987 will produce lasting accommodations in the area of bilateral trade remains to be seen. The agreement was concluded at a time of strong protectionist sentiment in the United States Congress. Many of the factors which generated that sentiment had little to do with Canada. Nonetheless, the failure of a declining dollar to turn around unfavorable trade balances external to North America, coupled with the loss of traditional markets for certain agricultural commodities and continuing fears about energy, has contributed to the emergence of a negative taxonomy vis-à-vis external economic relations. Adding to that taxonomy have been the very visible difficulties with Japan and other major trading partners. When the considerations cited above are added to the ever present concerns of special interest groups, the result is a climate that may be less than optimal for implementing an agreement that is both lasting and comprehensive.

Canada has its special interest groups as well, many of which must be described as wary of their larger neighbor to the south. Adjustments in traditional trading patterns made necessary by Britain's entry into the European Common Market resulted in the nation's becoming more closely aligned with the United States. Uneasiness regarding what seem to have been perceived as encroachments upon economic, if not political, sovereignty surfaced during the Trudeau Administration in the form of legislation to protect cultural industries and various other sectors of the Canadian economy. That the electorate may have been less concerned than the government, appears to be evidenced to some degree by a Progressive Conservative landslide in the most recent Canadian federal election.

It is ironic that the economic climate has deteriorated once again during the watch of a prime minister whose sympathies may be more pro-American than those of any of his post World War II predecessors and a president who has always been a vocal exponent of free trade. That such a deterioration is a reality has been highlighted by increasing media attention on both sides of the border. Recent discussions between the two nations have been carried out parallel to a series of increasingly public thrusts and parries, which may have been orchestrated to strengthen the bargaining positions of the protagonists but which in fact may produce a hardening of public attitudes, thereby diminishing the chances that the agreement that has been negotiated will be ratified by both countries and ultimately implemented.

Of course the issues relating directly to free trade are by no means coextensive with the entire menu of economic considerations facing the two nations. Prominent among those not included in the October accord are those relating to the environment. Nature is no respecter of national boundaries. That being so, it is almost inevitable that disputes should arise on environmental and resource-related issues. During the 1980s air pollution has become a contentious issue as forest and water resources have been damaged in New England and Eastern Canada by pollutants that are presumed to have come from the industrial heartland of the continent. In recent years Canada has been moving to control industrial emissions, but the Reagan administration has been somewhat reluctant to label the polluters involved in the problem cited above.

Under the best of circumstances, it would appear that two industrialized nations sharing a continent will face pollution-related issues from time to time. Issues with less general visibility may be those relating to natural resources. Prominent among those have been disputes relating to fisheries. As was the case with the winds aloft, fish are no respecters of national boundaries and/or territorial waters. Other resource and environmental issues relate to the Far North. Some of the latter are oil-related. Without attempting to enumerate all of the real or potential environmental and resource issues, suffice it to say that it seems inevitable that such considerations will impact relationships between the two countries from time to time.

The present volume makes no pretence of enumerating, let alone explaining, all of the economic issues that may face Canada and the United States. Instead, it is hoped that it will generate a better understanding of the strengths and weaknesses of the economic relationships between the two countries. First an overview of the economic structure of the two nations will be provided, with an emphasis on geography and economic positioning. Following that, a selection of environmental and national resource issues will be explored. The intent here is to give a well-considered, up-to-date view of energy and environmental issues, as they face the two countries, with an eye to generating an understanding of policy needs without getting immersed in the minutia of specific problem areas. However some shared problems with respect to continued competitiveness in agriculture will be discussed. The issues relating to trade will be explored in some depth, taking into account the October accord. An attempt will also be made to provide information concerning taxation and investment. The volume concludes with a brief overview of the trade issues and some final policy reflections.

2
Continental Restructuring:
U.S.–Canadian Comparisons
R. D. Norton

The talks on free trade between the U.S. and Canada have shown us how difficult it is even between two seemingly natural partners to open the door to economic change. It is difficult for the U.S., because its monumental trade deficit has bred a desire by politicians to seem to be "doing something" in defense of U.S. interests. And it is difficult for Canada because, despite projected national job gains in every region under free trade, genuine changes would have to occur. Moreover, the issue gives Canada's politicians and intellectuals an opportunity to affirm their nationalism by resisting the very real threat of U.S. cultural and financial domination.

A former Canadian diplomat observes, "Canada has never made economic sense, and Canadians have always had to pay an economic price for their political and cultural identity. The question now is whether Canadians are prepared to continue paying such a price." (John Halstead, quoted in Urquhart and Berkowitz, 1987.) Central to this formulation is the idea that economic inefficiency is the price of Canada's survival as a sovereign nation and distinct culture.

Clearly, Canada's need for cultural independence and for control of U.S. investment is compelling. Yet it may be that opposition to free trade, which tends to be loudest in Ontario, has additional wellsprings, sources relating to the maintenance of the region's industrial supremacy within Canada.

That is, there is more to the free-trade issue than economic rationality vs. cultural survival. If the autonomy question raises fears of domination from the south, it also spans an east-west axis—that is, among Canada's farflung regions, wary of domination by distant and more industrialized Ontario and Quebec.

Accordingly, this paper explores the free-trade issue from a regional angle. My conclusion will be that the U.S.' restructuring has entailed a regional revolution, while Canada's has turned back the clock, preserving a polarized regional structure.

SO CLOSE AND YET SO FAR: GEOGRAPHY AS DESTINY

Table 2.1 summarizes some of the main parallels and contrasts between the two countries. In addition to the common border, they share four other institutional traits. (1) English is the dominant language (rivaled by French in Canada and, increasingly, Spanish in the U.S.). (2) Each society has a large and well-defined ethnic minority, with historical grievances and separatist tendencies. (3) Each has a continental scale, of the kind sought after by Europe's economies in joining the European Community. (4) In contrast also to Europe, each uses federalism, a highly decentralized political structure, to deal with the administrative challenges of a vast geography. (5) And each enjoys one of the world's highest standards of living.

Canada and the U.S. also share certain recent political traits. (6) In both nations, massive study commissions (the Eighties Commission under President Carter, and the MacDonald Commission) explored strategic options for national development. (7) Both national governments have run unprecedentedly large federal budget deficits, with Canada's having loomed even larger proportionately than the U.S.' deficit. (8) At this writing, the two nations also share conservative, avowedly laissez-faire national administrations.

Now, given all these major institutional, demographic, and political traits in common, what is it that makes the U.S. and Canada so different from each other? Apart from the historical watershed of the American Revolution, one might suggest that much of the difference in national character and development reflects two key contrasts in demography:

1. The U.S. has 10 times the population (and market) of Canada. In its sheer population size, the U.S. is thus inevitably a Goliath to Canada's David.

2. The distribution of Canada's population is totally different from the U.S. pattern.

While most people focus on the first difference, size, the second—population distribution—is also a key to U.S.-Canadian trade arrangements.

Table 2.1
The U.S. and Canada: Institutional and Demographic Comparisons

A. STRUCTURAL PARALLELS

(1) English as the dominant but not sole language.

(2) Large and distinct ethnic minorities.

(3) Continental scale.

(4) Decentralized federalism.

(5) High living standards (but threatened).

B. POLITICAL TRENDS IN COMMON IN THE 1980S

(6) Strategic plans (the Eighties and Macdonald Commissions).

(7) Unprecedentedly large federal government deficits.

(8) Laissez-faire ideologies in command.

C. DEMOGRAPHIC CONTRASTS

(1) The U.S. has 10 times Canada's population.

(2) Canada's population is linear, America's is decentralizing.

The Importance of Being Linear

Some 90 percent of Canada's 25 million people live within less than 100 miles of the border. This ribbon of people is arrayed at "the common border . . . about 12 times as long as [Canada] is deep" in its settlement pattern. (*The Economist*, 1987, p. 16.). Hence the spatial orientation for much of the population is naturally south, to the U.S.

Historically, the ribbon pattern of development has posed a challenge to Canada's national identity matched only by the Quebec question:

Fears of U.S. domination are as old as Canada itself. In 1881, Canada, then a 14-year-old dominion, began building an east-west railroad. One big reason: to satisfy British Columbia and prevent its welcoming a threatened U.S. annexation. (John Urquhart and Peggy Berkowitz, 1987.)

To bolster the railroad link, Canada's National Policy of 1879 established tariff protection on infant-industries grounds and promoted trade along an east-west rather than a north-south axis.

As a consequence, there has been a form of regional specialization in Canada: the *Centre* (i.e., Ontario, and to a certain extent Quebec) has developed a fairly diversified manufacturing sector, while the West and the Maritimes have seen their development more concentrated in the agricultural and resource sectors. (Rodrique Tremblay, 1985, p. 85.)

As Tremblay observes, the resulting concentration of industry in the core, far from coastal markets, has meant higher prices for Canada's consumers. Transportation costs along the east-west corridor are one reason. The absence of economies of scale is another. The result is that Canada's consumers have historically subsidized the development of industry in the core.

As in the U.S. earlier in this century, the division of labor between the industrial central provinces and the resource-oriented periphery is not only economic but also political—not only a matter of efficiency but also a politically charged equity issue. In contrast to the U.S., however, Canada's regional division of labor remains intact and if anything is being reinforced by the present system of exchange rates and tariff arrangements.

The lesson? Canada's national identity depends intimately on its ability to maintain the east-west flow of products and ideas, in the face of enormous geographical pressure for a north-south reorientation. Putting it differently, the free-trade issue can only be understood in relation to Canada's regional structure, the key in turn to its cultural identity.

But in what sense has an opposite regional dynamic transformed the U.S. economy over the last generation?

REGIONS AND AMERICAN RENEWAL, 1965–1980

In the 1980s the U.S. has experienced an ever-deepening trade deficit. So it is easy to forget that during the 1970s, the U.S. had a regionally-driven restructuring of its manufacturing plant. (R. D. Norton, 1986.) The Frostbelt-Sunbelt shift was in this sense a decline of the older industrial heartland, and the emergence of a new and more regionally dispersed industrial system. A concomitant has been a Pacific tilt in the industrial system, away from Europe, and toward the Pacific Rim.

The industrial renewal was aided in the late 1970s by a depreciating dollar, a spur to rising U.S. exports of high-tech goods. And it was aided throughout by a more probusiness institutional setting in the South and interior West. Factor costs tended to range lower than in the North, notably for land, labor, and energy. Moreover, a city-building dynamic generated investment opportunities to spur the development of new industries and the filling in of the local industrial base in a pattern of import substitution that stripped the North of its former domestic export markets.

The upshot was an actual increase in U.S. manufacturing employment during the 1970s, despite the sharp job losses in the U.S. Manufacturing Belt—and in Europe's mature economies.

By the time the dollar began its long, steep rise against other currencies in the 1980s, the industrial system had thus been substantially modernized—recast into a new institutional structure and a new geographical array. Whatever the harshness this market-generated process of renewal brought with it, benefits can be discerned for the nation as a whole.

The national payoff from this regionally-driven restructuring shows up dramatically in Figure 2.1. It discloses that the South and West served not so much as a destination for the North's discards but as a spawning ground for growth industries. That is, all of the growth in the U.S. industries that expanded employment over the period took place within the South and West. In addition, virtually all of the growth in the younger regions stemmed from national growth industries, not declining ones.

To that extent, initially less-industrialized regions served as a matrix for restructuring the U.S. industrial base during the 1970s.

EXCHANGE RATES AND COMPETITIVENESS

But what about trade competitiveness, as measured by the balance of payments on goods and services? Here, too, the U.S. record was surprisingly successful until the Reagan Administration. The depreciation of the U.S. dollar in the late 1970s was accompanied by a move toward a surplus on the U.S. trade balance, a surplus that lasted until the dollar began its steep ascent in the early Reagan years. As the dollar climbed steadily through March of 1985, the positive trade balance of 1980 and 1981 turned into the huge deficit of the mid-1980s.

Despite the current widespread view that the U.S. is following Britain's path to industrial decline, some suggest an alternative view. That is, the U.S. trade deficit has macroeconomic, not long-term or structural sources. When the Reagan tax cuts were enacted, a gaping federal budget deficit opened, prompting continued higher real interest rates in the U.S. than abroad, which in turn triggered heavy demands for U.S. dollar-

Figure 2.1
Growth Industries by Region: 1969–85

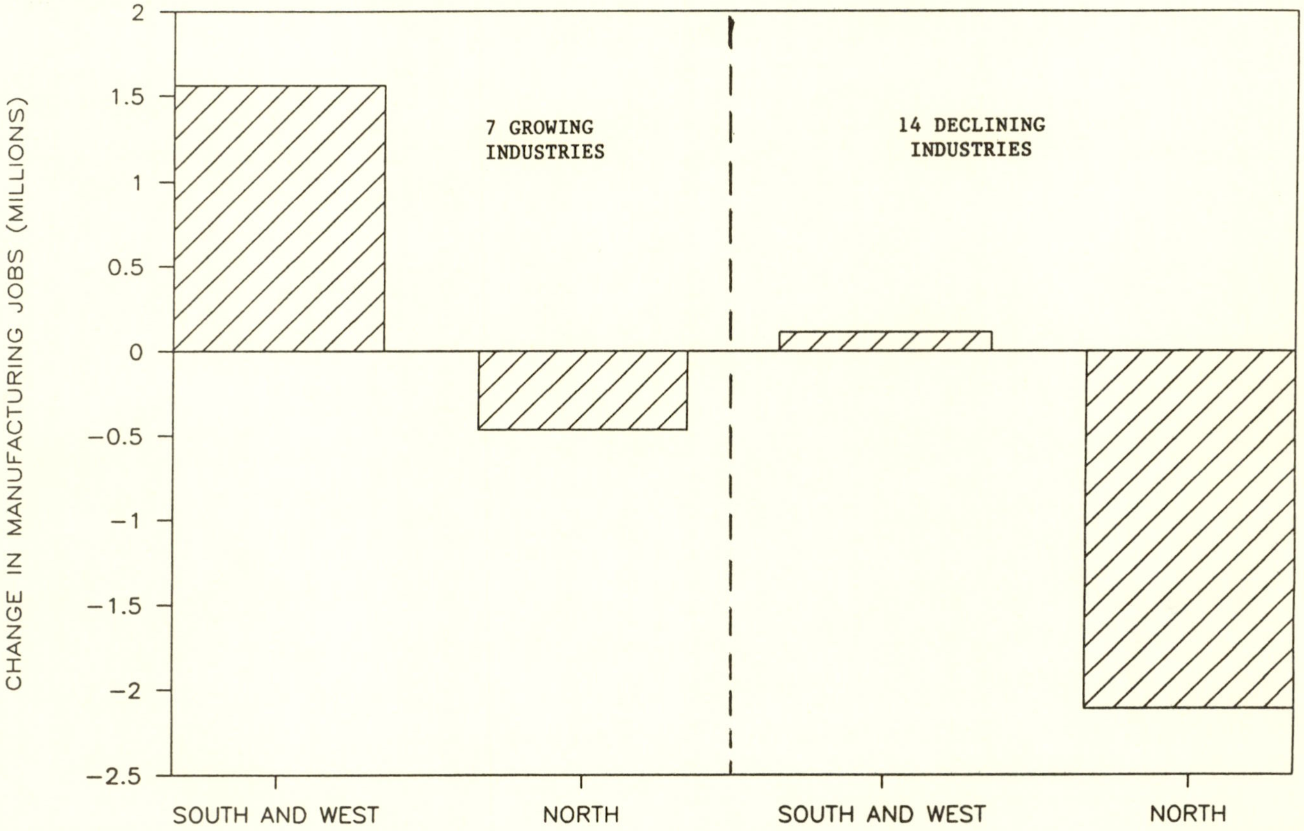

denominated securities and therefore for U.S. dollars. The result was to drive up the dollar, pricing U.S. exports out of markets.

By this macroeconomic interpretation, then, the U.S. trade deficit reflects less the long-term decline of the U.S. economy than a logical outcome of the Reagan administration's failed experiment in "supply-side" economics.

The Exchange Rate and Canada's Industrial Rebound

Why hasn't the fall in the U.S. dollar exchange rate reduced the trade deficit? One reason is that the U.S. dollar's decline has been highly selective: steep against the German mark, the yen, and the pound, but gentle against the East Asian Newly Industrialized Countries (NICs)— and mild indeed against the Canadian dollar.

In fact the Canadian dollar has fallen only 5 or 6 percent against the U.S. dollar since spring 1985, and stands today at about 76 U.S. cents. That places it down about 12 percent from its value in 1980.

This depreciation of the Canadian dollar, and its failure to rise perceptibly since 1985, have been as favorable to Canada's trade balance as the overvalued U.S. dollar was harmful to the U.S.'.

THE REGIONAL PRICE OF CANADA'S TRADE SUCCESS

Again, a U.S. comparison may be in order. In the U.S., the idea of two divergent regional systems, the declining Frostbelt and the rising Sunbelt, has given way in the 1980s to a different image entirely. Now the two divergent regional economies are alluded to via a "bicoastal" image. As reported in a Joint Economic Committee report in 1986, most of the growth in the U.S. economy in the first half of the 1980s was on the "two coasts": more accurately, California and the Atlantic seaboard.

In the bicoastal United States of the 1980s, then, the farmbelt, the Oil Patch, and the industrial heartland from Pennsylvania to Michigan are the new zones of economic stagnation.

In contrast, Canada's growth in the mid-1980s has been "non-coastal." Regional fortunes are similar in that the resource-reliant provinces of the periphery are hurting, just as in the U.S. farmbelt and Oil Patch. But it is opposite in that Canada's industrial heartland, Ontario and Quebec, are thriving.

The reason for the differing positions of the two nation's industrial regions seems clear enough. The exchange rate has hurt the old-line industrial regions of the U.S. during the 1980s, and helped trigger a Canadian industrial revival. And unlike the dispersed U.S. modernization from the 1970s, Canada's industrial comeback has occurred in the traditional industrial core: Ontario and Quebec.

A recent study helps place this division-of-labor issue at the center of Canada's stage. In "Regional Dynamics of Manufacturing and Non-Manufacturing Investment in Canada," Meric S. Gertler shows that provincial shares of the nation's capital stock have remained largely unchanged since the mid-1950s. Two exceptions prove the rule: Alberta's oil-based investment boom brought a steep rise in its share after 1976, and Quebec's separatist experiment brought a steep decline in the same period. Even so, the combined share of Quebec and Ontario in the nation's private capital stock fell only from 60.1 percent in 1956 to 52.5 percent in 1981. (Gertler, 1986, p. 528.)

The core provinces' shares of Canada's capital stock have risen again in the mid-1980s, apace with their export-led manufacturing boom (Edith Terry et al., 1987, p. 39.) This renewed concentration of manufacturing in the core is likely to reinforce the traditional polarization. Despite widespread assumptions about the services sector as being the wave of the future, Gertler finds that manufacturing investment remains the key engine of Canada's regional growth. He finds that the role of

. . . manufacturing investment has not declined significantly. . . . In fact, its pro-pulsive role in local economies . . . appears to bear up very well. . . . Manufac-turers may not generate many new local jobs . . . but their potential to stimulate the expansion in other sectors . . . deserves greater attention. (Gertler, p. 532.)

In turn, the concentration of the dynamic manufacturing sector in central Canada has kept resentment alive over the issue of "colonial" exploitation. In contrast to the truly continental industrialization that has marked the U.S. over the past generation, Canada's development has left the old regional divisions intact. As a development official from Nova Scotia writes,

The lament of both East and West for years has been along these lines: that the Canadian system has not integrated large parts of the country into a whole because the interaction among the geographic regions has been one of exploi-tation rather than of partnership. (James D. McNiven, 1986, p. 85.)

To that extent, the price of Canada's trade success has been a sharp-ening of regional disparities in the mid-1980s, at the very time when regional development programs are increasingly criticized. (Thomas J. Courchene and James R. Melvin, 1986.)

The Exchange Rate as a Means of Preserving the Status Quo

By the same token, one might expect free trade with the U.S. to reorient Canada's distant markets away from Ontario and Quebec toward the South. Both consumers and businesses in the periphery would tend to buy more from lower-cost U.S. suppliers. Meantime, Canada would specialize more in its resource lines (its area of comparative advantage in the free-trade confederation.) Whether or not the North-South shift would spur industrialization of the West and the Maritimes is open to conjecture.

To that extent, Ontario and Quebec might lose part of their distant markets within Canada to lower-cost, less distant U.S. firms. Hence it is not surprising that Ontario's premier should be reelected recently on a platform opposing free trade (*The Economist*, 1987, p. 51). The core is thriving from an "undervalued" Canadian dollar and a corresponding export boom. At the same time, fears of losing distant markets within Canada run high enough (and are plausible enough) to energize the campaign in Ontario against free trade.

Viewed from Canada's periphery, however, the Centre's preference for the status quo implies a continued subsidy of the Centre's industry (and labor) by the periphery's consumers. To both firms and consumers in the West and the Maritimes, free trade offers (1) lower consumer prices, (2) reduced U.S. barriers to resource exports, and (3) more subjectively, a weakening of the quasi-colonial relationship between the core and periphery.

In sum, then, how can Canada "afford" to avoid a basic restructuring to adapt to global competitive pressures? One reason seems clear. The undervalued Canadian dollar has created an industrial boom in the core region, though not elsewhere.

In turn, this boom has given central Canada an illusion that no basic (and uncomfortable) changes are required. And since the core region, the center of population and industry, also tends to set the tone in education, finance, media, and opinion making, much of the core's fashions will seem national. The upshot is that, whether consciously or not, the coalition defending the status quo may have dressed up a parochial regional interest as cultural nationalism.

REFERENCES

Atkins, Frank. "Free Trade, Economic Regions and the Foreign Exchange Rate." *Canadian Journal of Regional Science*, Autumn 1986, pp. 377–380.

Bergstrand, Jeffrey H. "The U.S. Trade Deficit: A Perspective from Selected Bilateral Trade Models." *New England Economic Review*, May/June 1987, pp. 19–31.

Courchene, Thomas J. and James R. Melvin. "Canadian Regional Policy: Lessons from the Past and Prospects for the Future." *Canadian Journal of Regional Science*, Spring 1986, pp. 49–67.

The Economist, September 19, 1987. "Go for it, Canada," pp. 16–19; "Ontario Mans a Roadblock," pp. 51–52.

Gertler, Meric S. "Regional Dynamics of Manufacturing and Non-Manufacturing Investment in Canada." *Regional Studies*, October 1986, pp. 523–534.

McNiven, James D. "Regional Development Policy in the Next Decade." *Canadian Journal of Regional Science*, Spring 1986, pp. 79–88.

Norton, R. D. "Industrial Policy and American Renewal." *Journal of Economic Literature*, March 1986, pp. 1–40.

Royal Commission on the Economic Union and Development Prospects for Canada. *Report*. Ottawa: Supply and Services, 1985.

Terry, Edith, Bill Javetski, and John Pearson. "Industry's Surprising Revival North of the Border." *Business Week*, July 27, 1987, pp. 38–39.

Tremblay, Rodrique. "The Regional Impact of Free Trade," *Canadian Journal of Regional Science*." Spring 1985, pp. 85–99.

Urquhart, John and Peggy Berkowitz. "Canada Worries Anew Over Loss of Identity to Its Big Neighbor." *The Wall Street Journal*, September 22, 1987.

PART II
NATURAL RESOURCES AND
RELATED ISSUES

3
Canada/U.S.: Cost Competitiveness in Agricultural Commodities
Norman Rask
Gerald F. Ortmann

Agriculture is an important sector for both the U.S. and Canadian economies, contributing significantly to total output and trade balances. Cost competitiveness in the production and marketing of specific agricultural commodities is important in determining the general pattern of cross-border trade between the two countries, as well as trade patterns with the rest of the world. Government policies enhance the competitiveness of some commodities (wheat), while in other instances they protect domestic sized, but less competitive enterprises (dairy).

The establishment of a Free Trade Agreement between Canada and the United States will result in less emphasis on the role of government and more reliance on true cost competitiveness for traded commodities. This should result in a greater volume of agricultural trade between the two countries. Exports of commodities that can meet international costs of production levels will increase, and by contrast, greater imports will occur where costs of production can not meet international standards. Both countries should gain, but each with a different set of commodities.

Trade patterns reflect unique production-marketing relationships. Both Canada and the United States are surplus producers of many agricultural commodities and compete in international markets, especially grain markets (wheat). More importantly, a long common border results in substantial cross-border traffic of regional agricultural products, principally livestock products and fruits and vegetables. Transportation costs associated with moving produce along this common border make it more economical in many instances to trade regionally, rather than ship over long distances within each country.

Despite substantial differences in population and size of economy,

Table 3.1
Principal U.S. Agricultural Trading Partners, 1986

Country	U.S. Agricultural Exports		U.S. Agricultural Imports		Total Agricultural Trade
		(Mil $ U.S.)			
Japan	$5,106	(1)	$ 213	(28)	$5,319
Canada	1,547	(3)	2,009	(2)	3,556
Mexico	1,074	(6)	2,018	(1)	3,092
Netherlands	2,069	(2)	681	(7)	2,750
Brazil	555	(13)	1,777	(3)	2,332
West Germany	1,042	(7)	634	(10)	1,676
South Korea	1,293	(4)	73	(45)	1,366
Taiwan	1,164	(5)	193	(31)	1,357
France	435	(15)	748	(6)	1,183
Spain	701	(10)	316	(21)	1,017
	14,986		8,662		23,648
All Countries	26,046		21,051		47,097

Source: USDA

the respective bilateral trade markets are important for both countries. In 1986, the U.S. was Canada's largest market for agricultural exports, and Canada was the second-largest agricultural trading partner for the U.S; second to Mexico in terms of U.S. imports, and third to Japan and the Netherlands as a market for U.S. agricultural exports (Table 3.1).

Government policies, transportation requirements, land resources, and climate, through their impact on costs of production, all contribute to the cost competitiveness, and hence trade importance, of specific commodities. Table 3.2 presents some key commodity flows. Transportation costs are especially important for Canada because major population centers and principal agricultural production areas of Canada are situated in a long narrow band just north of the border between the two countries. Severe climate as one moves north in Canada limits agricultural production, both in terms of the crop and livestock enterprises that can be undertaken, and through restricted yields, the level of competitiveness that can be achieved. Because of climate and topography problems, only about five percent of the Canadian land area is currently suitable for farming. Thus, in the absence of restrictive policies on cross-border movements of agricultural products, one would expect transportation cost differences alone to dictate considerable north-south movement of agricultural commodities rather than long-distance hauls along the border.

Table 3.2
U.S.-Canada Trade in Agricultural Products, 1986

Product Category	U.S. Exports To Canada	U.S. Imports From Canada	Net U.S. Exports to Canada
	(Mil $ U.S.)		
Livestock Products			
Live animals	37	240	-203
Meats	59	533	-474
Poultry	62	25	37
Dairy	10	72	-62
Hides and skins	102	50	52
Other	24	27	- 3
	294	947	-653
Vegetable Products			
Wheat & grain prods.	47	195	-148
Rice	29	---	29
Feed grains & prods.	54	---	54
Oilseeds & prods.	219	86	133
Other grains	41	160	-119
Feeds & fodder	51	77	- 26
Fruits & juices	301	57	244
Nuts	68	--	68
Vegetables	244	103	141
Sugar & prods.	45	125	- 80
Other	154	259	-105
	1,253	1,062	191
Total	1,547	2,009	-462

Source: USDA

PRODUCTION REGIONS

Geographic location (climate) favors agriculture of the United States in terms of levels of productivity and diversity of enterprise selection, as well as length of growing season for crops. For livestock production, cool summers of northern regions are an advantage, but can be over-shadowed by the additional housing and stored-feed requirements of the longer and colder winters. Since Canadian agriculture is situated at the northern edge of climate tolerance for most enterprises, the choice of production enterprises is limited. East-west differences in moisture availability effect enterprise selection in both countries as well.

Two principal Canadian production regions can be identified. They are, (1) the extensive semiarid region of the three Prairie Provinces, Saskatchewan, Alberta, and Manitoba, where much of the small grains (wheat) and range cattle are produced, and (2) the intensive agricultural region of southern Ontario, especially the area between the U.S. states of Michigan and New York, where corn, hogs, tobacco, and diary products are produced. Other specialized Canadian production regions involve dairy products and, to an increasing extent, hogs in southern Quebec, potatoes in New Brunswick, and fruit along the shores of the Great Lakes and in southern British Columbia.

On the U.S. side of the border, these production areas are mirrored, but on a larger scale. The cattle and wheat areas of the northern plains have many of the same production conditions as the Canadian Prairie Provinces. Washington State has important fruit-growing areas as does British Columbia (apples). Ontario agriculture represents a bridge between the eastern U.S. Corn Belt and the northeast dairy regions of the U.S. and Quebec. And, potato production in New Brunswick is carried out under soil and climate conditions similar to those of northern Maine.

Farther south, the U.S. enjoys a warmer climate and thus can produce a number of agricultural commodities, including semitropical fruits and vegetables that are not feasible to produce in Canada. Foremost among the U.S. agricultural regions is the Corn Belt, extending from central Ohio on the east through Iowa on the west. In terms of size, quality of soils, and growing season temperature and rainfall, the Corn Belt is the most naturally productive agricultural region in the world. In addition, seasonal production of fresh perishable commodities in several regions allows for defined cross-country market opportunities for each nation.

The existence of similar production environments in each country, or of more favorable natural production conditions in one country, however, does not necessarily signal equal or superior levels of competitiveness in either a cost-of-production or a market-access sense. There are a number of other variables that need to be considered, including government policies, exchange rates, and market size and location.

COMPETITIVENESS DEFINED

Competitiveness can be defined in many ways. Two definitions are widely used. The first, "true competitiveness," measures true costs of production based on opportunity costs of alternative resource use. Ideally, this measure should reflect cost situations with as few policy-induced market distortions as possible. Examples of farm level costs of production for selected crop and livestock products are presented in Tables 3.3 and 3.4.

The second definition, "market competitiveness," measures the ability of a country to sell in international markets. Under this definition, low production costs are helpful, but not necessarily determinate, in achieving market share. For example, market share can be "bought" if a country is willing to provide enough seller subsidy. Examples of current trade

Table 3.3
Crop Enterprise Costs - U.S./Canada

Crop	U.S. Northern Plains (1985)	Canadian Prairie Provinces (1987)	U.S. North Central (1985)	U.S. North East (1985)	Canadian Province Ontario (1987)
	($U.S./bushel)				
Corn	$2.41	–	$2.36	$2.53	$2.51
Soybeans	4.66	–	4.90	4.66	4.92
Oats	2.21	1.38	3.06	2.67	2.15
Barley	2.67	2.26	–	3.20	2.36
Spring Wheat	3.96	3.23	–	–	–
Winter Wheat	4.81	–	3.62	4.56	3.66

Sources: For the U.S. – McElroy
          For Canada – Driver
                      – Schoney

Table 3.4
Livestock Enterprise Costs - U.S./Canada, 1985

Enterprise	United States	Canada (Ontario)
	($U.S./cwt)	
Dairy (Milk)	$12.54	$13.79
(Northeast)	(12.91)	
Hogs (Pork)		
Farrow to finish	47.61	41.73
Beef		
Fed cattle	62.59	
Farmer feed lots	70.76	65.84
Commercial feed lots	60.77	
Cow-calf (per cow)	544.00	506.00

Sources: For the U.S. – USDA
         For Canada – Adapted from Driver

flows presented in Table 3.2 represent this definition. However, as will be noted later, with a few exceptions, both definitions lead to similar conclusions in the Canada/U.S. case. Market share for specific commodities is discussed in the following section on trade profiles.

Competitiveness can change over time and should be viewed as a dynamic concept. Prices, costs, exchange rates, technological efficiency, and competitor situation are all constantly changing variables. Thus, once having achieved competitiveness, remaining competitive is an on-going challenge of successfully adjusting to changing conditions. Finally, cost competitiveness does not necessarily determine trade, which is based more on comparative cost advantage than on absolute cost advantage. For example, the Corn Belt region of the U.S. may be the low-cost region for a number of commodities, but, it has a comparative advantage in corn and soybeans, and therefore specializes in these two crops.

In comparing competitiveness among various commodities produced in Canada and the U.S., the emphasis in this chapter is on farm production costs and, thus, more on the true costs of production rather than on market share. In the long run, costs of production determine the primary trade flows, though input subsidies and other forms of producer incentives, as well as border restrictions and/or incentives, can change short-run market share.

In this regard, Canada and the United States are in the early phases of consideration of a Free Trade Agreement (FTA) to liberalize bilateral trade. This agreement, when enacted, will reduce and in many cases eliminate market (trade) distortions due to agricultural subsidies, tariffs, and nontariff barriers. Thus, as these impediments to trade are reduced, true costs of production will emerge as the dominant force in the determination of competitive position for specific commodities.

U.S./CANADA TRADE PROFILE

Climate is a distinct advantage for the U.S. in the production of a number of commodities. As noted earlier, the U.S. can basically grow any Canadian crop along its northern border. However, because the U.S. has both temperate and semitropical regions, a much broader array of products is grown there, and in the case of fresh fruits and vegetables there is an early season advantage for the U.S.

With a distinct size and climate advantage for the U.S., it would be reasonable to assume that agricultural trade flows would occur principally from the south to the north. But this is not what happens. The U.S. does provide a much larger share of fruits and vegetables to Canada than it receives in return, principally for the climate reasons mentioned above (Table 3.2). However, this is more than offset by the very large livestock and livestock-product export flows from Canada to the U.S. Here, since the U.S. is a surplus producer of both feed grains and livestock products, a positive level of competitiveness on the part of Canadian producers exists. It is less meaningful to draw the same conclusion for fruit and vegetable production in the U.S. In this case, Canada simply cannot produce these commodities during a major portion of the year.

Even in the U.S., production of citrus fruits and fresh vegetables during the winter season is limited mainly to a few southern states and California, thus, necessitating regional product flows within the U.S. Therefore, one could hypothesize that U.S./Canada agricultural trade as presently constituted, may not be significantly different in product mix than internal U.S. north-south trade. And, in the absence of border restrictions, Canadian agricultural production and import and export patterns should be similar to those of northern-border U.S. states.

Within the various product categories, specific trade items are especially significant. Canada dominates the trade in live animals, and within this category cattle are by far the most important, including beef animals from the Prairie Provinces and dairy cattle from eastern Canada. Swine have been important Canadian live animal exports to the U.S. in the past but, because of U.S. producer action claiming unfair trade practices, a countervailing duty of $4.386 Can. per cwt. was applied and exports were reduced sharply in 1986, down 50 percent, and again in 1987, down 30 percent from 1986 levels.

A somewhat different picture is evident with trade in meat products. Here, Canadian swine products dominate, accounting for three-quarters of meat exports to the U.S. Beef accounts for most of the remainder. U.S. imports of Canadian swine products were up 32 percent in 1986, compensating in part for the reduced import of live animals, but reflecting also a rise in market share as Danish imports to the U.S. fell in response to their stronger currency valued against the U.S. dollar, thus giving Canada a greater competitive edge. In addition to the cost of production advantage noted in Table 3.4, Canadian swine producers have a location advantage over the traditional U.S. swine-producing areas of the Midwest in supplying northeastern U.S. markets.

The Free Trade Agreement (FTA) between the U.S. and Canada will likely restore the previous balance between Canadian live swine and pork-product exports to the U.S., assuming the countervailing duty on live swine is removed.

Poultry trade is less important and more balanced, both between the two countries and among the poultry products. U.S. exports are two and one-half times those of Canada. In both cases poultry meat accounts for about one-half of the trade, while eggs make up one-fourth. Dairy products, like poultry, are a minor component of trade and are principally from Canada.

In Canada, both poultry and dairy products are "sized" to the Canadian market by a series of market-protection and producer-incentive mechanisms. In the U.S., this is true for dairy also. With a FTA, more trade in both commodities groups can be expected, with a likely increase in poultry product exports from the U.S. to Canada. The direction of increased dairy product trade under a freer trade environment is less certain.

Trade in crop and vegetable products is more balanced in terms of total trade value between the two countries. However, as noted earlier, there are sharp differences among individual commodities. For example, wheat trade occurs principally from Canada to the U.S., while rice and feed grains (corn) go north. Soybeans and soybean products are U.S. exports to Canada also, and probably return in the form of livestock and livestock-products. Fruits and, to a lesser degree, vegetables are principally from the U.S. and represent an absolute and seasonal production advantage.

MEASURING COSTS OF PRODUCTION

International competitiveness generally reflects underlying production and marketing cost advantage, though, as noted above, these basic cost considerations are often distorted by swings in exchange rates and by import and/or export policies. For example, in the above-cited swine situation, Canadian exports of live swine to the U.S. were reduced because of countervailing duties, but swine product exports grew because of cost advantages vis-à-vis the U.S. and because of currency exchange advantage relative to Denmark, a principal competitor for the U.S. swine product market.

Also, caution is needed when comparing cost levels between countries, as there are often differences in the methods by which costs are determined, especially in relation to fixed costs such as depreciation. Finally, land rent, a principal cost component for both U.S. and Canadian crop production, is in part determined by rather significant farm price subsidies in both countries. These subsidies become swiftly capitalized into land values, which in turn raise costs of production for producers, either in terms of actual rents paid or in terms of opportunity costs for land owners.

It is difficult to make precise comparisons between countries concerning the level of market distortion for specific commodities that is caused by the many forms and types of producer and consumer subsidies and taxes, as well as tariffs and nontariff barriers. Although there is no single way of measuring the overall economic effect of these various support programs, "a set of metrics has been developed and estimated" (CBO, p. 88). They have been combined into a unit value termed "a producer subsidy equivalent" (PSE). A PSE "provides an estimate of the revenue that would be needed to compensate producers if existing government programs were eliminated."

When the PSE for a country is divided by total cash receipts for agriculture, a ratio is obtained that shows the percentage of income in agriculture that is attributable to government programs and, by extension, an estimate of the degree of market distortion that may be present in estimates of competitiveness. For Canada and the U.S. in the 1982–84 period these ratios were both 22 percent, an indication that on average each country was providing about one-fifth of farmer gross farm receipts from government programs.

Therefore, while there may be some minor differences between the two countries in specific commodity support, overall agricultural competitiveness should not be strongly influenced by government programs. For comparison of third-country farm program support, comparable ratios for several key market and/or competitor countries are as follows: Japan, 72 percent; EEC, 33 percent; Brazil, 7 percent; and Argentina, −22 percent. In the case of Argentina, rather than being subsidized, agriculture is taxed.

Exchange rate movements have favored Canada in the last few years. In 1980 the value of the Canadian dollar was U.S. $.85. It dropped to a low of U.S. $.72 in 1986 and in 1987 traded at a value of about U.S. $.75. Thus, relative to the other major agricultural trading partners for both countries, (Japan and the EEC), Canada has maintained a positive export position relative to its currency value.

COMMODITY COST COMPARISONS

Wheat is the only crop where Canada and the U.S. compete strongly in international markets. The U.S. exports about 60 percent of its production and supplies about 30 percent of all world-traded wheat, while Canada exports about 75 percent of production and provides about 20 percent of world wheat trade. Costs of farm production vary by region and generally favor Canada (Table 3.3). Production location, however, is important. Because of access to export ports on the Pacific coast, total Canadian costs (CIF) for serving Asian markets are marginally lower (Ortmann). The U.S. has a slight advantage in serving European markets.

Corn production costs favor the U.S. slightly in the principal Corn Belt regions. However, costs in the cooler Northeast are the same as in Ontario. Both regions, the northeast U.S. and Ontario, are deficit producers of corn, which they import from corn belt states. Cool-region crops such as oats and barley are produced at a lower cost in Canada and serve there as feed grain substitutes for corn. Barley is also a major export crop, with about 45 percent of annual Canadian production exported.

Livestock products have a cost advantage for Canada (Table 3.4). Canadian production costs are 7–14 percent lower for beef and swine products, which form the bulk of Canadian agricultural exports to the U.S. and account for the agricultural trade balance in favor of Canada.

Apples are a major production fruit for both Canada and the U.S. British Columbia (B.C.) and the state of Washington produce 40 percent and 30 percent, respectively, of their country's apple supplies. These production regions are contiguous, with B.C. experiencing somewhat greater climatic variability and lower yields. They supply similar markets; however, B.C. has somewhat greater production costs, primarily fixed costs. B.C. production growth has not kept pace with growth in Washington apple production in recent years.

SUMMARY

Canada and the United States are major agricultural trading partners. It is significant, however, that there is little bilateral trade in those commodities that each produces competitively for major international markets: grains and oilseeds. Rather, cross-border trade is concentrated in products that traditionally form normal regional trade patterns within the U.S.: fruits and vegetables from the south, and livestock and meat products from the north. Geographic location of production and consumption regions, and a relatively free flow of commodities, are responsible for the regional product specialization.

Cost competitiveness varies by commodity group. The U.S. has an advantage in fruits and vegetables dictated largely by climate. The U.S. also has a cost advantage in milk and poultry production, but protection of the Canadian poultry and dairy industries limits U.S. access to this market. Canada has a cost advantage in livestock and meat (beef and pork). This cost advantage is evident in a considerable trade surplus with the U.S. in these commodities.

A favorable exchange rate in recent years, has enhanced Canadian competitiveness resulting in a positive agricultural trade balance with the United States. Enactment of a Free Trade Agreement between the two countries should result in more regional specialization of production and a further increase in the already large volume of agricultural trade.

REFERENCES

Brinkman, G. L. "The Competitive Position of Canadian Agriculture," *Canadian Journal of Agricultural Economics*, vol. 5, no. 2, July, 1987.

Congressional Budget Office. "The GATT Negotiations and U.S. Trade Policy." The Congress of the United States, June, 1987.

deJong, A. "Ontario Farm Management Analysis Project—Feedlot Enterprise Analysis Report." Ontario Ministry of Agriculture and Food, Guelph, Ontario—January 16, 1987.

Ontario Ministry of Agriculture and Food. "1987—Crop Budgeting AID." Publication No. 60, Ontario Ministry of Agriculture and Food.

Driver, H., et al. "Ontario Farm Management Analysis Project 1985." University of Guelph, Guelph Ontario, July 25, 1986.

Lee, M. L. "Cost Competitiveness of Apple Production in British Columbia Versus Washington State." Working Paper 18/86, Department of Agricultural Economics, University of British Columbia, Vancouver, B.C., September, 1986.

McElroy, R. C. "State Level Costs of Production, 1985." USDA/ERS/NED, Washington D.C.; January, 1987.

McElroy, R. C., et al "Economic Indicators of the Farm sector, Costs of Production, 1985." ECIFS 5-1, USDA/ERS/NED, Washington D.C. August 1986.

Ortmann, G. F., V. J. Stulp, Rask, N. "Comparative Costs in Agricultural Commodities Among Major Exporting Countries." ESO 1325, Department of Agricultural Economics and Rural Sociology, Ohio State University, Columbus, Ohio, January 1987.

Schoney, R. A. "Results of the 1987 Saskatchewan Top Management Workshops" Bulletin FLB 87-01, Department of Agricultural Economics, University of Saskatchewan, June 15, 1987.

Warley, T. K., and R. R. Barichello." Agricultural Issues in a Comprehensive Canada–USA Trade Agreement: A Canadian Perspective." Paper, Department of Agricultural Economics, University of Guelph, Guelph, Ontario, 1987.

4
Energy Trade Shocks: The Impact on Canadian Economic Activity
Robert N. McRae

INTRODUCTION

The purpose of this chapter is to quantify the likely impact that changes in energy trade would have on the energy sector and macroeconomy of Canada.

This chapter is organized as follows: The first section is devoted to a description of historical energy-related trade patterns between Canada and the United States; the second section lists the trade shocks under consideration; the third section contains a very brief description of the linkages between the energy sector and the macroeconomy; the fourth section contains the results of the trade scenarios; and the final section provides a summary.

Historical Developments in Canada-U.S. Energy Trade

The analysis in this chapter will focus exclusively on oil and gas, even though under the term "energy trade," one should include Canada's large imports of U.S. coal, and Canada's net exports of electricity to the U.S.

Energy policy decisions in Canada and the U.S. have affected the volume and value of Canada-U.S. energy trade.[1] So have actions by OPEC, when world oil prices are affected.

Canadian oil and gas reserves[2] grew rapidly from 1947 to 1973. Energy taxation and trade policies actively encouraged development. In the 1950s the reserve base in western Canada was viewed as being plentiful enough to warrant the construction of both oil and gas pipelines from

Alberta to central Canada and to the export markets of the U.S., and a natural gas pipeline from British Columbia to the western U.S. At their peak, in 1973, oil exports accounted for 58 percent of Canadian production, and gas exports accounted for 32 percent of Canadian production. These large trade volumes played an important role in Canadian oil and gas development (Waverman [1974]).

Oil

The regional distribution of oil resources, and the cost of trans-Canada transportation, led to the establishment of an oil market in which oil is imported into eastern Canada (Quebec and the Atlantic provinces), and exported into the midwestern and western U.S.

Historically, this pattern was reinforced by the Borden Commission of 1958. It recommended the establishment of the "Ottawa Valley Line" or "Borden Line," which restricted the flow of crude oil, and eventually of oil products, into Ontario from offshore supplies. The Commission report also urged an expansion of oil exports to the U.S. as a means to ease the excess capacity prevalent in the industry. This policy became known as the National Oil Policy (Debanne [1974]).

During the 1960s and early 1970s the restrictions on oil imports into Canada fit in with the U.S. oil import quota program,[3] and allowed the North American market for oil to remain partially isolated from world events (Task Force on Oil Import Control [1970]). Prices for Canadian oil west of the Ottawa Valley Line reflected the U.S. oil prices, which were higher than the world price. Oil market-demand prorationing regulations in Canada and the U.S. provided further insurance against unwanted price fluctuations. These policies provided a stable sort of environment for oil development.

By the time of the first OPEC oil shock of 1973-74 there was a perception of a shortage of oil in Canada; the policy response was to phaseout exports of light crude oil to the US over the period of 1975–1977,[4] extend the Interprovincial Pipeline eastward from Sarnia to Montreal (and subsidize the tariff), establish a Crown petroleum corporation, PetroCanada, and encourage additional nonconventional supply, like synthetic oil from Syncrude (Canada, EMR [1976]). The National Oil Policy (Borden Line) was dismantled, and a "made-in-Canada" oil price was established, which was uniform across Canada (except for transportation costs) and lower than the world oil price. An export tax was levied on all oil shipments to the U.S., so that the export price was raised to the world price level.

The policy environment which affected oil trade remained in place until Canadian oil deregulation[5] in 1985. Deregulation eliminated all restrictions on the import and export of crude oil and oil products (unless the contracts are for terms longer than two years). The relaxation of oil trade restrictions has led to a shift in the marketing of domestic oil: less is being shipped to Montreal, via the Sarnia-Montreal pipeline extension, and more is being exported to the US.

For most of its history Canada has been a net importer of oil. Nevertheless, Canada has been, and continues to be, an important exporter of oil to the US.

Natural Gas

In 1959 the National Energy Board (NEB) was established, on the recommendation of the Borden Commission. One of the mandates of the NEB was the protection of Canadian interests involved in energy trade. Before the NEB could approve long-term natural gas exports, it must be satisfied "that the quantity of natural gas proposed to be exported does not exceed the surplus remaining after due allowance for the reasonable foreseeable requirements for use in Canada." To implement this policy the NEB established the "25A4 test": at the time of application for an export permit the gas reserves had to exceed 25 times the estimated demand in four years' time.[6] Consequently, the life index (reserves to production ratio) for natural gas has remained very high (and above 25). However, there was a period from about 1972 to 1982 when concern was expressed about the availability of future Canadian gas supplies[7]; hence no new gas export permits were issued during this period.

New long-term gas exports to the US were authorized as a result of the NEB's 1983 Gas Export Omnibus Decision, but by this time (1983) U.S. demand had declined to such an extent that only 40 percent of existing authorized exports was being shipped. Prior to this, authorization had been given for gas exports to flow through the Prebuild pipeline (Canadian portion of the Alaska Highway pipeline). Natural gas exports started flowing through the eastern leg of the Prebuild in 1982.

Until 1973, Canadian prices for natural gas were strongly determined by the export (U.S.) price. In the U.S., prices for interstate gas were held artificially low by the Federal Power Commission, which was granted control over such prices in 1954. Despite the low Canadian wellhead prices, it was still profitable to develop natural gas. After 1974, Canadian natural gas prices were held below the export price, and from 1980 to 1984 the export price was formally based on a full Btu equivalence with the world oil price. It was during this period that Canadian gas exports became overpriced, and hence volumes declined precipitously. Natural gas deregulation in 1986 has removed some of the barriers to gas trade, but not all.

POSSIBLE TRADE SHOCKS

To quantify the economic impact of various changes in Canada-U.S. trade, this section will concentrate on scenarios which will affect future trade. The following three scenarios will be analyzed:

1. an increase in natural gas exports to the US of 200 Bcf per year starting in 1986;
2. a reduction of $5 US in the OPEC oil price to $15 US per barrel[8] starting in 1987; and
3. a presumption that the Prebuild natural gas pipeline was not constructed.

Are these reasonable trade scenarios to consider? With the easing of the "gas bubble" in the US and with aggressive marketing by Canadian gas companies, it is quite likely that Canada will be able to increase its exports to the U.S. over the next decade.[9] If OPEC were to squabble over production shares and overproduce relative to market demand, then prices could decline to $15 U.S. per barrel. After all, oil prices temporarily dropped to about $9 U.S. per barrel in the summer of 1986. Foothills Pipeline (Yukon) Ltd. was granted permission by the Canadian government to build the southern portion of the Alaska Highway gas pipeline in 1979, before construction of the Alaska portion (hence the term prebuild), after US government officials gave assurances that the whole pipeline would be built. Canadian gas has been shipped through the Prebuild, and was to be replaced by gas from Alaska once the whole Alaska Highway pipeline was completed. It is doubtful if the northern portion of the pipeline will be completed in this century. With hindsight, it might be reasonable to suggest the Prebuild should not have been constructed. Had this been the case, energy investment and gas exports would have been lower than those actually observed—and future expansions in the capacity of the pipeline would not occur. Table 4.1 indicates the amount of investment expenditure and gas exports involved.

ENERGY-MACROECONOMIC LINKAGES

The economic performance of the Canadian macroeconomy and the energy sector is simulated up to the year 1995 under the three trade-related scenarios using the MACE (MACro-Energy) model of Canada.

The features of the macroeconomic component of the MACE model have been described in Helliwell et al. (1987). MACE consists of a small-scale annual macroeconomic model linked to a large regionally-based energy model. Energy is firmly entrenched in the structure of the macro component of the model: It is one of the factors in the nested production

Table 4.1
Investment Expenditure and Gas Exports Associated with the Prebuild Gas Pipeline

year	gas export revenue (million $)	gas by-product revenue (million $)	direct investment (million $)
1979	–	–	199.5
1980	–	–	518.0
1981	58.1	20.0	969.7
1982	703.4	233.6	411.0
1983	977.9	370.7	79.7
1984	919.0	339.1	2.3
1985	967.7	338.7	1.0
1986	615.6	209.3	0.9
1987	534.2	170.9	0.5
1988	603.9	193.2	23.5
1989	797.9	255.3	607.9
1990	1461.5	467.7	1178.3
1991	2108.8	673.2	250.5
1992	2295.2	734.5	70.5
1993	2423.1	775.4	0.5
1994	2589.2	828.5	0.5
1995	2791.3	893.2	0.5

Source: Wright-Mansell Research Ltd.

function, and its price affects the wage-price dynamics and profitability, which in turn affect output determination. The MACE model is fully able to simulate the often opposing effects of energy price changes in the energy-producing and energy-using sectors of the economy.

The following are the direct linkages between the energy sector and the macroeconomy which allow a change in the price of oil or energy trade to affect macroeconomic variables.

a. wage-price equations

b. import-export of energy products

c. factor demands and output determination

d. investment in the energy sector

e. government finance

The operation of these linkages will be explained below and as part of the section on the macroeconomic impact.

The demand for factors of production, including energy, is derived by the supply-side modeling in MACE. Output determination is based on a utilization rate decision, where actual output is measured relative to a synthetic variable, potential output. Potential output (qsv) is the level which would be produced if all currently-employed factors were operating at their average (normal) levels over the sample period. It is modelled as a set of nested constant-elasticity-of-substitution (CES) functions: qsv = f(g(K,E),L), where the factors are capital services (K), efficiency units of labor (L), and energy (E). Energy and capital are bundled together to capture their complementary relationship. The utilization rate decision (actual to potential level of output) is hypothesized to depend upon the level of unexpected sales, operating profitability, and unintended inventory accumulation.

The desired levels for factor demands are obtained from the production function for potential output, under the assumption that firms minimize anticipated production costs. Aggregate energy demand, derived in this way,[10] is split among seven regions according to the regional energy price index relative to the national average, and the regional share of real gross domestic product. Each region has a separate set of equations to disaggregate the regional energy demand into the fuel types (oil products, natural gas, and electricity) according to relative energy fuel prices.

Changes in the international oil price affect the domestic price of oil and natural gas, and these influence many components of the model. For instance, firms will adjust their optimal mix of capital, labour and energy—and the share of fuel types. The resulting change in fuel demand, and the value of imports and/or exports will alter the balance of trade, and consequently the exchange rate. If the change in energy price is felt worldwide, then Canada's balance of trade will be indirectly affected through the impact of energy prices on the economies of our trading partners. Energy prices are also an important determinant in the wage-price dynamics of the economy. Naturally, the induced changes in wages and output price index will have many channels of influence, and affect variables like consumption, nonenergy exports, and employment. Changes in energy prices will directly affect the level of investment in the energy sector.

The energy-producing component of MACE describes the supply side of the oil and gas industry (in the nonfrontier areas of Canada). This includes all upstream activity: exploration, development, production, and transportation. Within this sector, changes in domestic oil and gas prices or changes in energy trade lead to changes in energy demand, production, exploration and development investment, discoveries, and impacts. The fiscal systems for the producing provinces and the federal government are modeled, so MACE is capable of calculating government revenues and economic rents associated with oil and gas activity.

RESULTS OF THE TRADE SHOCKS

Background

The experiments with the MACE model are conducted with no changes in fiscal, monetary, or energy policies. This allows one to isolate the effects on the economy as having originated with the changes specified in each shock. The scenario with oil prices at $20/bbl is considered the base case, or the most likely outcome. The emphasis in the paper is on the impact of the three trade shocks relative to the base case.

The oil price shock should involve changes to exogenous variables which represent output, prices, and interest rates for both the world and the U.S. These exogenous variables have been modified, otherwise the Canadian macroeconomic impact (via the trade sector) would be exaggerated.

The next part of this section contains a description of the changes in economic rents and in certain key energy-related variables; it is followed by a discussion of the impact of the trade shocks on macroeconomic variables. Economic rents to the producers, consumers, federal and provincial governments are contained in Table 4.2. Results for selected energy variables are reported in Table 4.3. The values of key macroeconomic variables are displayed in Figures 4.1 to 4.5.

Energy Sector Results

The economic rents show the distribution of net benefits amongst the various participants, and are displayed in Table 4.2. They are measured in 1985, and again in 1995, at the end of the simulation period.[11] The increase in natural gas exports provides the oil and gas industry with a gain in economic rent of $1.6 billion relative to the base case. The resulting higher production values for natural gas provide the federal government with a gain of $1 billion, and the governments of the producing provinces with a gain of $1.7 billion.

A sustained drop in the world oil price of $5 U.S. per barrel starting in 1987 leads to a large decline in economic rents of about $23 billion for the oil and gas industry, about $8 billion for the federal government, and $11.5 billion for the governments of the producing provinces.

If the Prebuild pipeline had not been built, it would have meant a lower level of energy investment and a lower level of gas exports. This combination would result in the industry's losing $3.3 billion in economic rents, the federal government $3 billion, and the governments of the producing provinces $5 billion.

The impact of the trade shocks on key energy variables is contained in Table 4.3 for the years 1990 and 1995. The increase in the volume of natural gas exports by 200 bcf per year in Case 1 amounts to a 37 percent increase over the base-case volume in 1995. The relative impact is smaller in earlier years because the base volume of gas exports declines after 1990. The boost in gas export demand drives up production by 5 percent, and spurs exploration effort. There is virtually no cross-effect on the oil sector, except via a small change in the oil (and gas) price, lowered by an appreciation of the Canadian exchange rate.

Table 4.2
Present Value of Economic Rents Under Various Trade Scenarios
(billions end-1985 dollars)

	(1)	(2)	(3)	(4)	(5)	(6)
year	total rent	oil & gas industry	Cdn. users	(waste)	federal govt	provincial govts
1985	351.8	12.1	78.5	35.5	39.8	196.2
base case (oil price=$20 US)						
1995	407.2	15.9	71.3	39.4	44.0	250.4
shock 1: increase in gas exports of 200 bcf per year						
1995	411.4	17.5	71.1	39.4	45.0	252.1
shock 2: oil price decline to $15 US						
1995	359.7	-7.0	66.2	38.4	36.1	238.9
shock 3: no Prebuild gas pipeline						
1995	395.2	12.6	71.0	39.3	41.0	245.4

Notes: All rent calculations are based on an assumed real discount rate of 7 percent.The
1985 rents, which are the same in the fist two cases, are also reported in end-1985
dollars. The economic rents to producers are based on the wellhead revenues, less
all taxes and royalties, operating costs, land payments, economic depreciation, and
an after-tax charge on unamortized capital. Economic rents to domestic energy
users are the compensated consumer surpluses accruing between domestic and
world prices. Rents to provincial governments include income taxes and royalties
from conventional oil, natural gas, and synthetic oil, equity interest in Syncrude,
and land payments. Negative elements include various incentives and royalty abate-
ments, and a real tax opportunity cost of about 1 percent of invested capital. Rents
to the federal government include income and other taxes on the oil and gas industry
and energy consumers, less a real tax opportunity cost of about 2 percent of invested
capital. Total economic rents to the resource (Column 1) are the sum of producer
and consumer surpluses. Column 1 is the sum of Columns 2, 3, 5 and 6, and the
net economic rents captured by U.S. purchasers of Canadian natural gas. Column
4 is the present value of the increased consumption caused by pricing domestic
energy below world prices, net of consumer surpluses.

The decline in world oil price of $5 U.S. per barrel in Case 2 is suf-
ficiently large that by 1995 domestic oil and natural gas prices have fallen
by 25 and 22 percent respectively. This leads to relatively large increases
in oil demand (12 percent), gas demand (17 percent), and oil imports
(56 percent). On the other hand, oil and gas discoveries are significantly
reduced—by 38 percent and 23 percent, respectively. The increase in
demand for gas leads to an increase in production; however, by the
1990s, oil production is lower than in the base case because the limited
reserves are depleted more quickly.

If the Prebuild pipeline did not exist, then energy investment and
natural gas exports would have been lower than in the base case. This

Table 4.3
Energy Variables Under Various Trade Scenarios, 1990 and 1995

variable	base case 1990 (level)	shock 1 1990 %(S-C)/C	shock 2 1990 %(S-C)/C	shock 3 1990 %(S-C)/C
Canadian Oil Price	$32.75/bbl	-.5%	-23.7%	.4%
Canadian Gas Price	$5.16/Mcf	-.5%	-21.5%	.5%
Oil Demand	1460.0 Mb/d	-.1%	7.1%	-.2%
Oil Imports	322.9 Mb/d	-.2%	41.7%	-1.9%
Oil Production	1277.0 Mb/d	-.0%	-2.4%	.3%
Oil Discoveries	190.7 MMb	-.3%	-33.4%	.1%
Gas Demand	2.634 tcf	.1%	11.6%	-.2%
Gas Exports	1.484 tcf	13.5%	0%	-20.3%
Gas Production	11.3 bcf/d	4.9%	7.4%	-7.5%
Gas Discoveries	4.135 tcf	3.8%	-25.2%	-4.3%

variable	base case 1995 (level)	shock 1 1995 %(S-C)/C	shock 2 1995 %(S-C)/C	shock 3 1995 %(S-C)/C
Canadian Oil Price	$41.19/bbl	-1.6%	-24.8%	-.2%
Canadian Gas Price	$6.58/Mcf	-1.6%	-22.3%	-.3%
Oil Demand	1525.9 Mb/d	-.3%	12.1%	-1.1%
Oil Imports	503.8 Mb/d	-.7%	55.8%	-4.2%
Oil Production	981.4 Mb/d	-.1%	-9.8%	.5%
Oil Discoveries	181.9 MMb	-.3%	-38.0%	1.5%
Gas Demand	3.315 tcf	.1%	17.3%	-.8%
Gas Exports	.534 tcf	37.4%	0%	-86.3%
Gas Production	10.5 bcf/d	5.2%	14.9%	-12.7%
Gas Discoveries	3.990 tcf	2.4%	-23.4%	-7.2%

Notes: —%(SC)C is the percentage change in the shock solution relative to the control (base case) solution;
    —Shock 1 is an increase in gas exports to the US of 200 bcf per year;
    —Shock 2 is a reduction in the OPEC oil price to $15 US;
    —Shock 3 is a presumption that the Prebuild gas pipeline was not constructed;
    —bbl represents barrel;
    —Mcf (tcf) represent thousand (trillion) cubic feet;
    —mb/d represents thousand of barrels per day;
    —MMb represents millions of barrels;
    —bcf/d represents billion cubic feet per day.

scenario also accounts for the loss in planned investment and expected incremental exports associated with the Prebuild over the 1986 to 1995 period. The impact on the natural gas industry is opposite in direction but larger in magnitude to that experienced in Case 1 with the increase in gas exports. However, the fact that energy investment is directly affected in this case, leads to a more pronounced downturn in macroeconomic activity—and this leads to a decline in overall energy demand, and hence to a decline in oil and gas demand. The very small changes in oil and gas prices are also determined by a macroeconomic response: The mark-up equations, which are a component of energy user prices, are directly affected by changes in the overall price index.

Macroeconomic Results

A selection of macroeconomic variables representing aggregate output, consumption, investment, trade, employment, wages, prices, interest rate, exchange rate, balance of payments, and government finance is available from the author. These data represent the solution values for the base case, and the solution values for the energy trade shocks relative to the base case.

Macroeconomic Impact of an Increase in Gas Exports. The first shock entails an increase in natural gas exports of 200 bcf per annum, hence energy exports (XE) increase. This stimulates investment in the energy sector (IE). These effects provide a mild stimulus to aggregate output (UGNP) of up to .4 billion 1971 $ (.2 percent), and consequently to investment (INE) and consumption (C). Initially, a small drop in real energy prices leads to very small increases in energy demand (E) and energy imports (ME). This situation reverses in 1990.

Lower inflation (PGNP), initiated by the drop in energy prices (PE), is reflected in a lower export price index (PXNE); consequently, Canada's cost competitiveness in international trade improves, and exports (XNE) increase. But imports (MNE) also increase due to the rise in Canadian activity and the drop in import price index (PMNE)—the latter caused by the appreciation in the exchange rate (PFX). Overall, both the balance of trade in energy (BOTE) and the current account of the balance of payments (BOT) increase, and the foreign exchange rate (PFX) appreciates slightly.

Unemployment is virtually unchanged: it declines very slightly from 1986 to 1988 due to the drop in real wages, and thereafter increases slightly as real wages remain essentially unchanged, and the labor force grows. More gas exports and energy investment, and the more buoyant economy generally, cause an improvement to government finances (GBALE and GBAL).

Macroeconomic Impact of Decline in the World Oil Price. In Case 2 the decline in the world oil price of 5 $U.S./bbl leads to a decrease in the energy price index (PE) of about 14 percent, and an increase in industrial profitability and consequently in output (UGNP) of up to 7.3 billion 1971 $ (3.5 percent). Investment (INE), consumption (C), and employment also increase. Energy prices affect other price variables: Inflation (PGNP) declines by between 1 and 3 percent, and nominal wages decline initially by up to 1.4 percent. Higher output leads to a decline in unemployment (RNU), despite that fact that real wages have increased. Investment in the energy sector (IE) decreases, but this is more than offset by the increase in nonenergy investment (INE). Lower energy prices are beneficial to the energy-using sector, and this dominates the negative impact on the energy-producing sector.

The energy trade balance (BOTE) declines because Canada is a net exporter of energy, and because the sharply higher energy demand (E) leads to an increase in energy (oil) imports (ME). However, the non-energy trade balance improves, with the real value of exports (XNE) increasing by more than imports (MNE). The current account of the balance of payments (BOT) increases by up to $2.8 billion; hence the exchange rate appreciates.

Net provincial and federal government revenue from energy (GBALE) decreases by over $4 billion, but it is overwhelmed by the higher tax revenue from the buoyant state of the economy, and the government account balance (GBAL) increases.

Shock 3: Macroeconomic Impact of No Prebuild Pipeline. The results of Scenario 3 are similar to those of Scenario 1, except that most of the variables have the opposite sign. Like the first scenario, this case involves a change in the level of gas exports; however, in contrast, this case also involves direct changes to energy investment. Gas exports and investment associated with the Prebuild are lumpy (see Table 4.1), which tends to cause cycles in macroeconomic variables.

Energy exports (XE) and energy investment (IE) decrease, hence so does aggregate output (UGNP) by up to about 1 percent. The lumpy nature of the pipeline investment causes a cyclical response in output (UGNP) and nonenergy investment (INE), which temporarily increase between 1984 and 1986. Rising real energy prices and lower output leads to a small fall in energy demand (E), and a somewhat larger fall in energy imports (ME).

Changes in inflation (PGNP), which is lower for most of the period, lead directly to changes in other nonenergy price (like PXNE) and wage (WNE) variables. A fall in the export price (PXNE) relative to the import price (PMNE) leads to an increase in exports (XNE). The lower level of Canadian activity and rise in the import price (PMNE) for most of the period drives down imports (MNE). The balance of trade in energy (BOTE) is lower throughout the period, but the current account of the balance of payments (BOT) is sometimes higher and sometimes lower than the base case, depending upon the relative strength of changes in the energy and nonenergy sectors.

The very slight drop in real wages is not enough to offset the fact that changes in output are mirrored as changes in the unemployment rate, but with the opposite sign. The downturn in energy investment and

Figure 4.1
Real Gross National Product (UGNP) - Canada

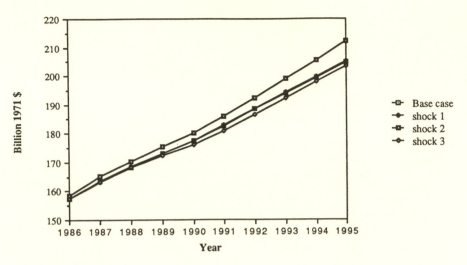

gas exports leads to a lower level of government revenue from the energy sector (GBALE); and when this is combined with the generally lower level of economic activity, government financial balances (GBAL) decline.

SUMMARY

Oil and gas deregulation in Canada has opened the door to relatively free trade with the U.S.–Canadian companies have been quick to seize the opportunity to expand in the spot market for gas and oil. Surprisingly, for the first half of 1987, Canada was the largest supplier of oil and oil products to the U.S. (Oilweek [1987]).

For ease of comparing the impact of the three scenarios relative to the base case, the values for real gross national product, inflation, unemployment, energy investment, and the balance of trade are graphically illustrated in Figures 4.1 to 4.5.

Figure 4.1 shows that the drop in world oil prices (Shock 2) has the largest effect on real gross national product (UGNP), such that by 1995 it has increased by 3.5 percent; the drop in gas exports and energy investment associated with the Prebuild (Shock 3) has a smaller but still significant impact on UGNP; and the increase in gas exports (Shock 1) has only a very small impact.

As expected, the largest change in the price index (PGNP) also occurs when oil prices decline: it declines between 1 and 3 percent. For the other cases, inflation does not change much.

Figure 4.2
Price Index for GNP (PGNP) - Canada

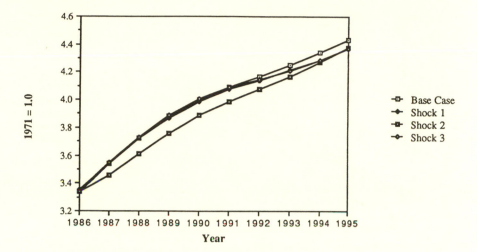

Figure 4.3
Unemployment Rate (RNU) - Canada

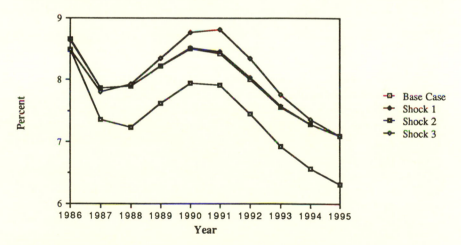

The changes in the unemployment rate (RNU), shown in Figure 4.3, are consistent with previous observations, in that by far the largest effect is from the decline in oil prices; the Prebuild shock is smaller; and the gas export shock is virtually indistinguishable from the base case. To get a perspective on the magnitudes, the unemployment rate in the oil price case falls by 0.78 percent points, which is equivalent to the creation of about 200,000 jobs.

Figure 4.4
Energy Investment (IE) - Canada

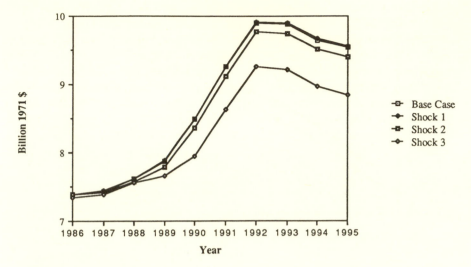

Figure 4.5
Balance of Trade (BOT) - Canada

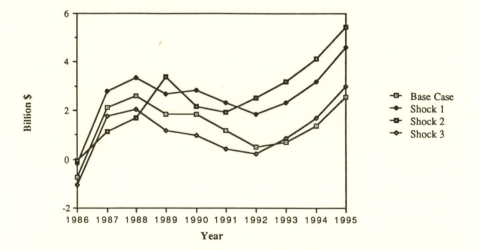

The Prebuild scenario causes the largest decline in energy investment (IE): it amounts to a decline of over 7 percent (700 million 1971$) in 1995.

Figure 4.5 shows that the increase in gas exports (Shock 1) has a large positive impact on the balance of trade (BOT)—in the order of $1-2 billion per year. As noted earlier in this discussion, the initial impact of the drop in world oil prices (Shock 2) is to lower the trade balance, but by

1989 the higher net exports from the nonenergy sector lead to a higher trade balance.

The three energy trade-related scenarios considered in this chapter have a differing but significant impact on the energy sector and macroeconomy of Canada. The impact on aggregate output of the economy is not too great, except with the world oil price shock, and in that case some of the increase in activity is due to the feedback from the exogenous boost given to the economies of the U.S. and the rest of the world. The macro impact of the Prebuild simulation, although cyclical, is also relatively large. However, this result would be lower if some of the export volumes shipped through the Prebuild could have been shipped through existing pipelines.

NOTES

1. Some of Canada's pricing and taxation policies during the last decade were the result of concern about rent capture, dividend flows and/or retained earnings by petroleum firms which had a high degree of foreign ownership. This concern was very evident in the National Energy Program of 1980 (see McRae [1982]). However, this discussion will not address such issues.

2. The distribution of oil and gas reserves is such that about 85 percent of oil and gas reserves are in Alberta. The remaining oil is mostly in Saskatchewan, and the remaining gas is mostly in British Columbia. Virtually all the reserves are in western Canada.

3. The most severe downturn in Canada export volumes of oil to the U.S. occurred because the U.S. initially included Canada in the mandatory import quota program in 1959. However, this did not last long, and by 1960 Canada (along with Mexico) had been granted an "overland exemption." While this exemption did not give Canadian oil unlimited access to the U.S., it did allow our export volumes to slowly increase throughout the 1960s.

4. Exports of heavy oil were not affected because Canadian refineries were unable to utilize them.

5. The policy document which enunciates deregulation is called the Western Accord. See Helliwell et al. [1986] for details.

6. In 1979 this requirement was revised to a "25A1 test," and a deliverability test was included.

7. Industry submissions to hearings before the NEB in the mid-1970s painted a picture of looming shortages for gas. This was in startling contrast to the optimistic reserve outlook at the end of the 1960s. A great deal of attention was focused on the arctic frontier gas as a source for southern Canada, and possibly the U.S. export market (Helliwell [1979]). Lengthy hearings ensued before the NEB in the 1970s regarding supply/demand and the feasibility of a pipeline to bring the arctic gas to market. The NEB decision in favor of the Alaska Highway pipeline (NEB [1977]) led to the Prebuild pipeline.

8. The OPEC oil price is crucial to the energy-using and energy-producing

components of the economy. It is assumed that the OPEC price will be $20 US/ bbl in 1987, and thereafter will grow at the US inflation rate plus 2 percent.

9. Although the impact of an increase in oil exports would be similar to that for gas exports, it was not considered because Canadian oil reserves are probably not sufficient to sustain a significant increase in exports over the next decade.

10. The inner function in the nested production function has energy tied to capital in a vintage framework. The demand for energy is dependent on the desired energy-capital ratio for new investment and for some of the vintage capital which MACE assumes can be retrofitted.

11. To get a complete picture of the impact on rents, the simulation should cover a time horizon long enough to completely exhaust the reserves.

REFERENCES

Canada, Department of Energy, Mines and Resources (1976), *An Energy Strategy for Canada: Policies for Self-Reliance*, Ottawa: Supply and Services Canada.

Debanne, J. G. (1974), "Oil and Canadian Policy", in E. Erickson and L. Waverman (eds.), *The Energy Question: North America, Vol. 2*, University of Toronto Press, pp. 125–147.

Helliwell, J. F. (1979), "Canadian Energy Policy", *Annual Review of Energy*, pp. 175–229.

Helliwell, J. F., M. E. MacGregor, R. N. McRae, and A. Plourde (1986), "The Western Accord and Lower World Oil Prices", *Canadian Public Policy*, June 1986, pp. 341–355.

Helliwell, J. F., M. E. MacGregor, R. N. McRae, A. Plourde, and A. Chung (1987), "Supply-Oriented Macroeconomics: the MACE Model of Canada", *Economic Modelling*, 4:3, July 1987, pp. 318–340.

McRae, R. N. (1982), "A Major Shift in Canada's Energy Policy: the Policies and Impact of the National Energy Program", *The Journal of Energy and Development*, VII, No. 2, pp. 173–198.

National Energy Board (1977), *Reasons for Decision: Northern Pipelines*, Ottawa: Supply and Services Canada.

National Energy Board (1986), *Canadian Energy: Supply and Demand 1985–2005*, Ottawa: Supply and Services Canada.

Oilweek (1987), Volume 83, No. 31, Calgary: Maclean Hunter.

United States, Cabinet Task Force on Oil Import Control (1970), *The Oil Import Question: A Report on the Relationship of Oil Imports to the National Security*, Washington: U.S. Government Printing Office.

Waverman, L. (1974), "The Reluctant Bride: Canadian and American Energy Relations", in E. Erickson and L. Waverman (eds.), *The Energy Question: North America, Vol. 2*, University of Toronto Press, pp. 216–237.

5
The Canada–U.S. Resource Connection: Minerals, Forest Products, Fish, and Water

Frank W. Millerd

This chapter reviews the Canada-United States relationship with respect to four natural resources: minerals, forest products, fish, and water. Other chapters in this volume examine energy and agricultural resources. The role of the Canadian resource industries is emphasized. These industries usually dominate Canada-U.S. resource trade and, consequently, are the resource industries most often discussed.

Some indication of the relative importance of natural resource industries in the two countries is given by value-added data. In 1984 the lumber and wood product, paper product, and primary metal industries were 2.7 percent of American Gross National Product and 6.5 percent of Canadian G.N.P. However, the absolute size of this group of resource industries in the United States was over six times the size in Canada. The Canadian natural resource sector is absolutely smaller but of greater relative importance.

Another indication of the importance of resource industries to Canada is the role they play in balancing Canada's trade. In 1986 the Canadian trade deficit of $29 billion in manufactured goods was offset by surpluses in each of agricultural, fishery, forest, mineral, and energy products. Forest products, with a $15 billion trade surplus, offset over half of this deficit.

Each of the resource sectors of minerals, forest products, fish, and water are reviewed. Comments are made on how each of these sectors contributes to the economic relationship between the two countries, particularly with respect to trade. In keeping with the Canadian perspective of this chapter, the difficulties and opportunities facing the Canadian resource industries are emphasized.

MINERALS

The most striking aspect of the trade in minerals is the dependence of the United States on Canadian sources of supply and the corresponding dependence of Canadian producers on the American market. In 1984, 26.6 percent of metal ores and scrap, 13.1 percent of iron and steel, and 31.4 percent of nonferrous metals, by value, were imported from Canada. As Table 5.1 indicates, for the 7 leading minerals and metals produced in Canada, between 13 and 35 percent of production is exported to the United States. Canada does export minerals and metals to other nations, but has an overwhelming and growing dependence on the American market. For example, between 1970 and 1986 the proportion of Canadian exports of nonferrous metals sent to the U.S. rose from 43.9% to 82.9%. A similar concentration of trade is evident for U.S. exports where, in 1984, 24.6 per cent, by value, went to Canada. However, the value of U.S. imports from Canada is about two and one-half times the value of Canadian imports from the U.S.

Perhaps more than any other resource industry discussed here, minerals are subject to world-wide supply and demand pressures, due to the widely diversified sources of supply and demand for minerals, the development of efficient bulk transport methods, and the lack of a high degree of concentration in the production of most minerals. Neither Canada nor the United States produces a relatively large percentage of any mineral and thus has little direct influence on price. World consumption of many minerals is derived from cyclical demands for capital goods and consumer durables with the result that many minerals also tend to have cyclical demands.

Many mineral markets have suffered from an overexpansion of world capacity. In the 1960s and early 1970s expectations of rapid economic growth, high resource prices, and fears of resource exhaustion led to plans to rapidly expand productive capacity on a world scale. These plans were largely fulfilled, facilitated by a favorable international banking climate and aid programs to less developed countries. However, the recession of the early 1980s and the effects of higher prices in increasing exploration and discovery and in lowering demand meant that prices, starting in 1980, declined sharply relative to the general price level. Additionally, despite lower prices, third-world countries tended to maintain production at high levels in order to generate foreign exchange earnings. The result of these forces is that, until recently, the relative price of industrial materials has remained weak, despite growth in the world economy and a depreciation of the U.S. dollar. Only in recent months are mineral prices recovering.

The conditions affecting individual minerals vary widely. Two of the more important minerals will be reviewed here, iron ore and potash.

Table 5.1

Percentage of Production Exported to U.S.A., Leading Minerals and Metals (All Stages of Production)

	76	77	78	79	80	81	82	83	84	Jan-Sep 85
Iron Ore	49.30	54.98	44.74	43.27	39.23	49.51	35.94	33.41	39.90	23.03
Copper: Ore and Alloys	19.13	14.19	10.61	12.36	18.13	12.49	18.41	13.01	27.81	13.40
Nickel: Ore and Alloys	42.81	52.17	85.35	60.30	37.84	43.66	58.90	42.50	31.50	22.93
Zinc: Ore, Matte & Refined	32.92	24.81	36.86	34.40	38.54	37.35	29.21	34.70	33.83	28.94
Asbestos: Unmanufactured	36.23	33.81	37.94	33.83	24.52	29.39	27.07	21.31	22.14	14.38
Radioactive[1] Uranium	X	20.86	26.54	56.38	31.05	19.20	41.42	3.80	32.80	X
Iron & Steel	18.09	22.55	22.81	22.73	22.24	28.05	21.18	22.60	26.13	35.41

Each illustrates features of the economic relationship. Iron ore mining is heavily dependent on export, particularly U.S., markets; 80 percent of production is exported, and 55 percent of exports are to the U.S. The Canadian iron ore mining industry was largely developed to replace the depleted Mesabi deposits, which supported the U.S. steel industry until shortly after World War II. The industry has a high degree of U.S. ownership, reflecting the backward integration of steel producers to gain a secure source of supply. According to an industry study, prices tend to be based on production costs plus normal profits rather than normal market forces, reflecting the degree of vertical integration.[1] A further consequence of this integration is that there is likely to be little bilateral conflict over this trade. Both Canadian producers and American consumers are protected from competition.

Potash, in contrast, is a mineral about which there has been considerable conflict. Saskatchewan, Canada's major producer, commenced production in 1962 and rapidly expanded output. By 1970 Saskatchewan produced 60 percent of North American potash and prices had declined from $40 per ton in 1965 to $20 per ton in 1969. U.S. protectionist measures were threatened. Saskatchewan, in response to this threat and because of declining prices introduced prorationing to control prices. Potash prices then increased.

American policy responded, but in a contradictory manner. The protectionist threat disappeared in 1974 when dumping charges against Canadian potash imports were dropped. However, in 1976, several Canadian producers and government officials were named as unindicated co-conspirators when six U.S. producers and two of their subsidiaries were charged with price fixing on the U.S. potash market. The Canadian connection recognized the role of the Saskatchewan prorationing scheme in raising prices. Again, in recent months, U.S. import duties are threatened and Saskatchewan has taken measures to limit its production.

This is perhaps an extreme illustration of the dilemma faced by many Canadian resource producers. If they compete vigorously, lowering prices and increasing market share, they may face U.S. protectionist measures. If they limit production, raising prices, there is a threat of antitrust pressure on U.S. subsidiaries operating in Canada or on Canadian government officials. Canadian producers clearly must keep in mind possible responses of U.S. competitors and policymakers, forcing them not to appear to be too aggressive nor appearing to collude. These are the problems that Canada will inevitably face in dealing with a single large trading partner. Canadian producers cannot be governed by market supply and demand alone when their price and output decisions are potentially subject to U.S. policy intervention.[2]

One factor that some have felt may have implications for Canadian producers of minerals is the concern for mineral security. Haglund, however, does not see how security concerns will translate into major direct gains for Canada as a mineral supplier. The Canadian mineral industry will do well when demand is strong, but slack demands are not likely to be offset by any purchases from the United States for security reasons. Canada is not particularly well endowed with those minerals most likely to be of strategic importance. Canada has no chromium, manganese, or vanadium production, and production of cobalt and the platinum-group metals cannot be expanded significantly unless nickel and copper production is expanded. With uranium, Saskatchewan producers have made a major penetration of the U.S. market. American producers have not successfully competed with the high-grade, low-cost Saskatchewan product, leading to an intensification of pressures for import restrictions.

The Canadian mineral industry's outlook is guardedly optimistic. The industry is strong in terms of resource base, management, labor force, and technology. However, as mentioned above, the recent expansion in economic activity has not been accompanied by the usual rise in mineral prices until very recently, due to worldwide oversupply. The industry is also burdened with high debt-equity ratios, due to its expansion in the early 1980s. This investment, however, improved productivity and reduced costs so that the industry has been able to maintain output although many producers are in a difficult financial position.[3]

One of the positive results of the slump in mineral prices is the postponement, maybe the elimination, of the threat of deep seabed mining. This source may have posed significant competition for Canadian land-based nickel and cobalt producers.

Nevertheless, future market conditions are predicted to be more competitive for Canada. Foreign producers will continue to expand and additional foreign sources will probably be found; Canadian output will grow slowly. Demand, although governed primarily by the overall rate of economic growth, will also be affected by trends in various industries. Products, such as automobiles, are being reduced in size and weight, slowing the demand for metals. Substitutions of nonmetals, such as plastics, for metals will also reduce demand.

FOREST PRODUCTS

Perhaps more than any other natural resource industry, the forest products industry may be viewed as a continental industry. There is both a complementarity of trade and a high degree of similarity between many aspects of the two industries. A high proportion of many forest products are exported from Canada and a high proportion of these exports go to the United States. Detailed data are available in Tables 5.2 and 5.3. For the major exports of lumber, pulp, and newsprint, most of

Table 5.2
Canadian Exports of Forest Products, 1984

Product	% of Production Exported	% of Exports to U.S.
Pulpwood	1.0	68.7
Pulpwood chips	8.7	43.1
Lumber - softwood	77.7	78.3
Lumber - hardwood	21.0	43.8
Shingles and shakes	n.a.	98.2
Veneer	45.7	82.9
Plywood	21.4	20.7
Wood pulp and similar	34.4	52.8
Newsprint	89.9	84.8
Other paper for printing	41.3	97.3
Paperboard	22.2	40.1
Other paper	41.8	73.6

Sources:

Statistics Canada, Canadian Forestry Statistics. Ottawa: Minister of
        Supply and Services, various years.

_____, Exports - Merchandise Trade. Ottawa: Minister of
        Supply and Services, various years.

_____, Sawmills, Planing Mills, and Shingle Mills.   Ottawa:
        Minister of Supply and Services, various years.

Canadian Pulp and Paper Association, 1985 Reference Tables, December 1985.

Canada's exports of these products go to the United States and nearly
all of American imports of these products are from Canada. In 1984, for
example, 95.1 percent of U.S. imports of wood pulp were from Canada
and 78.6 of paper and paperboard imports were from Canada.
Canada's imports of forest products are relatively minor compared to
exports, but ninety percent do come from the U.S.

Much of the Canadian industry developed in response to U.S. demands. Since early in the twentieth century, it has been quite clear that
American forests were incapable of satisfying the increasing American

Table 5.3
Canadian Exports by Destination

| | Wood and Paper Products | | | | | |
	UNITED STATES	UNITED KINGDOM	OTHER EFC %	JAPAN	OTHER COUNTRIES	TOTAL
1970	69.30	8.92	6.49	5.31	9.98	100
1976	67.25	7.94	11.02	5.21	8.57	100
1977	71.24	6.83	9.13	4.50	8.31	100
1978	73.73	5.59	8.09	4.97	7.61	100
1979	69.79	6.23	9.41	7.26	7.30	100
1980	63.11	6.77	12.09	8.11	9.92	100
1981	65.57	6.76	10.26	6.46	10.95	100
1982	67.70	6.63	8.99	6.72	9.96	100
1983	72.53	5.39	7.24	5.72	9.12	100
1984	74.18	4.70	6.96	5.66	8.49	100
1985	77.71	3.47	5.48	5.70	7.64	100
1986	74.58	4.10	6.90	6.77	7.65	100

NOTE: Percentages may not add to 100 due to rounding.

Source: Statistics Canada, Exports Merchandise Trade. Ottawa: Minister of Supply and Services (various years).

demand for forest products. Consequently certain forest products, particularly pulp, newsprint, and lumber were allowed duty-free access to the U.S. market. This has resulted in a three-sector development of the Canadian forest industry. The first sector is pulp, newsprint, and lumber which are produced in large quantities and mostly exported; sector two is plywood, waferboard, and some paper grades, produced for both internal and external markets and less heavily exported; sector three is millwork, cabinets, and converted paper products, produced mainly for a protected Canadian market.

Canada also exports significant amounts to European countries and Japan but these markets are becoming increasingly competitive. Western Europe is the largest net importer of forest products in the world, but Canada has experienced difficulties in this market in recent years as

Scandinavian producers have become more competitive due to gaining tariff-free access to the European Economic Community market, currency devaluations, resource upgrading, greater integration of pulp and paper production, and increasing industrial efficiency. According to some observers, Japan and other southeast Asian countries offer the best export prospects for Canada over the medium term. However, southern hemisphere countries such as New Zealand, Chile, and Brazil will become increasingly important suppliers to Europe and Japan in the 1990s.[4]

As might be expected, the forest industries in the United States and Canada are very similar. Similar products are produced with similar technologies and are sold in the same markets. Large portions of the two industries depend on similar resources, but there are important differences. Canada is more dependent on original natural stands and has no counterpart to the southern U.S. pine forests.

Segments of the industry are also linked through common ownership and control. This often takes the form of vertical integration, particularly in the pulp and paper industry, and results from the efforts of American firms to gain a secure supply of newsprint or pulp for their operations elsewhere.

Despite its success in exporting, the Canadian industry is not without problems. Canadian production has been competitive in world markets because of the relatively low wood costs which offset higher costs in other areas. In the past the supply of wood has come from using areas of virgin or first-growth timber. Inevitably the cost of this source of supply will increase as logging moves to more remote and inaccessible areas, and stands of lower density and quality are used. Forest management expenditures will increase as the lower-quality stands are used. Wood supply costs, to some extent, have been offset by technological changes, which have increased the utilization of wood and residues and have allowed the use of new species and sizes, but according to forest economists there is a limit to cost-reducing changes of this kind. A further constraint on timber supply arises from increasing demands for forest land for recreational and preservational purposes and from environmental restrictions on harvesting practices.

Supply restrictions are, to a large extent, a Canadian problem. Wood costs in the U.S. South and the Scandinavian countries are not expected to increase as rapidly as in Canada. Technological changes have favored the growth of the industry, particularly the pulp and paper segment, in these areas. Canada's comparative advantage derived from high-quality but slow-growing softwood is being eroded by technological advances in processing and shifts in product mix.[5]

Canada also suffers a competitive disadvantage because of the age of some of its processing plants. In newsprint production small scale and older machines are a higher percentage of capacity than in the United

States and Scandinavia. Older machines are also usually less energy efficient. In contrast, most Canadian market pulp mills and many lumber mills are modern and efficient. However those paper and paper product mills producing primarily for the domestic Canadian market lack economies of scale.

The forestry industry has recently been at the centre of trade disputes between Canada and the United States. In May 1986, President Reagan announced the imposition of a 35-percent duty on cedar shakes and shingles from British Columbia. It may be that this action was necessary in order to keep the Canada-U.S. free trade initiative going. Also in May 1986, U.S. softwood lumber interests asked U.S. authorities to rule on a charge of injury because of alleged subsidies to the Canadian industry. When it appeared that a tariff would be imposed, the Canadian government agreed to impose a 15-percent export tax. Later this tax was to be replaced by the equivalent increase in stumpage (or timber royalty) charges by each lumber-exporting province.

Despite the potential job loss due to an export tax of this type, there may be benefits to Canada. The export tax revenue and the stumpage fees are direct gains to provincial treasuries. British Columbia, the major lumber-producing province, is estimated to receive $350 million dollars a year. This will, no doubt, highlight the value of these resources to the citizens of these provinces. Most provincial stumpage fees are set as a residual after deducting estimated harvesting costs from estimated revenues. This procedure obviously encourages inefficient practices by allowing costs to be "passed through" by lower stumpage fees. Inadvertently the public is receiving a higher return or rent from these resources which have traditionally been under valued.

Despite a successful industry in the short term, long-term problems remain. They have been recognized and addressed by private producers and government authorities. Wansbrough, in examining the long-term prospects for the industry, feels that Canada's resource supply difficulties can be solved with a better use of existing resources. Better management of existing forests is required along with more prompt and effective regeneration of areas logged or burnt off. He also suggests increasing employment in the forest industry through improved processing technologies and upgrading the product mix to higher value-added products.

FISHERIES

The Canadian and American fishing industries are linked in several ways. There are trade linkages, both countries being highly dependent on the other for imports and exports. There is also a political linkage. Both are interested in limiting foreign exploitation of their waters and thus both were among the first countries to proclaim 200-mile fishing limits. Thirdly, the resource itself links the two countries. Many species of fish are not obliging enough to respect borders. As they migrate in common oceans and lakes, they are subject to exploitation by both countries.

The Canadian industry is highly dependent on exports. Well over three-quarters of Canadian seafish production, by value, is exported. The dependence on exports has been increasing in recent years, rising from 63 percent of output in 1976 to 76 percent in 1985. The United States has always taken the majority of exports, with Japan a distant second. The heavy dependence on the U.S. market is not true for all fishery products. Fresh or frozen fish fillets and blocks are almost exclusively produced for the American market whereas canned fish products have a relatively low dependence on the U.S. market.

Canada is also heavily dependent on the U.S. for the fish products it imports. In 1984 slightly over 55 percent of Canadian imports of fishery products came from the United States. However, Americans are not as relatively dependent on imports from Canada. In 1984 only 21.4 percent, by value, of fish imports came from Canada. The major species exported by Canada to the United States is cod, while the major species imported by Canada from the United States are shrimp and prawns. Canada exports those species that it has in abundance, but which are also often found in American waters, and imports those species not widely found in Canadian waters. The result is that Canadian exports sometimes compete with U.S.-produced fishery products, but Canadian imports generally do not compete directly with Canadian fish products.

As might be expected there is a significant regional dimension to the Canadian fishing industry. Three provinces, Newfoundland, Nova Scotia, and British Columbia each produce approximately one-quarter of the value of output. Approximately 70 percent of the value of output is from the Atlantic provinces of Newfoundland, Nova Scotia, New Brunswick, and Prince Edward Island. However, the type of output varies considerably between these regions. Fresh and frozen fillets and blocks are almost exclusively from the Atlantic provinces while the Pacific province of British Columbia produces the majority of the fresh and frozen whole or dressed fish, and the majority of canned fish. The regional variations in type of output are reflected in the varying regional dependencies on the U.S. market. The Atlantic provinces produce almost 80 percent of fishery exports to the United States. Only 7 percent of exports come from British Columbia. Not only are the Atlantic provinces heavily dependent on U.S. exports but their provincial economies are heavily dependent on the fishing industry. The most heavily dependent is Newfoundland, where 41.89 percent of manufacturing value added is from the fishing industry.

Table 5.4
Percentage of Canadian Seafish Production Exported

Type	1976	1977	1978	1979	1980	1981	1982	1983	1984	1985
Fish Whole or Dressed, Fresh or Frozen	66.66	90.35	92.52	92.73	93.92	(1)	98.83	(1)	88.25	89.83
Fish Fillets & Blocks, Fresh or Frozen	67.21	68.77	77.56	77.70	81.96	86.16	86.94	85.10	89.48	83.76
Fish Preserved, Not Canned	79.56	76.83	84.64	85.76	83.45	(1)	89.42	99.93	96.49	90.11
Fish Canned	38.18	40.03	47.66	49.51	47.44	49.75	50.86	47.07	54.39	31.70
Other Fishery Foods and Feeds	63.97	74.01	69.27	70.96	80.66	75.47	73.94	74.95	77.96	83.58
TOTAL	62.51	68.73	73.53	73.43	77.56	79.96	80.03	79.35	81.18	76.10

NOTES

(1) Value exceeds 100%, probably due to export sales out of inventory.

(2) Includes canned shellfish.

Sources:

Canada Department of Fisheries and Oceans, Canadian Fisheries Annual Statistical Review. Ottawa: Minister of Supply and Services, various years.

, Canadian Fisheries Statistical Highlights. Ottawa: Minister of Supply and Services, 1985 and 1986.

Table 5.5
Fishery Exports to U.S.A. as a Percentage of Total Exports

Type	1976	1977	1978	1979	1980	1981	1982	1983	1984	1985
Fish Whole or Dressed, Fresh or Frozen	45.17	37.35	28.82	28.64	34.11	35.05	30.43	43.45	43.19	45.90
Fish Fillets & Blocks, Fresh or Frozen	90.65	83.07	83.15	88.14	83.07	87.85	88.12	92.18	92.04	92.31
Fish Preserved, Not Canned	46.49	42.12	44.98	43.85	32.02	29.36	26.92	35.91	36.97	34.82
Fish Canned	14.31	9.70	10.22	10.18	13.74	10.84	14.15	15.13	11.90	13.81
Other Fishery Foods and Feeds	56.54	47.18	41.53	36.38	52.11	55.82	56.56	60.02	58.61	57.87
TOTAL	59.61	51.94	48.53	48.87	52.70	53.73	54.75	61.37	60.69	61.06

Sources:

Canada Department of Fisheries and Oceans, Canadian Fisheries Annual Statistical Review. Ottawa: Minister of Supply and Services, various years.

_____, Canadian Fisheries Statistical Highlights. Ottawa: Minister of Supply and Services, 1985 and 1986.

For many years the Atlantic provinces have had the lowest average incomes in Canada. Consequently, the fishing industry, as one of the major employers in the region, has often been the focus of economic development programs. Government assistance has been provided both to improve the viability of the industry and to support those engaged in it. In recent years particular emphasis has been placed on establishing a viable offshore fishery. New England fishermen, perhaps quite naturally, have viewed many of these programs as subsidies giving Canadian products an advantage in American markets. Various representations have been made for countervailing duties.

This issue, of course, is a point of controversy between the United States and Canada. No doubt Canadians would be more accepting of countervailing duties if they were properly applied and if they actually did what they were planned to do. Rugman and Anderson have examined the application of American trade law in the Atlantic groundfish case of 1985–86. They state that the U.S. International Trade Commission did not apply proper economic-based tests when it voted material injury as a result of subsidized Canadian fish imports. Also, no causal linkage between the alleged subsidies and injury to American producers was found.

Stephen Crutchfield, an American economist, has examined the impact of U.S. countervailing import duties on foreign groundfish. Through a computer simulation of an economic model of the fishing industry, he found that import duties would result in substantial increases in the wholesale and consumer prices of fillets, sticks, and portions, due to a reduction in the quantity imported. However, there was little evidence that any sizable benefits would accrue to the domestic fishing industry. The reason appears to be that domestic and foreign fish are commodities that do not compete directly in the same market. Most U.S.-caught fish are sold fresh to be consumed at home while foreign-caught fish are sold frozen to institutions and restaurants. However, as Crutchfield notes, it is not clear that higher U.S. ex-vessel prices would be of long-run benefit to U.S. fishermen. Most fisheries are regulated by quotas and thus have an inelastic supply. Higher prices would not result in increased landings, but could result in increased effort and inputs to the industry and thus the same average returns to individual fishermen.

One area of fisheries policy in which there is agreement between Canada and the United States is the necessity of the 200-mile limit. Both Canada and the United States, as a result of a substantial depletion of their offshore stocks, had a mutual interest in excluding foreign fleets from North American waters. Only the American tuna fleet is an offshore fleet, likely to be excluded from fishing areas if the 200-mile limit became widely adopted. It is fairly clear that Canada and the United States gained more in terms of net economic benefits by excluding foreign fishing fleets from their local waters than they lost by having to give up access to corresponding fishing areas. After some initial difficulties the 200-mile limit has stimulated modernization, expansion, and economies of scale in the Canadian fishing industry.

Canada perhaps had another reason for extending its economic zone and thereby encouraging others to do the same. As a major nickel producer, Canada did not wish to see the harvesting of manganese and mineral nodules from the ocean floor. In 1977 when 200-mile limits were introduced deep-sea mining appeared as a real possibility, although lower mineral prices have since made this form of mineral recovery uneconomical.

While the extension of fishing limits to 200 miles by Canada and the United States in 1977 may have removed some problems in each country's fishing industry, certain other problems were created. Offshore boundary extensions created a number of overlapping boundary claims on the Pacific, Atlantic, and Arctic coasts. The Atlantic maritime boundary was resolved by the International Court of Justice in 1984. The Pacific maritime boundary between British Columbia and Alaska is still a controversial matter. A further source of friction was the traditional access to the stocks of the other country which the fishermen of each country had enjoyed. After long negotiations Atlantic and Pacific coast agreements have been reached.

With proper biological, economic, and political management, the fishing industries in both countries can face a better future. Extended fisheries jurisdictions with 200-mile limits allow for improvements in conservation measures. Canada and the United States can manage their stocks without interference from foreign fishing fleets and depleted fish populations should be rebuilt. Several minor boundary issues remain although Canada's dispute with France may take time to resolve. A continuing problem in both countries is that of excess fishing capacity. Common property fisheries always attract too many inputs, resulting in low average fishermen's incomes and regulatory pressures. Canada and the United States are experimenting with ways to limit the number of fishermen in various fisheries. Only when this problem is resolved will there be economically sound fishing industries in both countries.

WATER

There is no doubt that Canada is generously endowed with fresh water, although not as well endowed as is sometimes reported. On an annual average basis, Canada's rivers discharge almost 9 percent of the world's renewable supply of fresh water. Since Canada comprises about 7 percent of the world's land mass, the 9-percent figure is not surprising and is roughly proportional to the area of Canada. Figures of 25 percent or more of the world's supply of fresh water in Canada are sometimes seen. These are proportions of the world's total surface water, including lakes, and make no distinction between renewable and non-renewable supplies of water. An important characteristic of Canada's water resources is that two-thirds of the flow is from south to north, with the result that the southern prairies form the major region in Canada without a generous water supply.

Excluding Alaska, the United States' renewable water supply is about 60 percent of Canada's renewable supply. This fact, plus indications of water shortages in certain regions of the United States, has spawned a number of plans for the transfer of water from Canada to the United States. The project most seriously discussed now is the Grand Canal scheme. It would involve the construction of a 160-kilometer-long dike across James Bay, which would then become a freshwater lake. Water would be pumped upstream to the Ottawa River and diverted to the Great Lakes via Georgian Bay. Pumps and canals would then transfer the water to five Canadian provinces and 25 American states. Costs are estimated to be 100 billion dollars.

Projects of this type have been opposed by both Canadians and Americans, particularly those Americans living adjacent to the Great Lakes. They argue that the water supply in the Great Lakes basin and for Canada as a whole is limited and should be reserved for future use in these areas and that expected future climate changes will probably result in a demand for irrigation water in the northern part of the continent. Opponents also point out that there has been no strong demand for Canadian water from water-short U.S. states. If this demand did materialize it would quickly be dissipated by the prices that would have to be charged for transferred water and alternative demand-reducing and/ or supply-increasing measures would quickly be examined.

There cannot be said to be any current Canadian policy on interbasin water transfers or exports. There is no framework to discuss or conduct water exports. All provinces, with the exception of Quebec, are opposed—an important consideration because the provinces have jurisdiction over water allocation and use. The most serious consideration of water exports was done by the Inquiry on Federal Water Policy, which reported in September 1985. The report of the Inquiry, while expressing skepticism about the viability of exports, suggested that water exporting would have to be a political decision.

A research study done for the Inquiry did examine the issue of water exports in considerable detail.[6] A water export policy, based on benefit-cost analyses of specific water export schemes, was proposed. A project would be approved if the greatest net benefits from the use of that particular water resource were achieved. The benefits to Canada must exceed the costs imposed on Canada when both costs and benefits are measured properly. Economic, environmental, and social benefits and costs should be included. All those affected by the project should be considered and, where appropriate, individual compensation should be provided. A further recommendation is that the project be flexible and reversible. There must be a way of altering the agreement, with the appropriate notice and compensation. If future conditions change, it must be possible to stop or reverse exports.

Any large-scale water exports will require a new framework agreement between Canada and the United States. Current international agreements are not adequate to deal with large-scale water transfers. The International Joint Commission, created by the Boundary Waters Treaty of 1909, has not exercised jurisdiction over existing small-scale diversions and does not have the mandate to consider water needs distant from the U.S.-Canada border or the diversion of water from a new lake, such as that created in James Bay. For large-scale diversions, new international agreements and institutions would be necessary to regulate the amounts of water to be transferred, water usage, and lake levels and riverflows.

It may be a surprise to Americans that water exports are a controversial issue in Canada. Other than a few engineering proposals, there has been no consistent pressure from U.S. sources for water. The debate appears to be mainly between Canadians. One group sees water sales as a way of starting a new export industry and the economic development associated with such an industry. Those opposed argue that no price can be put on water and that the water is now or will be needed in Canada. There is also an emotional and cultural dimension to water, not associated with other resources, even those that are not renewable. Early development in Canada was defined by its waterways. The lakes, streams, and rivers of Canada continue to have tremendous social, economic, environmental, aesthetic, and recreational significance.

CONCLUSIONS

Each of the resources discussed here illustrates unique features of the Canada-United States economic relationship. In all cases there is trade or, in the case of water, the potential for trade: trade where Canada is the dominant exporter and the United States the dominant importer. Many Canadian resources are exploited almost exclusively for American markets. Some of the resources are extensively traded throughout the world and thus are subject to world market conditions; some are dominated by U.S. and Canadian market conditions. The two countries' resource industries also interact in other ways. Technology, production methods, and processing patterns are similar; many are jointly owned; and the uncaptured resources themselves sometimes interact. The result is industries dependent on both countries and subject to the policies of both.

NOTES

1. This analysis of the industry is from W. Labys, *Market Structure, Bargaining Power, and Resource Price Information*. Lexington, Mass.: Heath, 1980 as reported by Anderson.
2. This discussion is based on Anderson.
3. See Brewer for a complete analysis of the industry.
4. See Wansbrough for a discussion of Canada's trade in forest products.
5. A thorough review of these concerns is presented by Pearce.
6. See Scott et al.

REFERENCES

√Anderson, F. J. *Natural Resources in Canada*. Toronto: Methuen, 1985.

Bank of Canada. "Commodity Prices and Canada's Resource Sector." *Bank of Canada Review* (September), 19–32, 1986.

Bourke, I. J. "Barriers to Trade in Forest Product." *Resources* (Summer, 1986) Wash. D.C.: Resources for the Future.

√Brewer, Keith. "Sectoral Views of the Longer Term: Mining" in *Long-Term Economic Prospects for Canada: A Symposium*. Toronto: University of Toronto Press, 1986.

Clarkson, Stephen. *Canada and the Reagan Challenge*. Toronto: James Lorimer, 1985.

Cruchfield, S. R. "The Impact of Groundfish Imports on the United States Fishing Industry: An Empirical Analysis." *Can. J. Agr. Econ.*, July 1985, 33(2), p. 195–207.

√Doran, Charles F. *Forgotten Partnership U.S.-Canada Relations Today*. Baltimore: Johns Hopkins, 1984.

√Haglund, David. "The West's Dependence on Imported Strategic Materials: Implications for Canada" in *Canada and International Trade*. Montreal: The Institute for Research on Public Policy, 1985.

√Haglund, D. G. "Protectionism and National Security: The Case of Canadian Uranium Exports to the United States," *Canadian Public Policy* XII, No. 3 (September), 459–472, 1986.

Maly, Stephen, and Lauren McKinsey. "Political Economy of Lumber Trade." *American Review of Canadian Studies*, No. 3, p. 265–78, Autumn '86.

Nord, Douglas C. "Managing a Regional Resource: The Case of the Great Lakes." *American Review of Canadian Studies*, XVI, 4, pp. 443–454.

Pearse, Peter H. "Forest Products" in Carl E. Beigie and Alfred O. Hero Jr. (eds.) *Natural Resources in U.S.-Canadian Relations* (Volume. II) Boulder, Col: Westview Press, 1980.

Rugman, Alan M., and Andrew Anderson. "A Fishy Business: The Abuse of American Trade Law in the Atlantic Groundfish Case of 1985–1986."

Halifax: Dalhousie University Centre for International Business Studies, 1987.

Scott, Anthony, John Olynyk, and Steven Renzetti. *The Design of Water-Export Policy in Canada's Resource Industries*, Vol. 14 of research studies prepared for the Royal Commission on the Economic Union and Development Prospects for Canada. Toronto: University of Toronto Press, 1986.

√Shaffner, Richard. "The Resource Sectors of the United States and Canada: An Overview" in Carl E. Beigie and Alfred O. Hero Jr. (eds.) *Natural Resources in U.S.-Canadian Relations* (Vol. I) Boulder, Col.: Westview Press, 1980.

Shaffner, Richard et al. "Other Replenishable Resources" in Carl E. Beigie and Alfred O. Hero Jr. (eds.) *Natural Resources in U.S.-Canadian Relations* (Vol. II) Boulder, Col.: Westview Press, 1980.

Wansbrough, John. "Sectoral Views of the Longer Term: Forest Products" in *Long-Term Economic Prospects for Canada: A Symposium*. Toronto: University of Toronto Press, 1986.

Weller, Geoffrey R. "Canadian Water Exports: A Controversy in the Making." *American Review of Canadian Studies* (XVI(4), pp. 425–441.

Whalley, John. *Canada's Resource Industries*. Toronto: University of Toronto Press, 1986.

Wilkinson, B. W. "Some Comments on Canada-U.S. Free Trade" in Whalley, John (ed.) *Canada-United States Free Trade*. Toronto: University of Toronto Press and the Royal Commission on the Economic Union and Development Prospects for Canada, 1985.

Wilkinson, Bruce W. "Canada's Resource Industries: A Survey" in *Canada's Resource Industries*, Vol. 14 of research studies prepared for the Royal Commission on the Economic Union and Development Prospects for Canada. Toronto: University of Toronto Press, 1986.

PART III
SOME PERSPECTIVES ON TRADE

6
Canada and the U.S. Balance of Payments Position
Donald J. Daly

One of the major international economic issues in the world economy since 1983 is the size of the United States deficit on merchandise trade and current account in its balance of payments. Thus far, this current account deficit has been largely financed by a capital inflow into the United States that is changing the U.S. balance of international indebtedness from that of a creditor country to that of the world's largest debtor country. This in turn implies that the United States will soon be paying a large and growing amount of investment income outpayments on this enlarged international indebtedness to other countries. This evolving pattern of developments on the U.S. current and capital account has contributed to a drop in the exchange value of the U.S. dollar of almost 40 per cent from its high point in early 1985 to a low in May 1987.[1] A drop of this magnitude in the key major world currency in less than 30 months, during a period of peacetime growth, is probably without precedent in international financial developments since 1800.

Such a large annual deficit on current account, the related large capital inflow, and rapidly growing U.S. international indebtedness do not appear to be sustainable or desirable from the point of view of either the U.S. or the world economy. The reasons for these developments and the possible policy solutions are still under active debate in universities, in government agencies, in international agencies, and at meetings between governments. It can make a major difference to the future of the world economy whether these problems can be resolved in a healthy and growing interdependent world economy, or whether they are resolved by new and intensified trade wars about tariff and nontariff barriers to trade, restrictive domestic policies, and the disintegration of the system of complete convertibility between major currencies that has existed for several decades.

This chapter does not intend to explore all the ramifications of this range of topics, many of which can only be explained and resolved in a multilateral context. The discussion will concentrate on the Canada-U.S. dimensions of the broader issue. This is important when each country is the largest trading partner of the other. Four topics will be dealt with, namely: the importance of two-way trade and investment between the two countries; a brief review of U.S. balance-of-payments developments; Canadian developments on uemployment and balance of payments; and the risks to Canada of potentially adverse U.S. economic and policy developments.

Many of these developments and themes are well recognized in Canada, and this material is aimed more at U.S. audiences. These Canadian developments and viewpoints are only a small part of U.S. interests and concerns, so they are usually less widely known to a U.S. audience. This is understandable when merchandise exports by the U.S. to Canada, for example, are only 1 percent of the U.S. GNP, compared to Canadian exports to the U.S. of 24 percent of Canadian GDP.

EXTENT OF U.S. AND CANADIAN TRADE AND INVESTMENT INTERCONNECTIONS

U.S. merchandise exports to Canada are larger than to any other country. Such exports to a country with a population approaching 26 million are thus greater than to such other countries as Japan, the United Kingdom, West Germany, France, and Italy, each with a much larger population than Canada. However, exports to Canada are still only about one-fifth of U.S. merchandise exports, reflecting the diversified nature of U.S. trade to a large number of countries.

Trade with the United States is much more important to Canada than is Canadian trade to the U.S. Merchandise exports to the United States are 24 percent of Canadian GDP, compared to only 1 percent for the comparable figure for the United States. This reflects the fact that exports to the United States are now approaching 80 percent of total Canadian exports. Exports to the U.S. have been tending upwards historically as a share of total Canadian exports, when it was only 35 percent in the opening decades of the present century.

Although Canada is the most important country to the U.S. for both exports and imports, trade with Canada plays nothing like the dominant role for the U.S. that U.S. trade has for Canada. Total U.S. merchandise exports are only 5 percent of U.S. GDP, and the Canadian share of U.S. exports is 20 percent of total exports. Both percentages are well below

Table 6.1
Selected Trade and Economic Statistics, United States and Canada, 1986

Item	United States	Canada
GNP/GDP (billion)	4,235.0	509.9
Total merchandise exports (billion)	217.3	120.6
Total exports of goods and services (billion)	372.8	138.3
Percent merchandise exports to GNP/GDP	5.1	23.7
Percent exports of goods and services to GNP/GDP	8.8	27.1
Merchandise exports to partner (billions)	45.3	93.8
Exports to partner as percent of total exports	20.8	77.8
Exports to partner as percent of GNP/GDP	1.1	23.7

Sources: U.S. Department of Commerce, <u>Business Conditions Digest</u>, July 1987, pp. 80 and 93; U.S. Department of Commerce, <u>1986 U.S. Foreign Trade Highlights</u> (Washington, D.C., March 1987, Tables A-1 and A-198 and Bank of Canada <u>Review</u>, Aug. 1987, pp. S116, S117 and S140.

the comparable ones for Canada. These comparisons can be seen in Table 6.1.

There are also some important structural differences in the composition of the trade and balance of payments flows between the two countries. For one thing, the composition of Canadian exports to the United States continues to be heavily oriented towards the export of primary and partially processed materials. Examples would include crude petroleum, natural gas, lumber and sawmill products, pulp and paper, metals and minerals, etc. Exports of manufactured products have become a larger share of Canadian exports in recent decades, but the share of manufactured exports in total exports is still well below that in the other high income countries. Exports of motor vehicles and parts form a striking example of increased exports, reflecting the increased two-way flow of trade made possible by the increased specialization associated with the Canada-U.S. Automotive Agreement of 1965. U.S. exports to Canadaof manufactured products continue to be far larger than the flow in the other direction. Thus Canada has a large net bilateral surplus on primary products to finance the large net bilateral deficit on manufactured products.

This difference in the composition of trade reflects Canada's traditional comparative advantage in primary products, when Canada has substantially larger resources of arable land and mineral resources in relation to total employment than other countries. Canada also had a higher level of output per employee in mining than the U.S. when the last comparison was made.[2] On the other hand, Canada continues to be a higher cost producer of a range of manufactured products, reflecting a continuing degree of greater product diversity at the plant level and the frequent slower adoption of new technology in Canada than in the U.S.[3] There are, however, some promising and important developments in small Canadian-owned manufacturing firms, which have specialized in some product niches that had been overlooked by the larger companies in the other countries and which are exporting a larger share of their domestic production than had taken place historically.

There are also significant differences in the two-way flow of trade in services and investment income between the two countries. Canada makes significant payments of interest and dividends on past portfolio borrowings and direct investment from abroad, and Canadian payments have exceeded receipts by a three-to-one margin in recent years. The Canadian net deficit on investment income has averaged more than $10 billion a year during the 1980s. Payments for other services (such as travel) also tend to exceed receipts for Canada. The Canadian nonmerchandise trade deficit with the United States has been about $11 billion for the last six years and this is expected to persist. Thus, Canada tends to run a surplus on merchandise trade to finance the continuing large net deficit on nonmerchandise transactions with the United States.

Although this discussion emphasizes the Canada-U.S. position, it should be noted that Canada has also traditionally had a deficit on its nonmerchandise trade balance with the rest of the world. An unusual development in 1985 and 1986 has been the emergence of a deficit on merchandise trade with the rest of the world as well. In 1986, Canada had a deficit on current account of $15.1 billion with the rest of the world. If this continues, Canada may have to retain its recent current account surpluses with the U.S. to cover its deficits in its non-U.S. transactions.

With this background of some of the key structural aspects of the trade and balance of payments interrelations between the two countries, we can now turn to the major recent U.S. balance of payments developments, the reasons for these developments, and what would be involved in a shift to a more sustainable pattern for the future.

THE RECENT U.S. BALANCE OF PAYMENTS DEFICIT

International monetary history of the earlier postwar period was dominated by a series of current account surpluses for the United States and extensive long-term capital outflows. For part of the period, the size of the capital outflows was larger than the current account surpluses, and there were periods of concern about such capital outflows and the extent to which the U.S. share of world exports was edging down from the earlier postwar highs.

Developments in the United States during the 1980s have departed significantly from the experience of the three previous decades. U.S. merchandise exports (adjusted) were about the same size in current dollars in the first half of 1987 as they had been in the first half of 1981 before the 1981–82 recession. In volume, U.S. exports are lower than six years ago. Merchandise imports, on the other hand, are up about 60 percent, leading to a merchandise trade deficit in the second quarter of 1987 in excess of $150 billion at an annual rate, and a balance of payments deficit of about $135 billion in early 1987. This is an unprecedented development for the highest real-income country in the world that has had an important role in world trade and finance for decades.

Such a massive change on current account has naturally been reflected in a major change in international capital flows. In a matter of a few years, the United States has shifted from the world's largest creditor country (with large private lending and direct foreign investment and large government loans and grants) to the world's largest debtor country.[4] Over a four-year period (1983 to 1987) the United States will have borrowed about $500 billion dollars from other countries. This will begin to be reflected in growing future interest payments abroad in the years ahead.

This brief review of the factual aspects of recent U.S. developments raises three related questions, namely: what are the major reasons for these new developments; are these developments sustainable and/or desirable; and what are the more promising remedies for both public policy and corporate strategies in the commodity-producing industries?

These three questions will be dealt with in turn.

Macro Influences On Capital Flows And Trade

Most U.S. economists have related the U.S. balance of payments deficit to the large federal budget deficit. The U.S. federal deficit has been running in excess of $100 billion since early 1982 and averaged about $200 billion a year during 1985 and 1986. These budget deficits were about 3.5 percent of GNP in 1985 and 1986. This is a fairly important shift from the 1960s and 1970s, as can be seen in Table 6.2. Gross do-

Table 6.2
Relationship Between Foreign Investment and National Saving and Investment, United States, Selected Years, 1966–1986, Percent of GNP

Year	Net foreign investment	= Gross private saving	+ Government budget surplus	- Gross domestic investment
1966	0.5	17.0	-0.2	16.7
1973	0.6	18.0	+0.6	17.6
1979	0.1	17.8	+0.5	18.1
1984	-2.4	15.1	-2.8	17.6
1985	-3.1	14.1	-3.5	17.0
1986	-3.4	12.6	-3.5	15.8

Source: Richard N. Cooper, "Dealing with the Trade Deficit in a Floating Rate System," Brookings Papers on Economic Activity, 1: 1986, p. 198 with 1984 to 1986 updated from Economic Report of the President, (Washington, D. C.:   U.S. Government Printing Office, 1987), p. 276 and U.S. Department of Commerce, Business Conditions Digest, (Washington, D.C.:   U.S. Government Printing Office, Aug. 1986), pp. 80-83.

mestic investment has been about the same percentage of GNP during 1984 to 1986 as in earlier decades, although investment in nonresidential structures in 1982 dollars has been declining for the last two years. Gross private saving has been a lower share of GNP in recent years, pulled down by a personal saving rate of less than 4 percent of personal disposable income, well below the peak rate of 10 percent reached in several quarters during the mid-1970s.

The net effect of a large federal government deficit and a lower rate of personal and gross private saving has been that the U.S. has not been able to finance the demand for funds from domestic sources. An important part of the U.S. domestic financial needs has had to be met by foreign borrowings. High nominal and real interest rates and other favorable developments and prospects in the U.S. have encouraged large foreign private purchases of U.S. government debt and increased investment in real estate, hotels, and stocks, and direct investment in manufacturing has also developed.

The large international capital flow into the United States has been a new initiating force, and the current account in the balance of payments has had to adjust to this capital inflow.[5]

Although the U.S. federal deficit has often been given priority in the analysis of the capital inflow and balance-of-payments deficit, those developments needed to be put into the context of the rest of a complete discussion of domestic savings and private investment. Canada, for example, has had an even larger federal and general government deficit as a percent of GDP, but with no comparable developments in the current and capital account of the balance of payments (as we will see later). Furthermore, Japan had budget deficits in the earlier 1980s that were even larger in relation to GNP than in the U.S., and yet Japan has had large surpluses on current account in recent years. Differences in domestic saving rates are an essential part of the whole story and the budget deficits can be an incomplete explanation if discussed in isolation.

The Sustainability Of Recent U.S. Balance Of Payments Developments

Such a large capital inflow into the U.S. and the associated current account deficit can only be sustained by rapid increases in U.S. international indebtedness. The extent of such international borrowing will involve larger U.S. payments of interest abroad in the future, which would contribute to further increases in the size of the current account balance of payments deficit from that influence alone.

The direction and size of capital flows among the industrialized countries has been so large and unstable that a continuation of such large inflows cannot be taken for granted. A decline in the extent of inflow could lead to a renewal of the decline in the international value of the U.S. dollar, that had been underway from early 1985 through the spring of 1987.

It is difficult for the United States to justify the highest real income country in the world as being the largest net importer of capital internationally to finance its federal budget deficit for any extended period. The 1986 current account deficit is equivalent to borrowing abroad at a rate of about $1,250 per person employed or $580 per person in the U.S. per year.

U.S. Public Policy Implications

Most U.S. observers would say that high priority should be given to reducing the size of the federal budget deficit, which would permit a reduction in the size of the international capital inflow.

Such a reduction in the deficit could only come from developments through three possible routes: an increase in private sector growth that would generate additional revenues from the existing tax structure, cuts in federal expenditures, or increases in tax rates. It is not appropriate as an economist from a neighboring country to either predict or recommend how these issues might be resolved. Gram-Rudman proposes declining deficit targets, but interest on the growing public debt, defense expenditures, and other commitments preclude sharp reductions in expenditures. Either defence or social security will have to be cut substantially, or some form of tax increase will be necessary. However, tax increases are difficult as President Reagan moves into the later stages of his term in office. These macro issues have been receiving a lot of discussion both domestically in the United States and internationally, but I would rather discuss the microeconomic implications of reducing the size of the current account deficit.

The current account deficit of a little less than $120 billion in the second quarter of 1987 is about 2.7 percent of GNP. A reduction of that to essentially zero would eliminate the need to import capital, but would still not permit the U.S. to return to the position of a net lender to the rest of the world, a function it had been filling for the last four decades. The minimum step of a current account balance would involve a net shift of real resources from use within the U.S. to making those resources available for use abroad. The major part of such a shift would have to take place in merchandise trade, as exports and imports of merchandise trade amount to about two-thirds of the total balance-of-payments receipts and payments. The service portion of the balance of payments (business services, international investment income, unilateral transfers, and other goods and services) are either small or relatively sluggish and not too likely to contribute in any major way to the large change in net receipts that would be required.

A major part of any adjustment on the trade side would have to come from a net increase in manufactured products and to some extent other goods-producing industries. A reduction of $120 billion in the current account deficit would amount to a net shift of about 9 percent of output in the commodity-producing industries (manufacturing, mining, agriculture and forestry). This is a fairly large shift to try to attain. Other countries are also wanting to get or maintain markets for manufactured products. The exchange rate declines for the European countries have brought their costs down from the extremely high levels of, say, 1980. At that time, unit labor costs in the U.K. were twice the U.S. level, Sweden was two-thirds higher, and France, Germany, and Italy were about one-third above the U.S.[6] Such cost differences permitted the U.S. to maintain export markets during those years, but subsequent exchange rate changes have brought unit labor costs in those countries down closer to U.S. levels again, and in some cases below.

There has also been an increase in competition from Japan and the newly industrialized countries in the Pacific Rim (South Korea, Taiwan, Hong Kong, and Singapore). Competition from these countries is no longer limited to the traditional exports of clothing, textiles, and shoes, but has moved into high-technology products, using best-practice techniques adopted from the industrialized countries at lower wage rates. The U.S. problems with international competition in manufacturing on a selective basis are coming more from the NICs rather than the other industrialized countries.[7] These developments have been reflected in the fall in the U.S. share of the world market for manufactured products. By 1985, U.S. imports of manufactured products had increased to more than 30 percent of gross national product in manufacturing, a significantly higher level than historically. U.S. firms are going to have to make adjustments to check this erosion of market share both domestically and internationally.

The option of a resort to increased tariff and non-tarrif barriers to trade, anti-dumping cases, etc., by the largest world-market and highest-income country would be a major setback to the freeing up of world trade and payments that has been going on for the last four decades. That would be an alternative way to reduce the current account deficit by curtailing imports. In discussing these issues Richard Cooper comments:

> The weak U.S. export markets and stiff competition from imports that resulted in the large trade deficit have been squeezing employment and profits in American manufacturing and mining. Firms and labor unions are seeking protectionist relief. . . . Such legislation would hurt U.S. consumers. . . .[8]

However, the problems that the U.S. may have in the competitive position of selected areas of manufacturing and in its overall balance of payments on current account do not arise primarily from its economic relations with Canada. We will now shift from a discussion of the United States situation to that in Canada, setting out the developments in a comparable manner.

DOMESTIC AND BALANCE OF PAYMENTS DEVELOPMENTS IN CANADA

Economic developments in the United States and Canada are very similar most of the time, primarily because we are essentially a common North American economy, with similar economic forces affecting growth trends, business cycles, and price and interest rate developments. One should expect similar developments, and if there are differences, it is the task of the economist to explain why any differences take place.

One similarity between Canada and the United States is the development of a large federal deficit. This can be seen as a percent of GDP in Table 6.3, with a presentation similar to that for the U.S. in Table 6.2 earlier. The government deficit has been even relatively larger as a share

Table 6.3

Relationship Between Foreign Investment and National Saving and Investment, Canada, Selected Years 1966–1986, Percent of GDP

Year	Net foreign investment	− Gross private saving	+ Government budget surplus	− Gross domestic investment
1966	+0.5	24.2	+5.1	22.4
1973	+0.4	24.1	+4.5	20.8
1979	+0.4	22.9	+0.9	22.1
1984	+1.9	25.4	-5.6	20.0
1985	0.0	25.1	-6.3	21.8
1986	+2.1	22.4	-4.5	20.7

Sources: Statistics Canada, CANSIM tapes for earlier years, last three years from *National income and expenditure accounts, first quarter 1987*, (Ottawa: Supply and Services), pp. 2, 3, 10 and 11. The residual error of estimate in the accounts has been omitted.

of GDP over the last three years in Canada than in the United States. However, Canada has had a small overall balance of payments surplus on a national accounts basis (net foreign investment in Tables 6.2 and 6.3).[9] On a macro basis, gross private saving has been sufficiently larger in Canada than in the United States that it has been possible to finance a higher ratio of gross domestic investment (based primarily on high residential investment), a larger budget deficit, and still permit net foreign investment abroad. Over the three years 1984 to 1986, gross private saving has run almost 25 percent of GDP in Canada compared to only 14 percent in the United States, a significant contrast.

There is one important difference in the economic performance of the two countries during the 1980s. Canada had a more severe recession in 1981–82, and the early stages of the recovery were slower and less complete. The rate of unemployment in Canada moved well above the U.S. in 1982 and has stayed consistently higher since. By the second quarter of 1987, the U.S. unemployment rate was down to 6.2 percent of the labor force, below the rate in the first half of 1981 before the last recession started. On the other hand, the rate in Canada was still 9.1 percent, almost three percentage points higher than in the U.S. in the same period, and still about two percentage points above the prerecession level. This is the largest difference in unemployment that has been present this far along in any business cycle expansion of the postwar period.

How does this relate to the Canadian balance of payments? This turns on how different the balance of payments would be if the Canadian unemployment rate was three percentage points lower and down to the U.S. rate. This would make a much larger difference to real GDP than just three percentage points more, as productivity would be higher, as would hours worked and more marginal workers would reenter the labor force. GDP in real terms would have been about 7.5 percent higher in the second quarter of 1987 if the Canadian unemployment rate had been about the same as then prevailed in the U.S.[10] Such a higher level of real GDP would have been reflected in a higher level of imports of goods and services. Imports might be expected to be about 10 percent higher for a 7.5 percent higher level of real GDP.[11] This would imply an additional level of imports of goods and services of about $13 billion, which would make a significant increase to the current account deficit of $8.0 billion in the second quarter of 1987. The balance of payments deficit consistent with an unemployment rate of 6.2 percent would have increased to about 4 percent of Canadian GNP, substantially higher than the similar ratio for the United States of 2.7 percent.

In other words, the Canadian balance of payments deficit would have been even larger in relation to GNP than in the United States, except that the higher unemployment rate and the larger gap between actual and potential output depress the level of imports of goods and services and mask the potential balance-of-payments vulnerability that currently prevails in Canada.

Why would Canada have a balance of payments deficit so much larger than that of the United States at a comparable rate of unemployment? The key reason is that the international competitive problems of Canadian manufacturing are much more widespread by industry than in the U.S. The U.S. is really only vulnerable in selected products and industries to competition from selected countries, but that is still creating concern and pressure from management and labor in the industries affected for more protectionist policies. Canada, on the other hand, has lower levels of output per hour in manufacturing than in the U.S. and higher levels of labor costs per unit.[12] In 1986, unit labor costs in Canadian manufacturing were about 20 percent above the U.S.[13]

By the mid-1980s, Canadian imports of manufactured products were about 80 percent of gross domestic product in manufacturing, while the comparable percentage for the United States was about 30 percent.[14] In both countries imports were high for certain products (such as television sets) and quite low for others (such as bakery products, beer, and cigarettes).

The pressure from high costs and low productivity in manufacturing has contributed to the low rates of return on investment in Canadian manufacturing (especially when depreciation, inventories, and the relevant balance-sheet items are valued at replacement costs). These developments have contributed to the plant closures and corporate bankruptcies in manufacturing (with effects on some related non-manufacturing industries), and the persistence of a higher unemployment rate in Canada than in the United States.[15]

This points up a serious policy dilemma for Canada. This structural problem in manufacturing has long historical roots, but there are some signs that it is beginning to be addressed by adjustments in corporate strategy in the private sector, especially in some of the smaller Canadian-owned establishments and in some of the Canadian subsidiaries.[16] However, as long as these problems persist, Canada has a conflict between the policy objectives of a lower unemployment rate or a larger deficit on current account in its balance of payments. During the mid-1980s Canada has been operating with a smaller deficit on current account as a percent of GDP than in the U.S., but at the domestic cost of a higher rate of unemployment than in the United States.

Although Canada always has such potential conflicts between domestic objectives (such as a low rate of unemployment) and its international objectives (such as a viable balance of payments), the conflicts are intensified by its persisting structural problems in manufacturing. A reduction in these problem areas would permit Canada to attain both *lower* unemployment and a *smaller* balance-of-payments deficit by reducing the size of the net deficit in manufactured products and increasing real incomes per person employed.

Even if Canada begins to accelerate these longer-term domestic adjustments within Canada, it could still be extremely vulnerable to some of the policy choices and dilemmas that the United States is currently facing that we explored in the first part of this chapter. We will now return to this topic.

ALTERNATIVE SCENARIOS FOR UNITED STATES DEVELOPMENTS

What everyone in the United States and in the rest of the world would like to see would be a renewed rate of economic growth closer to that of the 1950 to 1973 period than the experience since 1973, a reduction in the size of the federal budget deficit, and a reduction in the rate of international capital inflow into the United States and thus a decline in the size of the balance of payments deficit on current account. Such a pattern of developments would be sustainable and desirable from both U.S. and international perspectives.

In an uncertain world, such a desirable pattern of future developments cannot be taken as a certainty. There are four areas of future uncertainty that could make difficult or even prevent these favorable developments. We will briefly summarize them as some of these points have been developed in previous pages.

Persisting Large U.S. Budget Deficits

The U.S. budget deficits could continue to be large in relation to GNP, even if dropping somewhat from the high of 1986. Difficulty in reducing expenditures (including conflicting views on expenditure priorities between the president, the Senate, and House of Representatives little likelihood of tax increases before the second year of a new administration, and persisting slow economic growth would ensure the persistence of high budget deficits.

Persisting Balance of Payments Deficits

The previous analysis would suggest that the balance of payments deficits will likely continue for the balance of the 1980s, in spite of the extent of exchange rate adjustments that have taken place. It is recognized that the full effects of the adjustments to exchange rate changes can be long in coming, and the short-term effects can even be different in direction than the longer-term effects. This makes forecasting these developments an uncertain task, but the persistence of current account deficits should be recognized as a continuing problem until there is clearer evidence that this problem is being resolved.

How Much Longer Will the Expansion Last?

The low point in the 1981–82 recession was November 1982 in the United States and December 1982 in Canada. The expansion will thus have lasted five years by late 1987, more than twice as long as the average expansion in the last 130 years. Only two expansions (1938–45 and 1961–69) would have been longer. The evidence suggests that recessions have been milder since World War II than historically, and this tendency is expected to persist due to the changed institutional environment.[17] Even if the next recession is mild, it would lead to a further increase in the size of the U.S. budget deficit, as the drops in income and the tax base would lead to an automatic increase in the size of the budget deficit. (It would also lead to a drop in investment in inventory investment and other business investment and business savings as well. However, all these other effects cannot be explored here in a brief discussion.)

Potential Vulnerabilities in the U.S. Financial System

One of the new developments in the U.S. financial system has been the increase in international lending abroad, both to foreign governments and private financial and nonfinancial institutions. The size of some of this lending to third-world countries has been a source of concern, especially with the drop in oil and some commodity prices, and adverse exchange rate developments. These developments are affecting the profit and balance-sheet positions of some of the major financial institutions. Some of the institutions more heavily involved in international lending have been some of the major institutions in the leading financial centers (New York and California, for example). Although deposit insurance provides a degree of protection on deposits, losses on foreign loans could affect the U.S. domestic financial system if a number of other problems took place at the same time, such as a domestic recession that led to declines in profits and increased bankruptcies in companies in the commodity-producing industries.

A combination of a few of these potentially adverse developments could lead to further increases in protectionist pressure in the United States, especially when imports have become a larger share of U.S. gross product in manufacturing.

Potential Protectionist Pressures

A combination of a large balance-of-payments deficit, an increase in unemployment, and bankruptcies in U.S. manufacturing could lead to strong pressures on U.S. Congressmen and Senators to introduce tariff and nontariff barriers to trade. Even though these might be primarily directed at the products and countries that are the primary sources of import competition and the U.S. balance of payments deficit, these could have some repercussions on Canada, even though the previous analysis has suggested that Canada is *not* the primary source of the U.S. balance-of-payments problems. There is a long history of nondiscrimination in U.S. international policy, and Canada may not be able to receive special status (except under a successful Canada–U.S. free trade arrangement).

This is not a hypothetical academic possibility as far as Canada is concerned. In commenting on this issue, Richard D. Lipsey and Alan M. Rugman state:

Canadian exporters now face an ever-widening array of U.S. trade restrictions. . . . The unilateral U.S. decision making process reviews government subsidies and other industrial policies in the country that is exporting to the United States, but not U.S. subsidies and policies for its own domestic industry.[18]

A protectionist response to competitive pressures on a selective basis directed at other countries could have devastating effects on Canada when U.S. exports are so key in the Canadian economy, but when Canada is not really the source of the U.S. problems in either its balance of payments or in competition from imports of low-cost manufactured products. Such policies could intensify Canadian problems in the areas of both the balance of payments and the unemployment rate.

These issues can also be put into a broader multilateral perspective. There is a danger that protectionist steps in the United States could lead to a check and reversal of the whole system of reductions in tariffs and nontariff barriers to trade that have been the aim of international negotiations on a range of issues for decades.

It is my hope that the United States and Canada will be able to cope successfully with these problems in a world environment of growth, stability, and continued freeing up of trade and payments both on a Canada-U.S. and a multilateral basis. The possible scenarios from failure are so serious that I hope that they will encourage support for appropriate policies to reduce the risks of going the protectionist route.

However, the pressures for protectionist measures are the greatest since 1930, and a renewed business cycle recession could further intensify such pressures.

NOTES

1. This comparison is based on the weighted-average exchange value of the U.S. dollar against the other G-10 countries plus Switzerland. The 1972–76 global trade of each of the countries is used as weights. See U.S. Department of Commerce, *Business Conditions Digest*, (Washington, D.C., July 1987), p. 105.

2. D. J. Daly, *Canada's Comparative Advantage*. (Ottawa: Economic Council of Canada Discussion Paper No. 135, 1979).

3. D. J. Daly and D. C. MacCharles. *Canadian Manufactured Exports: Constraints and Opportunities*. (Montreal: Institute for Research on Public Policy, 1986) and D. J. Daly, "Technology Transfer and Canada's Competitive Performance," in Robert M. Stern, ed., *Current Issues in Trade and Investment in Service Industries: U.S.-Canadian Perspectives*. (Toronto: Ontario Economic Council, 1985), pp. 304–333.

4. It should be noted that the official statistics value the gold holdings in the foreign exchange reserves at $40.00 an ounce, well below current values of more than $400 an ounce. In addition, foreign direct investment by U.S. corporations is reported at book value historic cost, well below current replacement cost. U.S. foreign assets are thus undervalued compared to foreign liabilities. A. E. Safarian brought this point to my attention.

5. Richard N. Cooper, "Dealing with the Trade Deficit in a Floating Rate System." *Brookings Papers on Economic Activity* 1: 1986, pp. 195–207; Stephen Marris. *Deficits and the Dollar: The World Economy at Risk* (Washington, D.C.:

Institute for International Economics, 1985); Martin S. Feldstein and others have emphasized this interpretation.

6. D. J. Daly and D. C. MacCharles. *Focus on Real Wage Unemployment*. (Vancouver: The Fraser Institute, 1986), p. 70. This appendix describes the concepts and sources used to develop the data for manufacturing for nine major industrialized countries.

7. Bruce Scott and George C. Lodge, eds. *U.S. Competitiveness in the World Economy*. (Boston: Harvard Business School University Press, 1984), especially Chapter Two.

8. Richard N. Cooper, "Dealing with the Trade Deficit in a Floating Rate System," p. 196.

9. The shift from national product to domestic product in the 1986 revision of the national accounts has an important effect on the balance of payments presentation in the accounts. For example, the balance of payments shows a deficit in 1986 of $9.268 billion, while the national accounts shows a surplus of net exports of goods and services of $6.135 for the same year. The difference is the large net investment income payments to nonresidents.

10. This estimate is based on Okun's Law, which relates changes in unemployment and changes the gap between actual and potential unemployment. For a discussion of this applied to Canada see Donald J. Daly, *Managerial Macroeconomics: A Canadian Perspective*, (Homewood, Ill.: Richard D. Irwin, 1988), pp. 80–82.

11. This implied an income elasticity of imports of goods and services to real GDP of about 1.33. For discussion of this see Donald J. Daly, *Managerial Macroeconomics: A Canadian Perspective*, pp. 275–277.

12. D. J. Daly and D. C. MacCharles. *Focus on Real Wage Unemployment*. (Vancouver: The Fraser Institute, 1986), pp. 61–77.

13. This is based on an update of the sources in the study in the previous note, using U.S. Department of Labor *News* (Washington, D.C.: Bureau of Labor Statistics, June 15, 1987), "International Comparisons of Manufacturing Productivity and Labor Cost Trends." This Canadian data for output per hour in manufacturing does not yet incorporate the benchmark revisions.

14. U.S. Department of Commerce. *Survey of Current Business*, July 1987; General Agreement on Tariffs and Trade. *International Trade, 85–86*, pp. 145 and 147; and Statistics Canada, by telephone.

15. For a fuller discussion of the evidence and a discussion of the policy implications, see D. J. Daly and D. C. MacCharles. *Focus on Real Wage Unemployment* (Vancouver: The Fraser Institute, 1986).

16. D. J. Daly and D. C. MacCharles. *Canadian Manufactured Exports: Constraints and Opportunities*, (Montreal: Institute for Research on Public Policy, 1986).

17. Robert J. Gordon, ed., *The American Business Cycle: Continuity and Change*, (Chicago: University of Chicago Press, 1986), introduction by Robert J. Gordon and Chapter 9 by Victor Zarnowitz and Geoffrey H. Moore; Donald J. Daly. *Managerial Macroeconomics: A Canadian Perspective*, (Homewood, Ill.: Richard D. Irwin, 1988), pp. 154–160.

18. C. D. Howe Institute *Commentary*, "A Canadian-U.S. Dispute Settlement Mechanism: Binding or Effective?" No. 15, Sept. 1987.

7
The Canada–U.S. Free Trade Negotiations: An Assessment

Bruce W. Wilkinson

INTRODUCTION

Canada-U.S. negotiations for a bilateral free trade (BFT) arrangement commenced in May 1986. After 16 months, an agreement was reached on October 1987. This chapter will not attempt to assess the agreement in detail. Rather it will focus initially on the background leading up to the commencement of the bargaining, and then concentrate upon events that have transpired and clarifications that have occurred since negotiations began. The implications of these factors for the future of Canada-U.S. and world trade relations, as well as some policies Canada might follow in the future, will also be discussed.

BACKGROUND TO THE NEGOTIATIONS

Economies of Scale

A number of factors working together brought Canada to the point where it was prepared to enter BFT negotiations with the US. The first factor was a variety of studies done in Canada over a decade or so and concerned primarily with manufacturing.[1] These individually concluded that BFT would be a suitable way of enhancing the productivity of Canadian manufacturers through achieving greater economies of scale, encouraging more domestic research and development, and speeding up the adoption of the latest technology by industry. Consumers were expected to benefit from lower prices. (Agriculture, however, was given only limited attention in these studies,[2] and trade in services was virtually ignored.[3])

The Worsening World Situation

The second factor heavily influencing Canada's decision to approach the U.S. for a free-trade pact was the changing world situation. The developing countries were becoming more potent competitors in a wide range of labor-intensive goods; the newly industrialized nations were increasingly able to supply a range of mass-produced products varying from automobiles to TV sets and other electrical and electronic products. New sources of raw materials were being developed in many nations of the world, some of them of a developing status, hungry for the foreign exchange that resource exports could provide, even if such exports had to be subsidized. World economic growth was slowing down and simultaneously, because of the development of new materials technology as well as the downsizing and energy-efficiency trends that had been sparked by OPEC's initial successes, the close tie that had always existed between world growth and Canada's exports of raw and crudely-processed resources was severed. The accelerated pace of technological change; the increased protectionism by many countries, particularly through the use of non-tariff measures and the slowness with which GATT seemed to be moving to control or counter them; the expanded integration of world capital markets along with the massive indebtedness of many developing countries; and the heightened volatility of exchange rates not in accordance with the fundamentals determining the competitiveness of nations all increased Canadian (and the world's) sense of uncertainty about the future.

U.S. Protectionism

The third influence was the increase of U.S. protectionism as evidenced by the U.S. Trade Acts of 1974 and 1984, the increased frequency with which resort to the protection provided by these Acts was used, and the plethora of protectionist bills that found their way to Congress by legislators representing the vested interests of some of their electorates. It became apparent that increasing U.S. reliance upon "fair trade" laws or contingency protection as represented by their countervail, antidumping, and safeguard measures could become more troublesome for Canadian exporters than remaining tariffs. (Trade-weighted U.S. average tariffs on *all* imports from Canada, allowing for the Tokyo Round of reductions, amount to only .7 percent.[4] On *dutiable* products the U.S. average is 6.5 percent.[5] Apart from the special provisions of the Canada-U.S. Defence Production Sharing Programs, Canada was also excluded from U.S. government's purchase contracts through "Buy America" rules.

The Canadian Desire for Security

In general, then, Canadians (at least many of them) yearned for economic security in an insecure world. What better way to achieve this (they thought) than to tie their country more closely to the most powerful nation on earth—which already happened to be Canada's dominant trading partner, taking about 80 percent of Canada's exports and supplying nearly 70 percent of the nation's imports? The attractiveness of unhindered access for Canadian products to a country of 240 million people ensconced behind a wall of protectionism against the rest of the world seemed to be overwhelming—even if that nation's economic preeminence was being severely challenged by Japan.

All of these strands of thought were brought together in a Royal Commission report released in the summer of 1985—*The Report of the Royal Commission on the Economic Union and Development Prospects for Canada*[6] (The Macdonald Report). Whether the commissioners really believed that BFT was going to bring to Canada all the economic security and prosperity that they indicated, or whether it was simply that after sponsoring much research and years of meetings they had nothing else very dramatic to say, is an open question. They qualified fairly carefully, however, what they meant by free trade. Agriculture and the massive service sector were to be excluded from negotiations (even though it was well known by this time that these were two sectors that the U.S. would want included in the impending Uruguay Round of GATT liberalization talks). And Canada was to be able to retain the right to subsidize cultural activities; control the rate of exploitation as well as the pricing and taxing of its natural resource sectors; regulate U.S. capital inflows in accord with Canadian objectives; preserve its own regional and sectoral development policies, its own tax policy and social security and health care network, and the authority to set its own rules on imports from third countries.[7] Canada would also be given longer to reduce its tariffs than the U.S. and would preserve a flexible exchange rate as a final safety valve.

The whole issue was given some urgency through repeated statements by a variety of U.S. academics and officials that there was a small window of opportunity for Canada in the U.S., but that it was closing soon. Therefore, Canada ought to act quickly.

The Conservative Government in Ottawa, itself looking for something to restore its fast-waning popularity, thus decided in late September 1985 to notify the U.S. of its desire to open bilateral free trade negotiations. The government's key objective was to gain stable and assured access to U.S. markets. This meant gaining the removal of remaining tariffs and non-tariff measures such as "Buy-American" rules; reaching agreement on the rules regarding subsidies; and reducing the harassment of U.S. "fair trade" laws, in particular those relating to countervail, antidumping and safeguard measures.[8] It subsequently became clear that Canada wanted a dispute-settlement mechanism established involving equal representation from each country plus one independent member. Such a tribute was seen as preferable to permitting the U.S. to be both the petitioner as well as the judge. Another espoused advantage of BFT mentioned repeatedly by pro-BFT economists was that it would stem the flow of Canadian businesses setting up plants in the U.S. as a means of selling in that vast market when the U.S. curtain of protectionism descended.[9] The position taken by a number of Canadian economists, as well as Canada's chief negotiator prior to his being appointed to that position, was that Canada really had *no other option* if it was going to maintain its current level of prosperity, let alone improve its position in the future.[10]

The government recognized that they would have to go farther than the Macdonald Report suggested in that services, intellectual property rights, and agriculture would be included, although agricultural marketing boards (supply management systems) as well as the Auto Pact were not to be touched. The concept of "national treatment" was endorsed as the principle to follow in dealing with domestic and foreign firms and products, although precisely what was meant by this was never spelled out. Canadian political and cultural sovereignty was supposedly not to be threatened in any way.[11] All Canadian proponents of BFT placed much emphasis upon the idea that it was only free trade being negotiated and not a customs union or a common market.[12]

U.S. Indifference

The U.S. attitude towards BFT can only be labeled as indifferent at best. When the Senate Finance Committee finally assented to the fast track route for negotiations on April 23, 1986, the vote of ten to ten suggested little enthusiasm on the part of its members. And there were indications at the time that even this marginal endorsement was obtained by the Administration only after it made certain guarantees to take strong protective action against expanding Canadian lumber imports. Even when Canada walked out of the negotiations on September 23, 1987, after they had been continuing for nearly 16 months, only one U.S. television network (ABC) deigned to mention this. Reasons presented (by Canadians) for U.S. participation were that a strong Canada was of interest to it[13] and that BFT would demostrate to the world that the U.S. was genuinely interested in trade liberalization. If other major nations would not support the GATT Uruguay Round, the U.S. could show that at least it was prepared to go for bilateral arrangements from which many of them would be excluded. The US, however, made it clear that it expected substantive gains from BFT beyond these generalities if it was going to proceed.[14] Greater access to Canada for their services including those of a cultural nature, improved protection of their intellectual property rights in Canada, increased discipline over Canadian subsidies, removal of Canadian provincial restrictions on sales of U.S. alcoholic beverages, elimination of Canadian Wheat Board restrictions on imports of U.S. grains and products containing grains, were among the concessions that were mentioned by various U.S. representatives in the early stages when BFT was being considered.[15]

And so it was that in May of 1986 negotiations commenced, haltingly at first, but they commenced.

THE UNFOLDING OF NEGOTIATIONS

The Guarding of U.S. Legislative Authority

Since May 1986 five things have become increasingly clear. The first is that the U.S. Congress and Administration have been unwilling to surrender their powerful, and often protectionist, legislative authority over imports in order to achieve a free trade arrangement with Canada. Initial indications of this came right at the beginning of the negotiations when the President advised the U.S. Senate Finance Committee in writing that an agreement would not impinge upon authority of the U.S. to exercise its "fair trade" legislation. (The evidence was available even before this. In the 1984 hearings prior to the U.S.-Isreal free-trade arrangement Mr. Gibbons indicated that no alteration in or exemption from these laws would be entertained.[16]) Even when this position was expressed by the President to Mr. Mulroney in June 1987, the Prime Minister dismissed it as being a mere bargaining tactic.

Other indications of this stance have been there all along, too. Two days prior to when the two sides sat down for the first time to discuss negotiating procedures, the U.S. Coalition for Fair Lumber Imports petitioned their government for countervailing duties against Canadian softwood lumber—even though as recently as 1983 a similar case had been lost. As we know the U.S. Department of Commerce subsequently acted to support their domestic lumber interests in finding that Canadian stumpage practices were not in accord with their views of how such practices ought to be done, and that therefore lumber was countervailable.[17] On May 21, 1986, just one day after discussions commenced, the U.S. Administration levied 35 percent tariffs on Canadian shakes and shingles imports under Section 201 of their Trade Act.[18] For many Canadians, this action was an obvious violation of the joint statement made in March 1985 and repeated a year later that the two nations committed themselves "to halt protectionism in cross-border trade in goods and services."[19] But for U.S. officials the exercise of their own trade law took precedence over any agreed-upon pronouncement of this type.

Moreover, even though it is not uncommon for nations to suspend the application of their own trade laws while new arrangements are being worked out internationally (Canada, in fact did ask for this), since May 1986, U.S. officials have made it abundantly evident that nothing, not even what they have repeatedly referred to as the "historic" free trade negotiations between themselves and Canada, were to thwart in any way their battery of "fair trade" laws. In addition to softwood lumber, the U.S. either introduced or brought to completion in 1986 and 1987 actions against Canada with respect to such items as steel products for gas wells and oil wells, gas pricing, oil imports, salmon and herring fisheries, some flowers, brass sheet and strip, live hogs, uranium, and potash.

The final manifestation of the importance that the U.S. authorities have placed on their contingency legislation is the two trade bills that were approved during the spring and summer of 1987 by the House of Representatives and the Senate, respectively, and which are now being reconciled prior to being submitted to the President. Each of these is about 1000 pages and each one has many clauses which expand the protectionist nature of the existing law. For example, the 1986 Department of Commerce preliminary ruling in the Canadian softwood lumber case, which made judgments about the appropriateness of Canadian stumpage policies and resource management methods generally, is being codified in both versions of the new bill. The consequence will be that almost any practice or regulation by foreign governments regarding the development of their own domestic industries may be interpreted as providing countervailable subsidies to those industries. And even though a subsidy or other grant is *generally* available, this fact will no longer make it noncountervailable. Rather, as in the lumber case, if only a specific group is deemed to have received the subsidy, then countervail can be applied.[20] Although there is permission given in the bills for the President to negotiate a trade agreement with Canada (e.g., Section 109 of the Senate bill) nowhere in either of these trade bills is there any indication that Canada would or should be exempted from the legislation, should a BFT arrangement be negotiated. One of the sections that is of interest to Canada is the specific condemnation in the Senate bill of Canada's countervailable duties on U.S. corn imports—the first (and as we shall see later, probably not the last) such action by a foreign power against the U.S.

The agreement that has now been signed by both countries, pending final approval by Congress and Parliament, does not alter the argument developed in the preceding paragraphs. The binational dispute settlement panels to be established when disagreements arise will only have the authority to ensure that the country objecting to imports applies its own laws, regulations, and administrative practices correctly. The panels cannot judge the fairness or appropriateness of the established laws and procedures.

There is provision in the agreement, however, for the two nations to negotiate over a period of up to seven years a new set of rules in each country on antidumping and countervailing duties. But there is no assurance that the U.S. will change any of its existing or incipient protectionist laws as a consequence of these negotiations. Canada certainly has little left to offer to the U.S. in return for it's altering its statutes and administrative practices. The U.S. knows in turn that although the agreement provides for the free trade arrangement to be terminated by either party if rules satisfactory to both nations are not agreed upon, Canada, after seven years of increased integration with the U.S. would not be in any position to terminate. Canada would be locked in and would have to live with the U.S. laws and practices as they were at that time, regardless of whether it deemed them satisfactory.

U.S. Demands on Canada

The second major fact that has been forcefully driven home to Canadians is that the U.S. demands upon Canada in the negotiations have been much more than many (not all) Canadians initially expected, and that these demands have clear and adverse implications for Canadian cultural and economic sovereignty. But what does not seem to have registered for many ardent Canadian advocates of BFT is that these demands have gone further than a mere free trade agreement which they repeatedly said was all that was being negotiated, and that they also have gone further than the U.S. would expect to attain out of the multilateral GATT negotiations.

Culture. The U.S. already dominates Canadian cultural industries. Over 75 percent of book sales, nearly 90 percent of records and tapes, 97 percent of movie screen time, 75 percent of magazine sales at newsstands, and over 95 percent of TV drama in English are accounted for by foreign products, almost all of which are from the U.S.[21] Yet, although it would be unlikely to tolerate such a high degree of foreign content in its own consumption of cultural-type products, the U.S. has expected Canada to remove all remaining restraints on its activities in Canada as well as assistance to Canadian producers designed to retain a Canadian element to domestic cultural industries. Such insistence clearly is a new infringement on Canadian cultural sovereignty.

The new agreement, although still incomplete as to details, indicates that although cultural industries are essentially exempted from the provisions for almost complete freedom of U.S. investment in Canada, the

U.S. has had considerable success on cultural matters. Canada will no longer be able to encourage Canadian magazines by restricting deductibility for income tax purposes to those advertising expenditures made in publications printed in Canada. All Canadian tariffs on printed material and recordings are to be removed. Finally, the U.S. may retaliate with measures of an "equivalent commercial effect" against any measures Canada may take to encourage its cultural industries.

Even within the EEC the individual nations have been able to retain many controls over and subsidies of their own cultural industries—such as the BBC in Britain to mention but one obvious example. And under GATT Article IV there are express provisions for nations to require a "specified minimum proportion of movie-screen time to be for films of domestic origin." In Canada, because of U.S. ownership of movie theatre franchises, it is extremely difficult for Canadian films to get a fair showing in domestic theatres.

Investment. Canada already has more foreign ownership of its industry than any country in the world, with over 75 percent of this ownership held by Americans. Yet, the U.S. has wanted removed all remaining Canadian restrictions on U.S. foreign investment in Canada, saying that " . . . a free trade agreement must also cover investment if it is to work properly . . . Trade cannot be free if investment is restrained."[22] This statement is untrue and woefully misleading. First, free factor flows are not a characteristic of a free trade area. They are not even a characteristic of a customs union, which is the next step after a free trade area in terms of the degree of integration involved between participants. Rather, they are a characteristic of a common market which is the integrative stage *beyond* a customs union. The European Economic Community, which has been in existence for nearly 30 years, still does *not* have absolutely unrestrained capital flows such as the U.S. has been demanding from Canada. Thus, why should the U.S. believe or expect that all investment must be unrestrained to have a free trade area? The answer is that the U.S. seems to have in mind something much more comprehensive than a mere free trade area.

A second reason the quote cited above is inaccurate is that, as any economist familiar with the Heckscher–Ohlin or factor-endowments theory of trade flows is aware, commodity flows are often an important substitute for factor flows.[23] You do not need both in the standard factor-endowments situation. It is true, where economies of scale or technological differences exist between countries, that factor flows may be complementary to commodity flows in bringing about factor-price-equalization.[24] But all this theoretical conclusion tells us is that if a country is relatively short of capital or labor (as measured by its relative factor prices compared with its trading partner), then it may find it appropriate on occasion either to allow capital inflows or immigration. This, of course, Canada already does. In fact the huge extent of Canadian debt capital borrowings in recent years is all too evident from its burgeoning net international indebtedness and annual service payments. (For 1986 Canada's official net foreign indebtedness was 37 percent of GNP—compared to 6 percent for the U.S. This Canadian net debt would be 49 percent of GNP if market value of physical assets were used rather than book value.[25]) But surely when a country chooses to acquire foreign capital, whether that capital is of a debt or direct investment nature, the rules that investment must follow when entering the country must involve the sovereign decisions of that country itself with such decisions not being forced upon it by another nation.

The U.S. itself has a wide range of restrictions on foreign direct investment. Direct federal restraints exist for coastal and freshwater shipping; dredging and salvage operations; shipbuilding; fishing; air carriers; radio, television, telegraph and telephones; nuclear power; hydroelectric facilities; transmission of natural gas and electricity; transfers of federally-owned land; mineral rights; and defense supplies. Indirect regulations particularly with respect to antitrust matters and securities, as exist under the Clayton Act, the Sherman Act, the Federal Trade Commission Act, and the Securities Exchange Act, can pose major legal hurdles for, or restrictions on, foreign firms attempting to invest in the U.S. In addition many states have laws banning or restricting foreign ownership in a variety of sectors.[26]

What does the new agreement state regarding investment? Both parties are to be bound not to introduce policies necessitating new minimum proportions of domestic ownership in firms, or forcing divestiture of existing ownership. They are both prohibited from requiring the other country's firms within their borders to meet new performance obligations on exporting, local sourcing, or import-substitution; and from even requiring investors from third-countries to meet such commitments if it might significantly affect U.S. Canadian trade. Because Canada is by far the smaller country and already has far more foreign direct investment as a proportion of the economy than does the U.S., these rules will place a much greater restraint upon Canadian policy freedom than they will on the U.S. Already, for example, Canada must face the fact that foreign-owned firms within its boundaries import 2.4 times as many imports as a proportion of sales than do domestically-owned firms. For the service sector this ratio is much higher.[27] The above twenty-seven provisions mean that Canada will be prevented from taking any future steps to alter this higher propensity to import of foreign-owned firms, or in any other way to encourage greater sourcing of purchases in Canada to the promotion of Canadian production and employment.

The pact also specifies that in four years from implementation of the agreement Canada will not be able to review any direct U.S. acquisitions in Canada of less than $150 millions, and that in only three years Canada will not be able to review *any* indirect acquisitions of Canadian firms by U.S. investors or even any acquisitions by third countries of firms in Canada under U.S. control. At the same time as all these new restraints are put on Canadian actions, *all existing U.S. laws, regulations and practices such as those mentioned above to restrain foreign investment in the U.S. remain intact.* They are, to use a technical term, grandfathered by the agreement.

Again, Canada even before the agreement was negotiated had liberalized its rules on the ownership by foreign banks and other financial institutions beyond what is permitted in the U.S. Yet in the agreement it has gone further to exempt U.S. bank subsidiaries from *any* limitations on the ownership of Canadian controlled financial institutions by U.S. nationals other than those also facing Canadians, and the foreign bank sector is no longer limited to 16 percent for U.S. bank subsidiaries in Canada. The stage is set for substantial growth in the ownership and control of the Canadian financial sector by the U.S. Clearly, the Canada-U.S. agreement goes much beyond a simple trade liberalization pact.

Regional and Industrial Development. The U.S. view in the negotiations was that Canada needed to be "disciplined" with regard to its developmental policies[28] in spite of the fact that many of Canada's policies are similar to those being propounded by industrial strategy advocates in the U.S. Subsidies have been the major issue in this context. Lipsey and Smith[29] suggested a variety of possibilities such as the negotiators' developing a list of subsidies acceptable to each country providing they are not above some agreed-upon level, or having Canada gain permission to use subsidies for regional or local development that would not give Canada a cost advantage above what it would have had if production had been located in the lowest-cost Canadian location.

Obviously no meeting of minds occurred on these issues. As indicated earlier, the two nations agreed that arbitration panels should be established to examine disputes as they arise, but in themselves they will change nothing. Canada will still be subject as before to U.S. rules and definitions regarding subsidies, dumping, or other trade practices not in keeping with the U.S. view of how the world should be organized.

In the EEC the individual nations are permitted the use of tax concessions, special depreciation rules, special investment funds or nationalized industries to assist individual industries or regions.[30] The restraints that the U.S. wishes to put upon Canada seem to go beyond what already exists in that long-standing customs union. The argument may be put that even if what the U.S. wanted from Canada goes beyond even what exists in GATT now or in the EEC, it is no more than what the U.S. would expect of third countries in the Uruguay Round of GATT negotiations. This argument does not stand up. On May 28, 1987, U.S. Commerce Secretary, Malcolm Baldrige, had this to say: "Many are calling a U.S./Canada bilateral agreement a model for the Uruguay round of multilateral trade negotiations. *That view may go too far*"[31] (emphasis is mine). He went on to suggest that the agreement to be negotiated with Canada would be closer than anything that the U.S. could expect in the incipient GATT round!

Canadian Strategic Errors

Overstatement of net gains. The third major observation one can make about the negotiations is that ardent Canadian advocates of BFT have committed a number of serious tactical errors. The most important of these errors is the overstatement of the possible gains from BFT that Canada would achieve. The numbers most often quoted were in the order of 7 to 10 percent of GNP. These percentages were based on a variety of studies which invariably emphasized the economies of scale that might be achieved in Canadian manufacturing.[32] In spite of words of caution raised repeatedly about whether these sorts of numbers were realistic,[33] it has been common to see all such cautions ignored by proponents arguing the case for BFT.[34] It is true that in the last year or so, some advocates of BFT have modified their claims to about 2 or 2.5 percent of GNP. But even numbers of this magnitude have to be questioned. Hazeldine has argued that 1 percent or thereabouts may be more likely, and that compared with the margin of error that can exist in economic forecasts, one should not be placing much weight on it.[35] And as some of us have argued, if the U.S. were to obtain many of its demands with respect to investment services (including cultural industries), resource development and pricing—as they seem to have done—then the gains could quite easily be negative.[36]

The cited benefits in employment for Canada are questionable too. Because of differing assumptions, the estimating models have produced exaggerated or contradictory, often improbable, results so that one can have little confidence in them.[37] The strong advocates of free trade tend to have ignored these difficulties.

Another dimension of the overstatement of net gains has to do with the location of industry. The argument cited earlier that an agreement will be of great benefit to Canada because it will stop the flow of Canadian producers setting up plants in the U.S. to serve that market behind the U.S. protectionist wall, is no more than an opinion, a value judgement, certainly not an established fact. Even if it were true, it would not necessarily be desirable. This is not the place to go into a full-scale discussion of this issue. I leave that for another occasion.[38] It is sufficient to point out that most of the studies on recent Canadian investment in the U.S. do *not* indicate that U.S. trade barriers, actual or expected, are the major reason for that investment.[39] Hence BFT, even with some watered-down form of "secure access" to the U.S. is unlikely to cause any major change in this economic process.

One should not be surprised or alarmed (as the bilateral free traders want to make us[40]) that Canadian firms are investing in the U.S. What is surprising is that it has taken many of them, both large and small, so long to realize that they are perfectly capable of getting into the foreign direct investment business, and that such investment is an important way of developing foreign markets. It also provides new possibilities for sales of Canadian-made parts and components, expansion of head office employment in Canada, and the repatriation of profits. Also, operating in the U.S. market is a useful learning experience before moving further afield. These are pluses to Canada in the long run, not minuses.

The problem with all of the studies overstating the benefits from free trade has been threefold: (1) Canadian negotiators and politicians have been misled into believing that Canada has more leeway to give away certain things than the country really has; (2) the expectations of the public regarding the benefits they will receive have been inflated—so that they are set up for disappointment even if the deal is finally approved by both countries; and (3) the U.S. has been given the incentive to ask for much more from Canada than they otherwise might have done if the espoused net benefits to Canada had not been placed so misleadingly high.

The "no-other-options" scenario. The second serious tactical error by Canadian proponents of BFT, including Canada's chief negotiator, is repeatedly stating that Canada has had no other options, and that any Canadian prosperity we have now will cease if BFT is not negotiated.[41] Even as the negotiations broke down, Prime Minister Mulroney[42] as well as the Business Council on National Issues reiterated the hard time Canada was going to have without making any mention of other avenues or strategies that might be followed. As with inflated estimates of gain, such a position has encouraged the U.S. to press its demands much harder than it otherwise might have done. Some may submit that Canada really has had no other option, so why try to hide it. I do not accept this view but will leave discussion of it until the next section of the chapter.

Giving away of bargaining points. The third error for Canada was to give away a number of important bargaining chips well before the negotiations had commenced, or at least without specifically tying them to the negotiations. These include the relaxing of our foreign investment laws; the dismantling of Bill C-22 to give U.S. pharmaceutical firms far greater patent protection in Canada, beyond that recommended by the Royal Commission established to study this issue (although this bill has not passed the Canadian Senate at the time of writing); and the easing of restrictions on foreign financial firms in Canada.

This type of naivety may be a consequence of many Canadians having overstated the net gains from BFT, or it may simply reflect two other strategic mistakes: a failure by Canadians to recognize the unlikelihood of reaching a BFT agreement on their terms, or alternately, a failure to recognize the full extent of historic U.S. nationalism.

The worst time for negotiations. This last comment leads us to the final negotiating error: Canada allowed itself to be rushed into attempting to negotiate a free trade agreement with the U.S. at the *worst* possible time in the last 45–47 years. Because of the large U.S. trade deficit, which has shown no signs of abating this year (for April-June 1987 it attained a new record of US $41.1 billion), and the need for Congressmen hoping to be elected next year to be seen taking a firm stand to protect the interests of their constituents, U.S. protectionist sentiments are at their zenith. What an inappropriate time to be trying to extract concessions from U.S. officials! At the time of revising this paper we also have great turbulence in world stock markets and exchange markets.

U.S. States Have More Influence Than Canada

The fourth thing that is so evident from the events of the past eighteen months is that even a single, relatively small state in the U.S. union has much more political clout in Washington than does all of Canada. New Mexico, where most potash in the U.S. is produced, has been able to get antidumping duties levied against imports of Saskatchewan potash, even though such action raises the cost of fertilizer for most of the farm community throughout the rest of the country.[43] Five lumber-producing states were able to influence the Administration to find Canada guilty of subsidizing softwood lumber exports. As a consequence lumber costs for homebuilders and other consumers throughout the rest of the U.S. have been raised.

The Canadian Situation: Of Historical Origin

The fifth and final observation regarding the current negotiations is that Canada's difficulties in reaching a suitable agreement with the U.S. are not just the result of intransigence or excessive demands on the part of the U.S., or miscalculations and tactical errors in bargaining on the part of Canada. They go back about a century.

This information is not well known, so it is worth spending some time elaborating on it.[44] At that time four major countries, Britain, France, Germany, and the U.S., as well as two minor ones, Belgium and Switzerland, had already moved into their first phase of industrialization and dominated world production. But a group of late-follower countries had already begun to industrialize. These included the Czech states, Italy, Japan, Russia, Sweden, and Canada (The Netherlands might be included here, too). (The "white dominions" like Australia and Argentina were well behind Canada and the rest at this time.) Towards the close of the 19th century Canada ranked well up among these late-follower nations in terms of industrial production and exports, in the ratio of finished to primary good exports, and in the diversified nature of its finished manufactured goods exports. Between the turn of the century and World War I, however, Canada regressed in relation to these other late-follower nations. It became more and more dependent upon imported finished goods and technology, primarily from the U.S. and saw far less growth of exports of fully-fabricated products than did the other late-follower nations. The more dynamic manufacturing sectors became increasingly dominated by American firms "often by taking over the Canadian firms that had started out by licensing American technology,"[45] and were focused only upon production for the domestic market, not for export.

The usual Canadian explanation of the expansion of foreign (particularly U.S.) ownership is that it was an *inevitable* consequence of Canada having put on high tariffs in 1879. But this is invalid. The majority of the industrialized and industrializing nations increased their tariffs during the late 1870s, the 1880s, and early 1890s.[46] (Even U.S. duties measured as duties to total imports for consumption were almost invariably above those of Canada for the years from Confederation to 1900.) Tariffs alone, therefore, do not provide a satisfactory explanation. The major difference was that unlike Canada, which welcomed foreign direct investment, many of the other nations encouraged domestic ownership in the face of U.S., and in Europe, German expansion. "It was not proximity to an expansionist industrial giant that accounted for Canadian exceptionalism but rather a different reaction to the threat of external domination."[47] Canada's banking system was geared more toward short-term loans for commercial purposes than to long-term ones more suitable for encouraging new, innovative domestically-owned manufacturing. Reliance was placed upon British military technology so that engineering firms, which often rely on military expenditures for support, particularly in generating new technology, did not receive the encouragement that they did in countries like Sweden. Also, Canada emphasized the building of railways—beyond actual economic needs—which increased debt capital inflows, encouraged imports and the entrance of U.S. branch plants, and pushed the economy more toward natural resource exports.

In general, government policies over time have resulted in economic activity in Canada being heavily influenced by the interests of U.S. transnational firms. And as George Grant pointed out over two decades ago, even Canadian-owned large businesses have tended to adopt views similar to those of their American counterparts.[48] Witness today the group of about 500 companies in the U.S. and Canada committed to pushing strongly for a BFT agreement. The Canadian government is obviously under great pressure to satisfy the North American industrial complex in this regard.

Why do I take the space to develop this theme? Is it not just past history? Not at all. Consider which of our most industrialized provinces is most disposed to BFT at this time—Quebec. Why is this? Quebec has, over the last decade or so developed a strong cadre of largely Quebec-owned and controlled manufacturing and service-oriented companies. This did not happen by accident, but was a well-orchestrated policy of the Parti-Quebecois government, which assisted in various ways, including helping to arrange the provision of adequate supplies of capital for these developing firms. Many of these firms have already begun exporting to the U.S. (aided over the years by the depreciation of the Canadian dollar). Their nationalism and loyalties are clear, and they see the possibilities of greater exports to the U.S. if restrictions on imports to that market are further removed via BFT.[19] Yet, if the BFT agreement goes through, other provinces may not have the option of encouraging domestic industry as Quebec has done. (Quebec, of course, could easily become less enamored with free trade if it finds the U.S. beginning to interfere aggressively with the Quebec policy of differential pricing between domestic and U.S. sales of electricity.

IMPLICATIONS

The unwillingness of the U.S. to negotiate in any substantive way at this time regarding the application to Canada of its "fair trade" laws, coupled with its strong demands for greater control over the Canadian economy, Canadian overestimates of the net gains to Canada from free trade, the common Canadian belief that the country has no other options available, the fact that Canada gave away important bargaining points prior to or apart from the negotiations, the pressures of big business on each side of the border for an agreement to be reached, and the fact that this is the worst possible time for Canada to be negotiating with the U.S. add up to an agreement which, if approved by both nations, is likely to result in the inflated Canadian expectations of the benefits from BFT being far from realized. This result plus the knowledge that even a small state in the U.S. union has more political power to influence decisions in Washington than the Canadian government, could easily cause some Canadians to think that the only way of achieving the benefits they had anticipated, including guaranteed access to the U.S. market, is for Canada to apply for membership in the U.S. This is far from an impossibility, given what we know of Canadian naivety and U.S. nationalism. Canadians should not forget that the U.S. has refused to recognize Canadian sovereignty in the Arctic, that the U.S. has unilaterally decided to alter in its own favor the traditional border between Alaska and the Yukon (the 141st meridian) as it extends into the oil-rich Beaufort Sea, and desires to bend the historical dividing line between Canadian and U.S. territory off the Queen Charlotte Islands so as to acquire a greater share of the salmon and possible oil resources there. This is the same U.S. with which Canada has now negotiated an agreement. In its coverage this agreement, in a number of ways, goes beyond the degree of integration that exists in the European Economic Community. It is a pity (for Canada) that enthusiastic supporters of BFT so often fail to see that recent U.S. behavior toward Canada as indicated above has much to tell us about U.S. attitudes toward Canada in general and U.S. aspirations for the continent we share.[50] Canada could be absorbed into the American union just as that independent nation, Hawaii, was, only 23 years after it signed a free-trade treaty with the U.S. in 1875 in order to have "assured access" for its products in the huge U.S. market. The price was high—political independence.[51] There are already key figures in the U.S., such as the newspaper magnate, W. R. Hearst, Jr., who are seeing the recent economic integration agreement as a major step toward political integration.[52]

In my judgment, there are a number of steps that Canada could have taken, and which even now it might follow in order to strengthen its position, regardless of whether the current economic integration agreement is given approval by both countries.

A Change in Viewpoint

The most obvious step would be to educate the Canadian public to the effect that the net gains from BFT are not likely to be nearly as great as was once thought, particularly given the nature of the agreement now negotiated. This point needs no more elaboration.

In addition many ardent Canadian advocates of free trade need to stop making sweeping, nonspecific statements about the terrible things that will happen to Canada if an agreement is not given final approval by both governments. These people remind one of Chicken Licken in the children's story, who created panic among the farmyard animals by telling them the sky was falling and the world was coming to an end. More careful analysis of the situation revealed that acorns were beginning to fall from the oak tree, that he had been hit by one, and that there were steps which he and the others could take to avoid this in the future. In the current trading environment the solution will not be as simple as for Chicken Licken and his friends, but there are, nevertheless, a number of other positive things that Canada can do, by itself and in conjunction with others. These are to adopt policies which will (1) improve the nation's productivity and competitiveness; (2) minimize the scope for U.S. contingency laws to be applied; and (3) increase the possibilities for international solutions to U.S. protectionism. Consider these in turn.

Domestic Policies for Enhanced Productivity and Competitiveness

On the domestic scene, Canada needs first of all to see the negotiations as a positive learning experience. Provincial politicians, having been regularly involved in briefings on the progress in negotiations, undoubtedly have had it brought home to them more clearly than ever before that narrow provincial protectionism, while possibly gaining some votes in the short run, discourages efficiency-improving change and adaptation, reduces the entire nation's ability to compete both internally and abroad, and inevitably will lead to the disintegration of Canada as a separate country. The incentive should thus exist for provinces to begin such measures as removing "buy-provincial" policies for goods and services; liberalizing interprovincial trucking regulations; reducing interprovincial restrictions on liquor sales; lowering competitive provincial subsidy programs for both agricultural and industrial sectors; and finding new ways to assist in the survival of small agricultural producers of dairy products, poultry, eggs and the like (assuming that is our society's desire) without the use of supply management systems which also subsidize very large producers who do not need the assistance and may discourage productivity improvement.

These adjustments will not be easy. Ontario, being the dominant province, may be tempted to take the same attitude in the working out of new, interprovincial arrangements that the U.S. has tended to take in the BFT negotiations. This would not be productive. Instead new approaches may be necessary. To illustrate, Canadians may have to begin integrating their system of equalization payments with the reduction of provincial trade barriers, rather than seeing the equalization system merely as a means of providing citizens in each province with some reasonably comparable level of government services. Discussion of the possibilities and difficulties in this regard could command a long essay unto itself. All that needs to be emphasized in this context is that internal adjustments of this type are feasible without having to "give up" anything internationally—although they will improve our productivity and competitiveness and enable us to bargain internationally more effectively in the future.

Minimizing the Scope for the Application of U.S. "Fair Trade" Laws

Another policy direction Canada might pursue relates both to the improvement of the nation's internal productivity and to the reduction of the scope for U.S. contingency laws to be applied. This would involve the complete reassessment of federal and provincial regional and industrial development policies not only from the traditional viewpoints regarding whether they have been effective (which they frequently have not been), or biased regionally (which they often have been),[53] but from the viewpoint of how encouragement to industry can be given which minimizes the potential for the U.S. to levy countervailing duties or other defensive measures. Some may take the hard line that Canada is a sovereign nation and should not have to amend its policies simply to suit the U.S. But the fact is that even from a purely Canadian perspective many of our policies leave much to be desired and need to be revamped. Most Canadians, for example, would not want to see a repeat of the $220 million assistance to General Motors to retain and update an aging plant in Quebec.

And from an international viewpoint, a careful domestic assessment could have a number of advantages, not just with respect to the U.S. In the Tokyo Round of GATT negotiations five particular codes of behavior were developed and signed by various subsets of nations. These applied to customs valuation, import licensing, procurement, standards, and subsidies. They were not successful at providing greater trade liberalization, but they were a move in the direction of greater harmonization and transparency of rules, and have helped to prevent greater decoordination of policies.[54] The next stage would be for the nations in the Uruguay Round to begin trading concessions so as to expand the number adhering to each code and reduce the protectionist nature of the codes.[55] Just as the earlier GATT rounds entailed a certain amount of "squeezing the water out of the tariff," so we might expect that at first there would be some squeezing of water out of subsidies or other nontariff measures. Thus in relation to subsidies, for example, if Canada were to research carefully the full extent of its grants or other assistance (both federal and provincial) to domestic industry over the past half-dozen years or so, the nation would be in a much more knowledgeable position than it is at present to negotiate multilaterally on amendments to existing codes or on developing new codes of behavior.

With regard to the U.S., this exercise might be done in two ways: working with "the facts" as known fully from government and corporate records, and working with a range of interpretations that might be applied to these facts in accordance with the way the U.S. Department of Commerce establishes "constructed values," when determining whether or not to retaliate against other countries. By relating this information to the extent of each industry's exports to the U.S. as a proportion of its total production, Canada would have a clearer understanding of which industries are currently and realistically vulnerable to U.S. "fair trade" laws and what degree of U.S. retaliation, if any, there might be.

Concurrently, this analysis would set the stage for devising new, acceptable ways of encouraging technological advance and other productivity-improvement in Canadian industry. Several possibilities come to mind. Some variant of the Quebec approach is one. That is, governments rather than giving grants or below-market-interest-rate loans, might simply purchase some shares of companies or give loans at market rates for part of the financing, thereby enabling the companies involved to gain greater credibility and obtain the rest of their financing for new projects from the market. From a purely domestic viewpoint, this approach would seem to be more equitable than large subsidies at the expense of the average taxpayer. Again, some research corporations are being established across the country using a combination of university professors, senior undergraduate and graduate students, and industry personnel. These are a means of funding universities, developing new technology, and facilitating the transfer of that technology to industry capable of utilizing it commercially. More of these could be encouraged. After all, Route 128, encircling Boston, and Silicon Valley in California have involved a combination of business and university expertise plus government assistance through defense contracts and otherwise. Notice also that it may be easier to do these things without the current economic integration agreement than with it.

Another very important possibility is for Canada to reduce its interest rates relative to U.S. rates, and let the Canadian dollar decline from its current rate of about $.76 U.S. The policy that Canada has been pursuing over the last decade of maintaining the value of its currency vis-à-vis the U.S. by keeping its interest rates well above those in the U.S. has resulted in substantial debt capital inflows to Canada, greatly increased Canadian net international indebtedness (now about $185 billion, second only to the U.S.) and hence annual service charges on this debt (now running in net terms at 12 percent of exports excluding retained earnings), and resulted in a higher cost of capital for domestic borrowers. In 1986 the interest rate spreads were at record levels. The money market spread, for example, was 2.5 percent, or 40 percent above U.S. costs. This is a significant extra cost of doing business in Canada. Also continuing growth of the net international indebtedness means that an ever-greater proportion of Canadian exports will have to go to servicing this debt. Thus, retaining higher interest rates than the U.S. as a method of establishing a sound international currency is a self-defeating policy. It places a drag on the economy and will lead eventually to a lack of confidence in the currency.[56] More important for the present discussion, the decline in the Canadian currency value in terms of U.S. dollars that would result from ceasing this approach, plus the lower capital costs for businesses in Canada, would help compensate any Canadian businesses that have been or might be hit with new U.S. duties under one or the other of U.S. contingency laws. Certainly, where those duties are in the 5 or 6 percent range, this policy move could be an effective antidote.

The Canadian government might also provide much technical assistance to business, especially to smaller Canadian firms and industries, faced with new allegations under U.S. "fair trade" laws. This may be in the form of helping them in establishing the facts; preparing their defence; and identifying U.S. consumer or producer groups which have an interest in supporting the Canadian position. These might be groups buying the Canadian products or others who would be hurt through reduced sales to Canada if Canadian producers have to cut back on their production and therefore their imports from the U.S., of components, parts, materials, or capital equipment. Once they are identified, they could be educated as to the situation and encouraged to put pressure on their Congressmen with regard to their interests. (One would hope that these efforts would not be interpreted by the U.S. Department of Commerce as new types of countervailable subsidies. It would be ironic if they were.)

There may also be occasions where Canada can respond to U.S. protectionist action in ways that quickly cause groups in the U.S. to put political pressure on their government representatives to alter U.S. policies. Saskatchewan's response in passing legislation to control potash production and the raising of price on sales to the U.S. by 60 percent by the Potash Company of Saskatchewan (and followed by the other major Canadian producers), is a good example of this. The farm community is a powerful lobby. Saskatchewan in this instance has considerable monopoly power and would be foolish not to use it.[57]

Another possibility, though one not likely to be used very frequently, might be for large Canadian firms to monitor conceivable sources of objection to Canadian imports arising from smaller U.S. firms and simply buy them out. Then some form of cooperative division of the market might then be more feasible, and the result could readily be greater stability of employment patterns in this industry on both sides of the border. The purchase by Bombardier of design plans from Budd Co. of Michigan for rapid transit vehicles would seem to be of this type of strategy.

Increase International Cooperation to Reduce
U.S. Protectionism

The final dimension of Canada's response if no agreement is finally approved by both countries, would be for Canada to recognize that it is not alone. The opportunity of working with third nations in response to the U.S. was mentioned briefly in the preceding section, but it deserves some elaboration.

It is true that Canada is much more dependent upon trade with the U.S. than any other country in the world. To that extent, it is much more vulnerable. But other nations are also very concerned with the increasingly aggressive U.S. contingency law and the enlarged scope for its use that is implied by the impending trade bill. The consequence could be that these other nations, such as those in the EEC and Japan will have a greater incentive to see the Uruguay Round bring forth a reduction in nontariff measures and in some cases a codification of measures that will be multilaterally acceptable and not countervailable or subject to antidumping charges. In other instances, because of close intercorporate arrangements between European and U.S. firms, especially in sophisticated manufacturing, the result may simply be agreements between them not to intrude too much in each other's home market. This type of response could generate a growing number of arrangements among countries and companies to agree upon market shares, in each other's markets and third countries as well, just as the U.S. has done with regard to steel imports, the EEC has done for Canadian pulp and paper, and so on. While such agreements may discourage the growth of world trade and reduce the possibilities for additional countries or firms having newly-developed technological or other sources of comparative advantage to gain access to existing markets, it is not nearly as frightening a scenario as a complete collapse of world trade as some pundits prophesy. In all such negotiations, Canada will need both to find support from other nations wherever it can and ensure that it exercises its full rights under GATT (this latter option being something that it has not always done—as it did not do in the softwood lumber case).

Probably the most important source of conflict between the U.S. and the EEC will continue to be respecting agricultural products. A reduction of protectionism in this sector is where the U.S. stands to gain the most, both with regard to the EEC as well as Japan. It would be appropriate for Canada to remind the U.S. that the major reason for the U.S. problems with European agricultural protectionism and subsidization of exports is that the U.S. Congress, as a condition of joining GATT, chose to have agriculture exempted so as to permit the continuation of its own agricultural support policies developed in the 1930s. The U.S. also got one or two other subsequent changes made with regard to GATT so as to protect its agricultural sector.[58] The point then needs to be emphasized that if the U.S. leads the way now in establishing new avenues of protectionism through its trade bill providing enhanced opportunity for U.S. producers to commence and win relief actions against imports, other countries may follow this pattern. Thus, in the years to come, when the U.S. wants to generate huge trade surpluses in order to reduce the massive indebtedness that it is presently piling up, it will have difficulty doing so. In the long run, then, it could easily be the greatest loser from its current protectionist stance.[59]

Canada's cooperation with third countries could take other forms too. It has already led the way in raising potash prices on exports to the U.S. The strong likelihood is that other potash-producing nations will be quite willing to accept Saskatchewan's price leadership at this time and in the years ahead.[60] More generally, however, Canada, because of its close relationship with and export sales to the U.S., has been reluctant to consider cartels in resource products such as minerals (uranium is an exception and involved very special circumstances).[61] But there is obviously no longer any reason why Canada should not explore such possibilities with other major world producers. The U.S.S.R., the most important producer of a wide range of minerals, may not be disposed to join any such group. Then again, neither is the U.S. likely to want to become increasingly dependent upon the U.S.S.R. for its mineral supplies. There are, of course, limits to what cartels for minerals might accomplish today because of the rapid development of new-materials technology. Yet they are something that Canada should not completely ignore.

There may be other sources of cooperation between Canada and other nations that would help to bring political pressure within the U.S. against the protectionist fervor of the moment. Consider the huge exports of U.S. entertainment that occur in the form of movies, T.V. shows, and videos. U.S. sales abroad are at much less than the U.S. cost of production. This is clearly dumping. The prices charged are also much less than the cost of producing substitute material in other countries. (This is the main reason, of course, why Canada has so much difficulty in developing its own television programs.) Suppose Canada and other nations were to argue that such dumping warranted significant anti-dumping duties? It may well be a worthwhile negotiating point.

Conclusion

To conclude, a failure to finalize the Canada-U.S. agreement as currently negotiated need not be the national catastrophe that many supporters of those negotiations have been painting it to be. Yes, there will be difficulties and adjustments. Canadians will have to develop a new sense of oneness in their dealings with the U.S. and not allow themselves to be divided—the federal government versus the provinces, Central Canada versus the outlying regions, or business versus labor—as has so often occurred throughout the nation's history—and even now is occurring in the free trade debate. If this is done, Canada can continue to be a land very much worth living in. This conclusion assumes of course that the majority of Canadians, and particularly those with power and influence, are interested in preserving the nation. If this is an unjustified assumption, then there need be no debate in Canada. The nation can simply move full speed ahead with the agreement—and quite possibly end up in due course as another addition to the American empire.[62]

NOTES

1. The classic studies were by (a) Ron and Paul Wonnacott, *Free Trade Between the United States and Canada: The Potential Economic Effects* (Cambridge, Massachusetts: Harvard University Press, 1967) and (b) H. C. Eastman and S. Stykolt, *The Tariff and Competition in Canada* (Toronto: Macmillan of Canada, 1967). There was also a series of studies produced about the same time by the Private Planning Association of Canada, the predecessor of the C. D. Howe Institute. This series was followed by the Economic Council's report *Looking Outward* (Ottawa: 1975) and its accompanying research papers; by Jim R. Williams, *The Canadian-United States Tariff and Canadian Industry: A Multisectoral Analysis* (Toronto: University of Toronto Press, 1978); and by the Senate of Canada, The Standing Senate Committee on Foreign Affairs, *Canada United States Relations, Vol II and III Canada's Trade Relations With the United States* (Ottawa: Queen's Printer, 1978 and 1982 respectively). Other papers have been written on these issues from time to time, but these were the ones receiving the most attention.

2. The Private Planning Association's work considered agriculture as did that of the Economic Council and J. R. Williams, but the other studies excluded it.

3. For more detail on what the various studies contained, see B. W. Wilkinson, "Canada-United States Free Trade: Setting the Dimensions," in *Knocking at the Back Door: The Political Economy of Canada-U.S. Free Trade.* (Ottawa: The Institute for Research on Public Policy, 1987.)

4. Brown, Drucilla. "Testimony Regarding United States-Canada Free Trade" before the Subcommittee on Economic Stabilization of the Committee on Banking, Finance, and Urban Affairs. (U.S. House of Representatives, August 5, 1985.)

5. Magun, Sunder, Someshwar Rao, and Bimal Lodh. *Impact of Canada-U.S. Free Trade on the Canadian Economy*, Discussion Paper No. 331. (Ottawa: Economic Council of Canada, 1987.)

6. Ottawa: Minister of Supply and Services, 1985.

7. Ibid., Vol I, pp. 309–313.

8. James Kelleher, "Notes for an address to the Canada-California Chamber of Commerce for the California Council for International Trade," January 16, 1986.

9. One of the more recent statements to this effect is by R. Lipsey in "Canada's Trade Options," *Canadian-American Free Trade: Historical Political and Economic Dimensions*, ed. by A. R. Riggs and Tom Velk. (Halifax: The Institute for Research on Public Policy, 1987), 73.

10. Crispo, John. "The Case for Free Trade With the United States," in *Canadian Trade at a Crossroads: Options for New International Agreements*, eds. David W. Conklin and Thomas J. Courchene. (Toronto: Ontario Economic Council, 1985), 312; Reisman, Simon. "Trade Policy Options in Perspective," in Conklin and Courchene, p. 389; also Lipsey, Richard G. "Canada's Trade Options," in *Canadian-American Free Trade: Historical, Political and Economic Dimensions*, eds. A. R. Riggs and Tom Velk. (Halifax: The Institute for Research on Public Policy, 1987), 72–73.

11. Joe Clark, Minister of External Affairs, Government of Canada, "A Speech to the Foreign Policy Association in New York," Nov. 18, 1985, and also B. W. Wilkinson, "Canada-United States Free Trade: The Current Debate," *International Journal*, Vol. XLII, No. 1 (Winter 1986–7), 212–213.

12. J. Crispo, "The Case for Free Trade . . . ", pp. 308-310; also Peyton V. Lyon, "CUFTA And Canadian Independence," in *Canadian-American Free Trade: Historical, Political and Economic Dimensions*, pp. 195–198.

13. Senate of Canada, The Standing Senate Committee on Foreign Affairs. *Canada United States Relations*, Vol. III, pp. 39–41.

14. Allen Wallis, "Prosperity Is The Goal of U.S. Trade Policy," a Speech to the Economic Policy Council of the United Nations Association of the USA, January 17, 1986, in *Department of State Bulletin* 86 (March, 1986), 35.

15. B. W. Wilkinson "Canada-United States Free Trade: Setting the Dimensions . . . ".

16. Sam Gibbons. "Statement to the Deputy U.S. Trade Representative and the Deputy Undersecretary of Agriculture for International Affairs and Commodity Programs." Proposed United States-Israel Free Trade Area: Hearing Before the Subcommittee on Trade of the House Committee on Ways and Means, 98th Congress, 2nd Session: 26.

17. For a detailed analysis of this ease, see Mike Percy and C. Yoder, *The Softwood Lumber Dispute and Canada-U.S. Trade in Natural Resources*. (Halifax: Institute for Research in Public Policy, 1987.)

18. This is an "escape clause" provision. The tariff was for five years, declining from 35 percent to 8 percent in the final period.

19. Christopher Waddell. "Free Trade Pessimism Could Presage Retreat," *Globe and Mail*, September 16, 1987.

20. Section 333 (B) of H.R. 3, House of Representatives.

21. David Crane. "Canada-U.S. Free Trade Negotiations and the Cultural Industries: A Canadian View," notes for a presentation to the Council on Foreign Relations, New York, March 26, 1987.

22. Malcolm Baldridge, "Remarks by Commerce Secretary Malcolm Baldridge. Before the Merrill Lynch International Advisory Council Program," Toronto, Canada, May 28, 1987.

23. Robert A. Mundell, "International Trade and Factor Mobility," *American Economic Review*, 47 (June, 1957); 321–335.

24. J. R. Markusen, "Factor Movements and Commodity Trade as Complements," *Journal of International Economics* 13; 341–356.

25. B. W. Wilkinson, "A Review of Studies of Canadian Direct Foreign Investment and Free Trade," in preparation.

26. Foreign Investment Review Agency, Policy Research and Communications Branch. "Barriers to Foreign Investment in the United States," mimeographed, 1982.

27. Statistics Canada. *Canadian Imports by Domestic and Foreign-Controlled Firms: 1978* (Ottawa: Minister of Supply and Services, 1981).

28. The concept of "bringing discipline" to Canadian policies was repeatedly mentioned by William H. Cavitt, a U.S. Coordinator of the U.S. Canada Free Trade Negotiations, U.S. Department of Commerce, in a speech on July 27, 1987.

29. Richard Lipsey and Murray Smith. *Taking the Initiative: Canada's Trade Options in a Turbulent World*. (Toronto: C. D. Howe Institute, 1985), 152–156.

30. A. W. A. Lane. "Economic Integration—Some Aspects of European Experience," mimeographed 1985, p. 14.

31. M. Baldridge, "Remarks . . . "

32. See references in n.1; also R. Harris and D. Cox, "Summary of a Project of the General Equilibrium Evaluation of Canadian Trade Policy: Appendix Further Calculations on Sectoral and Bilateral Free Trade," in *Canada-United States Free Trade*, eds. John Whalley and Rod Hill. (Toronto: University of Toronto Press), 171–177.

33. See B. Wilkinson, *Canada in the Changing World Economy* (Toronto: C. D. Howe Institute, 1980), Appendix D. for early questioning of the numbers, see also B. Wilkinson, "Canada/U.S. Free Trade and Some Options," *Canadian Public Policy*, VIII, 1982 (Supplement): 428–439; and B. Wilkinson, "Canada-United States Free Trade. Setting the Dimensions . . . "; and most recently Tim Hazeldine, "What Do Economists Know About Free Trade?" in *Canadian-American Free Trade: Historical, Political and Economic Dimensions, . . .* , and references cited there.

34. Even the most recent edition of the textbook by A. Blomqvist, P. Wonnacott, and R. Wonnacott cites the gain from bilateral free trade to be in the order of 8–9 percent of GNP without alerting students to the fact that these numbers are greatly exaggerated. See *Economics*, Second Canadian Edition, Toronto: McGraw Hill Ryerson Ltd, 1987, p. 690.

35. Tim Hazeldine, "What Do Economists Know About Free Trade . . . "

36. B. Wilkinson, "Canada-United States Free Trade: Setting the Dimensions . . . "

37. Ibid. See also Tim Hazeldine, "What Do Economists Know About Free Trade?" Also note that in the most recent study of the gains from free trade the Economic Council of Canada concluded that 65 percent of the employment gains from bilateral free trade would arise in the service sector—even though the possibility of free trade in service was excluded in making the calculations! See Sunder Magun, Someshwar Rao and Bimal Lodh, *Impact of Canada-U.S. Free Trade on the Canadian Economy*. Discussion Paper no. 331. (Ottawa: Economic Council of Canada, 1987.)

38. B. W. Wilkinson, "A Review of Studies of Canadian Direct Foreign Investment and Free Trade," in preparation.

39. Although Rugman suggests that they are. See Alan Rugman, *Outward Bound Canadian Direct Investment in the United States*. (Toronto: C. D. Howe Institute, 1987.)

40. See R. Lipsey, "Canada's Trade Options" in *Canadian-American Free Trade* ..., p. 72–73.

41. See references in n. 10.

42. *Globe and Mail*, September 26, 1987.

43. The potash case is unique, however, for it is working out to Canada's advantage. See B. Wilkinson, "Canada-U.S. Trade Relations and the Exercise of U.S. 'Fair-Trade' Law with respect to Canadian Potash," a paper prepared for the Conference on Unequal Partners: A Comparison of Relations Between Austria–Federal Republic of Germany/Canada–U.S. Carleton University, September 24–25, 1987.

44. This section relies on the important work by Gordon Laxer, "Foreign Ownership and Myths About Canadian Development," *The Canadian Review of Sociology and Anthropology*, 22:3 (August, 1985): 311–345. See also Gordon Laxer, "Class, Nationality and the Roots of the Branch Plant Economy," *Studies in Political Economy*, 21 (Autumn, 1986); 7–56.

45. Laxer, "Foreign Ownership," p. 332.

46. The most noteworthy exception was Britain, which was still following the free trade policy adopted in the 1840s. But Britain, too, industrialized initially under an umbrella of protection.

47. Gordon Laxer, "Class, Nationality and the Roots of the Branch Plant Economy," p. 333.

48. George Grant, *Lament for a Nation: The Defeat of Canadian Nationalism*. (Toronto: McClelland and Stewart Limited, 1965.)

49. J. Parizeau, "Parizeau on Trade," in *Canadian-American Free Trade* ..., pp. 213–217.

50. R. Lipsey, for example, fails to see any relationship between recent U.S. actions and their attitudes and behavior in the free trade talks. See "Canada's Trade Options" in *Canadian-American Free Trade* ..., p. 68.

51. It is amusing to read that Peyton Lyon in "CUFTA and Canadian Independence ..." wants to apply for a research grant so he can spend next year in Hawaii to determine whether it is true that the free trade agreement signed between the U.S. and Hawaii in 1875 eventually led to political integration of the two independent states! Many books and papers have already been written on this phenomenon—which perusal of any good university library would reveal. See also B. Wilkinson, "Canada/US Free Trade and Canadian Economic, Cultural and Political Sovereignty" in *Canadian Trade at a Crossroads: Options for New International Agreements*, eds. D. Conklin and T. Courchene. (Toronto: Ontario Economic Council, 1985), 291–307.

52. *Globe and Mail*, October 14, 1987, A-4.

53. See, for example, Marsha Gordon, *Government in Business* (Toronto: C. D. Howe Institute, 1981) and Richard D. French, *How Ottawa Decides: Planning and Industrial Policy-Making, 1968–1980* (Ottawa: Canadian Institute for Economic Policy, 1980).

54. J. David Richardson "International Coordination of Trade Policy." (Cambridge, MA: National Bureau of Economic Research, 1987), 43–44.

55. Ibid.

56. William Mackness, "Defending the Canadian Dollar: Our High Interest Rate Policy Pays No Dividends," *Policy Options* (May, 1987) 4–6. For the first seven months of 1987, the Federal Reserve Bank of New York discount rate was 2.6 percentage points below the Bank of Canada's Bank Rate (5.50% versus 8.09%).

57. B. Wilkinson, "Canada-U.S. Trade Relations and the Exercise of U.S. 'Fair-Trade' Law With Respect to Canadian Potash."

58. Frank Stone. *Canada, the GATT and the International Trade System.* (Halifax: The Institute for Research on Public Policy, 1984), 155–163.

59. Richard Lipsey and Murray Smith. *Global Imbalances and U.S. Policy Responses: A Canadian Perspective.* (Toronto: C. D. Howe Institute, 1987.)

60. B. Wilkinson, "Canada-U.S. Trade Relations and the Exercise of U.S. 'Fair Trade' Law with Respect to Potash."

61. D. G. Haglund, "Protectionism and National Security: The Case of Canadian Uranium Exports to the United States," *Canadian Public Policy,* XII, No. 3, (September 1986): 459–472.

62. As this chapter was being completed, the chaos in the stock markets, commodity markets, and foreign exchange markets of the world suggest that the world may be in for a very difficult time. U.S. protectionism could rise even more and other nations could retaliate. World trade would be greatly reduced. Even if Canada signs an economic integration agreement with the U.S., it will not be immune to U.S. protectionism under U.S. trade laws. And because of the agreement, Canada may well find its hands tied more than it would like in taking measures that could alleviate its own situation. It could even find itself worse off with the agreement than without it.

8

Expanding Both Canadian and U.S. Trade

Warren J. Bilkey

"Mercantilist" and "physiocratic" concepts still appear to dominate international trade thinking. The former implicitly assumes that money and near-money is a country's true wealth. It can be illustrated by the Keynesian equation, $Y = C + I + G + T$ (where Y is net national product, C is aggregate consumption, I is net investment, G is the government's budgetary balance and T is the country's trade balance—all in real terms). This equation implies that where all else remains equal a country's best interest is to obtain a foreign trade surplus (a positive T). The "Mercantilist" concept focuses only on the interests of a single country. That pits each country against all others, because for one country to have a trade surplus some other country or combination of countries must have a corresponding trade deficit. Those having trade deficits become worse-off than they otherwise would have been; this gives them an incentive to restrict imports unilaterally. I do not know of a single country that has politically tolerated a long-term trade deficit that would have allowed trade surplus countries to acquire its assets.

The "mercantilist" concept creates an incentive for governments to seek free entry in foreign markets and to restrict foreign entry to their own markets in order to obtain an export surplus. Yet, no means have been found for a government to adequately police the foreign trade restrictions and subsidies of another country. For example, countries usually are unwilling to permit their firms' books to be checked by foreign governments who wish to determine whether or not those firms are dumping. In other instances governments claimed that they have no import restrictions when in fact they restrained trade indirectly by authorizing private associations to limit the import of products that relate to those associations.

Theoretically, the "mercantilist" concept of international trade can yield a zero trade balance for every trading partner if each is able to counteract the others' self-interests. That requires: (1) tight prohibitions against subsidies and restrictions that lead to trade imbalances among trading partners, (2) each partner accurately monitoring the other partners' trade actions to ascertain whether or not the agreed-on prohibitions against trade unbalancing actions are being violated, and (3) punishing whichever trading partner breaks an agreed-on trade unbalancing prohibition. If power is equally distributed among trading partners and they follow the above requirements, they theoretically could obtain mutually beneficial trade with each having a zero trade balance. But, if one country gains dominance over its trade partners, that country logically could dictate trade policies and practices that are in its own interests. In short, implementing a mutually beneficial "mercantilist" international trade policy appears possible, but difficult.

The "physiocratic" concept of international trade holds that a country's true wealth is its consumable products, rather than its money and near-money. The Ricardian theory of comparative advantage illustrates the "physiocratic" concept of international trade by focusing on gains from trade where the value of every country's total imports and exports are equal. This concept recognizes that all trading partners must perceive themselves as being better off with trade than by being self-sufficient, or they will stop trading. Accordingly, the "physiocratic" trade concept focuses on maximizing the total amount of mutually beneficial trade, rather than on maximizing any one country's own export surplus. Unresolved, however, are the unrealistic assumptions which underlie the Ricardian theory of comparative advantage.[1] That could cause many people to question whether or not there really are gains from trade, despite Professor Friedman's theory of positive economics.[2]

The "physiocratic" concept of international trade provides a foundation for negotiating mutually beneficial trade with a zero trade balance for each trading partner. However, it will not yield both free trade and a zero trade balance for trading partners unless there is near-identity in certain of their economic institutions plus coordination of their major economic policies plus agreement on their balance of trade accounting definitions. As an illustration, let us assume that Country I has achieved what at a full employment level would be equality between its aggregate internal production and its aggregate internal consumption—which typically requires substantial *equality* of income distribution. Assume also that at a full employment level Country II would have less aggregate internal consumption than aggregate internal production—which typically results from substantial *inequality* of income distribution. All else equal, that would tend to make Country I a high wage rate—high consumption economy, and Country II a low wage rate—low consumption economy. Then, *ceteris paribus*, free trade would have the effect of Country II exporting its excess production to Country I. In other words, free trade would allow Country II to use Country I's market to compensate for its high inequality of income distribution, and Country I would experience rising unemployment because of its trade deficit. Similar results could occur if Country II's population has a higher propensity to save than does Country I's population. This situation would tend to result in Country II having lower capital costs than Country I—which, all else equal, would tend to make Country II's products cheaper than Country I's products. Free trade would enable Country II to develop a trade surplus with Country I.

As a second illustration, assume that Country II uses the value-added tax (VAT) as its primary revenue source, while Country I uses corporate and personal income taxes as its primary revenue sources. Then, for Country I firms to export to Country II they must pay Country I's corporate income taxes on profits from those exports, plus the Country II's tariffs, plus Country II's VAT tax on the full value of those exports. Alternatively, a Country II exporter to Country I is reimbursed Country II's accumulated VAT taxes on the exported items and pays Country I's import tariff on those exports. In other words, exporting from Country I to Country II would require more total tax payments than does exporting from Country II to Country I. With free trade, all else equal, that would result in Country I having a trade deficit with Country II. It would be unrealistic to argue that currency exchange rates automatically adjust to compensate for such policy differences, because currency exchange rates are a function of many variables—not merely of comparative trade balances.

As a third illustration, assume that Country I uses a governmental budgetary deficit to stimulate its economy, and Country II gives its economy *no* economic stimulus. *Ceteris paribus*, that should cause Country I's economy to grow faster than Country II's economy, which with free trade would cause Country II to have a balance of trade surplus with Country I. In other words, without coordinated economic policies, free trade would lead to a trade imbalance between the two countries.

As a fourth illustration, assume that Country I has a large military budget for protecting both itself and Country II, and that Country II contributes nothing to defense. Then, *ceteris paribus*, Country I will have higher taxes and/or a greater government budget deficit than Country II, either of which under free trade would tend to cause Country I to have a balance of trade deficit with Country II.

In short, failure to eliminate differences in economic policies and institutions, such as those illustrated above, will result in one of the trading partners having a trade deficit. Ultimately, that would induce the trade deficit country to impose protectionist measures, which will not be eliminated by merely calling for free trade.

ALTERNATIVE TRADE POLICIES

The "mercantilist" concept implies that trade negotiators should adopt a confrontational approach, tightly specifying what each trading partner must and must not do. (Arms control negotiations between the U.S.A. and the U.S.S.R. suggest that such an approach can be very long with distressingly little progress.) The "physiocratic" concept implies that achieving free trade plus a zero trade balance for every trading partner requires that their institutions and economic policies be carefully harmonized. These include military expenditures, types of welfare programs (e.g., subsidizing firms to create jobs vs. providing direct welfare payments), tax methods (e.g., a VAT as opposed to corporate income taxes), government budgetary deficits, etc. Attitude and value differences among trading partners may make such coordination difficult.

Logic suggests that the "physiocratic" concept is consistent with two types of negotiating approaches. One, is to place priority on free trade (i.e., create a "level playing field"), and secondarily seek agreement on whatever institutional and economic adjustments will yield approximately a zero trade balance for each trading partner. The other negotiating approach is to place priority on achieving a nearly zero trade balance for all of the trading partners, and secondarily to seek to make trade among them as free as possible.

Under ideal conditions both approaches should yield the same results, but in a less-than-perfect world the results will differ. As an example, assume that Countries I and II are trading partners, and that Country I has a trade surplus with Country II. If their negotiations focus on free trade, Country I's firms who wish to export would have no incentive to promote importing from Country II. Rather, Country I's firms would have an incentive to pressure Country II to allow completely free trade. On the other hand, if the countries' negotiations focus on every partner having a nearly zero trade balance, Country I's firms who wish to export to Country II would have an incentive to encourage imports from Country II so that they in turn can export more to Country II. Furthermore, Country I's negotiators probably would refuse to reduce trade barriers if that could lead to worsening trade deficits with Country II, but might be willing to negotiate for freer trade if trade deficits could be avoided.

Definitional issues also need to be agreed upon by all trading partners if free trade with a nearly zero trade balance for every trading partner is to be achieved. *One* is the equivalence between exporting, foreign licensing, foreign franchising, foreign investment and foreign services (which include foreign finance, foreign management contracts, foreign consulting, foreign construction contracts, educational and medical services for foreigners, tourism, etc.). The issue goes far beyond mere balance-of-trade accounting. For example, is it economically equivalent for Country I to have an investment surplus with Country II if the latter has an equal value of export surplus with Country I? As another example, is one million dollars worth of exports from Country I to Country II economically equivalent to one million dollars worth of licensing by Country II to Country I? A *second* type of trade issue is the handling of three-way trade—where Country I has an export surplus with Country II, which has an equal export surplus with Country III, which has an equal export surplus with Country I—with the result that each country's foreign trade has a zero balance. How then should Countries I and II calculate their trade accounts with each other? A *third* issue is the trade accounting period. If Country II has a trade surplus with Country I during a particular year, should Country II's exports to Country I be curtailed the next year by an import quota or a tariff surcharge? Or should the trade period be a running average trade balance over a five year time period? Or should a limited margin for trade fluctuations be allowed—e.g., so that a tariff penalty against Country II will not be imposed by Country I unless Country II's export surplus to Country I is greater than a specified percentage of their total trade with each other? What is an acceptable margin?

Thus far Canadian–U.S. trade negotiations have focused on free trade. Progress has been made, but much opposition to further concessions are being voiced. As a political-economy effort to reduce the power of special interest groups it may be well to consider whether our countries' negotiating focus should shift to seeking, primarily, a nearly zero trade balance for each trading partner, and, secondarily, the elimination of all trade restrictions that are consonant with trade balance.

PROMOTING TRADE

The Ricardian theory of comparative advantage (which underlies the "physiocratic" concept of international trade) holds that all trading partners can gain from trade where each country's total exports and imports are equal, i.e., that increased free trade between Canada and the U.S. with a zero trade balance for each would be beneficial to both countries. One means for increasing total trade between Canada and the U.S. would be for both countries to promote exporting by their own firms provided that both countries use the same export stimulation methods. Research in Canada, the U.S. and Western Europe over the past fifteen years has convinced analysts that many more firms in each of those countries could export than now do. Most of those studies obtained survey data from firms, and used regression analysis for analyzing those data. Typically, the dependent variable was (a) whether or not the firm exports, or (b) the percent of the firms' sales exported. The independent variables typically were characteristics of the firm and its management (e.g., firm size, type of product, the firms' organizational structure, management's goals, managements' attitudes regarding exporting, management's perceived obstacles to exporting, etc.). Those studies indicate that there are great similarities in export behavior among firms in all of those countries. They also indicate that the most important export determinant tends to be management's attitudes regarding exporting—which can be influenced. Additional determinants of exporting were found to be: management's information regarding foreign markets, information available to management regarding how to export (export channels, export documentation, obtaining payment, etc.), and financial and legal assistance. In addition, those studies imply that the kind of export assistance needed by management differs according to the firm's size, the firm's export experience, the type of product exported, etc. Governments can use those research findings for developing export promotion programs, and for profiling firms that have good export potential. By identifying which firm would be most likely to respond to export promotion efforts, exporter profiles enable a government to maximize results from their export promotion efforts.

Another line of research for stimulating exports focuses on firms' export marketing practices. Survey data have been classified according to firm characteristics (type of product exported, firm size, firm's export experience, annual amounts exported to each country, perceived competition to exporting, etc.). For each combination of those characteristics, firms' export marketing practices have been related to their export profits. Research indicates that firms using the "best" (meaning the most profitable) combination of export marketing practices tend to average approximately 40 percentage points higher export profit than firms using the "worst" (meaning the least profitable) combination of export marketing practices. Yet, the "best" combination of export marketing practices are not the most frequently used, nor are the "worst" export marketing practices the least frequently used. The apparent reason is that managements tend to use "satisficing" criteria for selecting their export marketing practices, because they lack information as to which export marketing practices indeed are best for their particular situations. Survey studies could be systematized, and the findings provided to firms as guides for selecting their own export marketing practices. That should increase export profitability—thereby stimulating greater export effort.

In short, much can be done by Canada and by the U.S. to stimulate their exports to each other and to other countries. The "physiocratic" concept of international trade implies that with proper governmental policies both countries can gain by increasing their trade with each other.

SUMMARY

The following argument has been presented. Trading partners cannot achieve both free trade and zero trade balances unless their relevant institutions and economic policies are harmonized. This is politically difficult, because of differing economic ideologies and because of vested interests who resist change. Therefore, an appropriate trade strategy is needed. A suggested strategy is: (a) that trade negotiations between Canada and the U.S. focus primarily on achieving a nearly zero trade balance for each country and secondarily seek as much free trade between our countries as is consonant with such trade balance, and (b) that both countries seek, by using agreed-on methods, to stimulate their firms to export as much as possible to all countries, including each other. The purpose of these suggestions is to create political pressure from would-be exporters to nullify protectionist pressures by vested interests in both countries.

NOTES

1. Unrealistic assumptions underlying the Ricardian theory of comparative advantage are that: pure competition exists, currency exchange rates are determined primarily by relative trade balances, and a two country–two product model adequately explains mutually advantageous multilateral trade relationships. If the Heckscher–Ohlin explanation for comparative advantage is included, the following unrealistic assumptions must be added: that products move across national boundaries but factors of production do not, and that identical production functions for each traded product are used by all trading partners.

2. Milton Friedman's theory of positive economics argues that unrealistic assumptions in a theory do not matter so long as the theory's results conform with actual experience. Unfortunately, the absence of an objective measure of comparative advantage makes comparisons between actual experiences and the theory of comparative advantage uncertain.

PART IV
TAXES, FINANCIAL MARKETS, AND BILATERAL INVESTMENT

9
The Impacts of Tax and Tariff Reform on U.S. Direct Investment in Canadian Manufacturing

Lorraine Eden

INTRODUCTION

In the Canadian manufacturing sector in 1981, U.S.-controlled enterprises generated 38.2 percent of shipments (i.e. $83.5 billion), 34.2 percent of value added ($26.8 billion) and 36.9 percent of investment ($4.7 billion). Foreign-controlled (mainly U.S.) firms owned 44.9 percent of the assets ($167.9 billion) and generated 76.2 percent of the imports of this sector. Since the largest U.S.-controlled manufacturing firms bought more than 70 percent of their imports from, and sold over 76 percent of their exports to parents and affiliates, probably 60 percent of traded goods and services in the Canadian manufacturing sector could be classified as intrafirm, moving between countries at transfer prices set within multinational corporations.[1]

Given the close links between the U.S. and Canadian manufacturing sectors, it is not surprising that the current changes in U.S. and Canadian corporate income tax and tariff rules should be causing much uncertainty and controversy on both sides of the border. Tariff rates have been falling in response to the Tokyo Round; by 1988 close to 90 percent of U.S. exports will enter Canada with levies of less than 5 percent (Lush, 1987). A new GATT round is now underway in Uruguay. Declining tariffs, if not offset by increasing nontariff barriers to trade imposed by a protectionist U.S. Congress, are expected to bring Canadian and U.S. commodity and factor prices more closely in line and stimulate trade and output in both countries. In addition, the two countries are currently engaged in talks to create a bilateral free trade area where tariffs would be eliminated, nontariff barriers severely constrained, and investment flows liberalized. If this happens, trade flows between the two countries could be further enhanced with some trade diversion against third countries. The net impact on U.S. foreign investment in Canadian manufacturing is unclear. Labor unions and the Canadian public expect a large outflow as branch plants close down and production is shifted to the United States; however, most specialists in the area expect net movements to be small, although within certain industries there may be large dislocations (Burgess, 1985b; Rugman, 1987). If the talks fail, rising U.S. protectionism may offset much of the earlier gains under the Tokyo Round, causing increased dislocations in intrafirm trade flows between Canada and the United States.

Coupled with tariff reductions under the Tokyo Round, the United States is reforming its personal and corporate income tax structure, shifting its emphasis from an instrument of social and economic policy to one of revenue collection and neutrality.[2] Statutory rates are being lowered, the numbers of rates reduced and tax exemptions severely restricted. The U.S. federal statutory rate of corporate income tax (CIT) will fall from 46 percent to 34 percent by 1988 with estimates of a combined federal/state CIT of 40.6 percent across all industries. Because many tax exemptions are also being reduced, most commentators expect the average burden of CIT to rise, particularly in those industries where exemptions are large, such as oil and mining, although the burden could fall for manufacturing. In addition, the lower statutory rate reduces the U.S. foreign tax credit available to offset foreign taxes on dividends remitted from abroad. Coupled with the change from an overall to a per-country limitation on the credit, countries like Canada with high tax rates are widely expected to lose U.S. investments.[3] With lower tax rates in the United States there is an incentive to take interest deductions in Canada, price intrafirm imports higher and exports lower and allocate more management fees to Canada, in order to shift profits to the U.S. As tariff rates fall, the incentive to price Canadian imports high will be accentuated.

These predicted effects on Canada may be less likely in the manufacturing sector, because manufacturing and processing profits are currently subject to a 40 percent Canadian CIT rate, compared to the general statutory rate of 46 percent. However, although Canadian CIT rates have been lower than U.S. ones on manufacturing, the gap between statutory rates falls substantially after U.S. reform which may strengthen the incentive to shift profits and investments to the U.S. For example, *The Globe and Mail*, Nov. 11, 1986, argued that the gap between Canadian and U.S. tax rates was "unlikely to provoke a wholesale exodus of manufacturing operations from Canada. . . . U.S. parents (however) might want to raise the price they charge to their Canadian subsidiaries on intercompany transfers of goods or services." (p. B9)

Partly as a result of U.S. tax reform, the Canadian government announced its own tax reform package on June 18, 1987. The statutory CIT rate is to be reduced from 46 percent to 38 percent (34 percent by 1990 on manufacturing profits). Some exemptions such as capital cost allowances are to be reduced and certain tax credits such as the investment tax credit eliminated. The federal government justified these measures on the grounds that statutory rate reductions were necessary to keep the Canadian fiscal system competitive with its major trading partners, especially the U.S. "Without tax rate cuts, income-earning activity in Canada could be diverted elsewhere and corporations . . . could arrange their activities in such a way as to earn more income taxable abroad and less in Canada. The tax rate cuts . . . are designed to avoid these undesirable effects." (*Income Tax Reform*, p. 99)

The purpose of this chapter is to analyze the net effects of these corporate income tax and tariff rate changes on U.S.-controlled manufacturing firms in Canada. We restrict our analysis to a first-order approximation to the net impact, taking a partial-equilibrium approach so that second-round exchange rate and income effects are ignored. We concentrate only on the impacts of reform on manufacturing intrafirm trade and investment flows between the two countries.[4] In the first section of the chapter we explain the impacts of corporate income taxes on international capital flows and relate this to current U.S. and Canadian taxation of U.S.-owned subsidiaries in Canada. In the second section we develop a partial-equilibrium theory of a horizontally-integrated multinational (MNE) and predict the impact of tax and tariff changes on capital, intrafirm trade and financial flows within the MNE. The fourth section uses data for the period 1978–81 to estimate effective marginal CIT rates on capital flows and effective average CIT rates on book profits for the U.S. manufacturing parents and their Canadian subsidiaries. We then reestimate these effective marginal and average rates under the following scenarios: U.S. reform only, Canadian reform only, and U.S. plus Canadian tax reform. Based on the theories presented in the second and third sections, the marginal and average tax rates are then used to predict the impact of Canadian and U.S. tax and tariff reform on capital, trade, and financial flows of U.S.-controlled manufacturing subsidiaries in Canada. The fifth section sums up.

The chapter concludes that U.S. tax reform should generate an investment boom in Canadian manufacturing; however, both effective marginal and average corporate income tax rates rise so sharply under the Canadian tax proposals that an overall net decline in new investment by U.S.-controlled subsidiaries in the Canadian manufacturing sector of between 16 and 28 percent is predicted. Since tax reform should increase financial outflows and imports while the reduction in Canadian tariffs should reduce the incentive to underinvoice, the net impact is likely to worsen the Canadian balance of payments in this sector.

THE IMPACTS OF CORPORATE INCOME TAXES ON INTERNATIONAL CAPITAL FLOWS

Current Rules on the International Taxation of Capital Income

Taxation of multinational capital income by either the home or host country has complicated effects that spill over internationally. These spillovers occur because taxation of MNEs affects not only the international allocation of capital, but also the distribution of gains from foreign investment between home and host countries, the returns to residents and nonresidents in the host country, and the treatment in the home country of local residents with foreign-source income relative to those with domestic income. As a result of these international complications, the OECD has a Model Tax Treaty Convention on Income and Capital which countries are urged to follow in taxing MNE income.

Under the OECD Convention the host country has the primary right to tax business income earned within its borders. The MNEs tax base is allocated internationally according to the concept of a permanent establishment, with affiliates treated as separate legal entities and income apportioned between them assuming intrafirm transactions take place at arm's length prices. The home country has the right to tax remitted income, with the host country having the prior right to levy a withholding tax. Since the host is considered to have the primary right to tax, the home country is expected to modify its rules to take account of host taxation. Usually the home country defers taxation of foreign retained earnings and taxes only repatriated profits, giving a foreign tax credit for the CIT and withholding taxes paid in the host country.

With respect to U.S.-controlled manufacturing affiliates in Canada, both the Canadian and U.S. governments basically follow the OECD convention. In Canada foreign-controlled permanent establishments are taxed at a federal plus provincial statutory CIT rate with most tax deductions and credits available to domestic firms also available to foreign establishments. Manufacturing and processing firms benefit from a reduced CIT rate. Foreign-owned branches pay an additional 25 percent of taxable income, from which the CIT is deductible, as a branch tax. Withholding taxes on remittances (except interest payments) are levied when these funds are repatriated. In the United States, the CIT applies to domestic income of U.S. MNEs plus accrued foreign branch profits plus head-office fees and interest payments remitted from foreign affiliates. Remitted dividends are grossed up by the amount of foreign CIT

Figure 9.1
The Impacts of U.S. and Canadian Corporate Income Taxes on Capital Flows

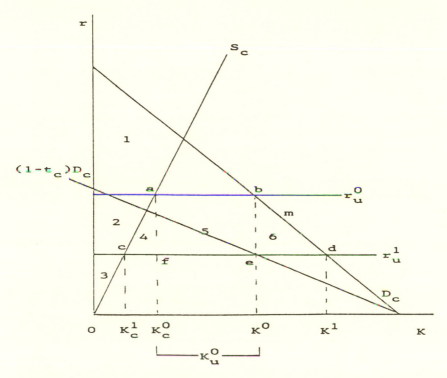

and also brought into taxable income. Foreign tax credits are provided for withholding taxes on remitted interest, head office payments and dividends, foreign branch taxes, and foreign CITs on dividends. The credit on dividends for the foreign CIT plus withholding tax is limited to the U.S. tax due on these profits.

A Simple Model of U.S.-Canada Capital Flows

We can explain the impacts of these U.S. and Canadian taxes using a simple model of capital flows between the two countries. We assume the net return to capital is determined in the U.S. market so that Canada treats the net return as given. Assume initially that neither country taxes domestic profits. Figure 9.1 shows the Canadian demand for capital curve, D_C the Canadian supply of savings curve, S_C, and the supply of U.S. capital curve, S_U, which is horizontal at the going U.S. net return to capital, r_u^0. Equilibrium occurs at point b with total investment in Canadian manufacturing of K^0, consisting of K_C^0 in resident-controlled capital and $K^0 - K_C^0 = K_u^0$ (the distance ab) in U.S.-controlled foreign direct investment (FDI). National income is measured by labor income equal to area 1 plus resident capital surplus (the excess over the opportunity cost of capital) of area 2 + 3, for a total Canadian welfare level of area 1 + 2 + 3.

We examine several possible tax cases organized under three headings according to whether the Canadian government does not tax U.S.-controlled capital income, taxes it at the same rate as in the U.S. or taxes it at a higher rate. In each case we compare exemption of foreign-source income by the U.S. with taxation of foreign income accompanied by a foreign tax credit up to the U.S. tax. We examine the impacts of the Canadian government levying either a nondiscriminatory CIT or a separate withholding tax on FDI income.

Canada Does Not Tax Capital Income

The U.S. Exempts Foreign-Source Income. Assume that the U.S. decides to tax domestic capital income at rate t_u, leaving an after-tax return of r_u^0 to local investors, but exempts all foreign affiliate profits from tax. Since the net return to capital invested in the U.S. falls, foreign direct investment in Canada expands to the distance cd, equal to $K^1 - K_c^1$ in Figure 9.1. National welfare rises by area 4 + 5 + 6 since the decline in the opportunity cost of capital causes producer surplus to fall by area 2 and labour income to rise by area 2 + 4 + 5 + 6. Areas 4 + 6 represent the traditional specialization and exchange gains that accompany increased trade while area 5 is a revenue transfer from foreign capitalists to Canadian labour because the opportunity cost of capital has fallen.

The U.S. Taxes Foreign-Source Income and Provides a Foreign Tax Credit. If the U.S. government taxes both domestic and foreign-earned returns to capital at the same rate t_u, the analysis is quite different. The U.S. tax on foreign-source income acts like a tariff, raising the cost of U.S. investments in Canada. Now all U.S. capital wherever invested is taxed at the same rate, ensuring capital export neutrality. In Figure 9.1 the price of foreign capital in Canada shifts back to r_u^0 and K_u returns to its initial level K_u^0 (the distance ab). Canadian welfare returns to area 1 + 2 + 3 as Canada loses area 4 + 5 + 6. The only difference compared to the zero-tax case is that area 5 goes to the U.S. government instead of the foreign investor.

Canada Taxes Capital Income at the U.S. Rate.

The U.S. Exempts Foreign-Source Income. (a) Assume that all capital in Canada is taxed at rate $t_C = t_u$ and that the U.S. exempts foreign source income from taxation. Before the Canadian tax the economy is importing cd of foreign capital at price r_u^0. The Canadian tax causes the demand for capital curve in Figure 9.1 to rotate downward to $(1 - t_C) D_C$. Assume t_C initially equals t_U so that the new demand curve must pass through point e directly below point b. Thus total capital investment falls from K^1 to K^0, resident investment is unchanged while FDI contracts to $K^0 - K_c^1$. Total Canadian tax revenue equals area 2 + 4 + 5. Since labor income falls by area 2 + 4 + 5 + 6 while resident capital surplus is unaffected, national welfare falls by area 6, the deadweight loss (DWL) in exchange, the net loss due to the lower capital/labor ratio.[5]

(b) If the Canadian government places a discriminatory tax on non-resident capital income the results are slightly different. A discriminatory tax such as the withholding tax acts as a tariff, raising the price of imported capital. Since the tax does not apply to resident capital, its net return rises by the tax. In Figure 9.1, a withholding tax at rate $w = t_U$ causes the price of capital to rise to point b, K_U to shrink to $K^0 - K_C^0$, generating area 5 in tax revenue. The welfare loss to Canada is identical to a tariff loss; i.e., area 4 (the DWL in specialization) + 6 (the DWL in exchange). Note that the discriminatory withholding tax causes a larger welfare loss than a nondiscriminatory CIT.

The U.S. Taxes Foreign-Source Income and Provides a Foreign Tax Credit
(a) Assume that Canada levies a CIT and the U.S. government also taxes MNE income earned in Canada on an accrual basis (i.e. the foreign affiliate is a branch). We assume the U.S. credits Canadian taxes on MNE profits up to the level of the U.S. tax. With only the U.S. tax in place, the initial position is represented by the distance ab in Figure 9.1 and U.S. tax revenue by area 5. Imposing the Canadian CIT at rate $t_C = t_U$ generates a new equilibrium at point e. Total capital investment is unchanged at K^0, resident investment falls to K_C^0 while FDI expands to $K^0 - K_C^1$. The total Canadian tax, equal to area 2 + 4 + 5, has two effects. First, the tax generates a revenue transfer equal to area 5 from the U.S. to the Canadian government, because the U.S. government credits the Canadian tax. Secondly, the nondiscriminatory CIT tax lowers the net return to Canadian savers to r_u^0, causing a fall in resident capital equal to $K_C^0 - K_C^1$ and an equal-sized inflow of U.S. capital. Since the opportunity cost of U.S. capital is r_u^0 while the opportunity cost of resident capital is the area under the S_C curve, a specialization gain is generated equal to area 4. The Canadian CIT, if credited in the U.S., causes national welfare to increase by area 4 + 5. Thus, if the U.S. exempts foreign-source income from taxation, the Canadian CIT causes a fall in national welfare equal to area 6; whereas U.S. taxation with a foreign tax credit implies that the Canadian CIT raises welfare by area 4 + 5.

(b) If the Canadian government places a discriminatory tax on non-resident capital and the U.S. taxes foreign-source income but credits the Canadian tax, the gains are not as large. The new equilibrium is at point b, with Canadian revenue of area 5 and foreign capital of $K^0 - K_C^0$. The welfare gain to Canada is simply the revenue transfer area 5. Thus the withholding tax, if the U.S. exempts foreign income, lowers Canadian welfare by area $4 + 6$; whereas if the U.S. taxes and credits, Canadian welfare rises by area 5.

Note that, if Canada does tax capital income, a nondiscriminatory tax like the CIT is preferred to an equivalent discriminatory tax such as the withholding tax because the CIT generates a larger welfare gain than the withholding tax. From Figure 9.1 we also see that, if the U.S. provides a credit up to the U.S. tax rate, it is in Canada's interest to set its rate at the U.S. rate. Any rate lower than that reduces the Canadian welfare gain.

Canada Taxes Capital Income at a Rate Higher Than the U.S. Rate

The U.S. Exempts Foreign-Source Income. This analysis is similar to that in B.1, except the losses are larger.

The U.S. Taxes Foreign-Source Income and Provides a Foreign Tax Credit. (a) Assume that the Canadian government levies a nondiscriminatory CIT at a rate higher than in the U.S. so that a deficit of foreign tax credits occurs. This is represented in Figure 9.2, which is based on Figure 9.1. A Canadian CIT at the same rate as in the U.S. generates a welfare gain equal to area $4 + 5$ in Figure 9.1 and area $8 + 9 + 10 + 11$ in Figure 9.2. If the Canadian tax rate rises, the demand curve rotates again to $(1 - t_C^1) D_C$ and total investment is determined by point g with the gross price of capital represented by point h. Capital flows shrink to K^2, with unchanged resident investment and a smaller amount of foreign capital inflows, $K^2 - K_C^1$. The new tax revenue is area $2 + 3 + 4 + 6 + 8 + 9 + 10$ compared to the earlier revenue of area $6 + 8 + 9 + 10 + 11$, for a net change of area $2 + 3 + 4 - 11$. Since labour income falls by area $2 + 3 + 4 + 5$ while resident capital surplus is unchanged, the net impact is a loss of area $5 + 11$. Area 5 is the DWL in exchange caused by the fall in investment, while area 11 is the foregone revenue transfer on foreign capital. Thus, raising the Canadian CIT rate above the creditable level in the U.S. causes an outflow of FDI, generating a DWL in exchange and a smaller revenue transfer that lowers Canadian welfare.

(b) If the Canadian tax is discriminatory, the welfare losses are larger. Suppose the only Canadian tax is a withholding tax on foreign capital

Figure 9.2
The Effects of Setting the Canadian Tax Rate Above the U.S. CIT Rate

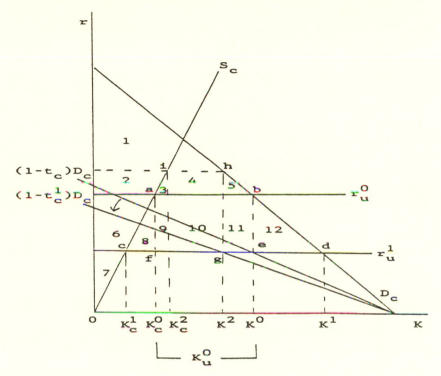

levied at a rate greater than t_u. The tax acts like an import tariff, raising the price of capital to point h, and lowering FDI to $K^2 - K_c^2$ (the distance ih). Compared to a withholding tax equal to t_u, the higher tax causes tax revenue to change by area 4 + 10 minus area 9 + 10 + 11 for a net change of area 4 − 9 − 11. Since labour income falls by area 2 + 3 + 4 + 5 and resident capital surplus rises by area 2, the net change in Canadian welfare is a loss of area 3 + 9 + 5 + 11. Area 3 represents the specialization DWL, area 5 the exchange DWL, while area 9 + 1 is the foregone revenue transfer. Note that the losses, as before, are larger under a discriminatory tax.

Implications for Current U.S. and Canadian Taxation of Capital Income

In practice, the U.S. and Canadian tax structures fall somewhere in the middle of the above cases. Canada levies both a nondiscriminatory CIT and a discriminatory withholding tax. However, since the current withholding tax on dividends is low (10–15 percent) and levied only on remitted profits net of the CIT, the effective rate is even lower (6–9 percent on dividends), compared to a statutory CIT rate on all manufacturing profits of 40 percent. Thus, in general, Canadian taxes on nonresident capital income can be considered as nondiscriminatory. Since the United States taxes branch profits as accrued and provides a full foreign tax credit up to the U.S. tax rate, we consider cases (B)(2)(a) and (C)(2)(a) as appropriate for branches depending on whether the Canadian tax rate is higher, lower, or equal to the U.S. rate. The implicit policy implication for Canadian taxation of U.S. branches is that the Canadian government should keep Canadian taxation of American branches is that the Canadian government should keep Canadian taxation of American branches at rates creditable in the U.S. in order to generate welfare gains for Canada.[6]

The implications for U.S. subsidiaries in Canada are not straightforward since the U.S. defers taxation of subsidiary income until it is remitted. There is a large literature on the economic effects of tax deferral,[7] with the standard view being that tax deferral lowers the effective tax rate on foreign subsidiary earnings, encouraging capital outflows from the home country. The effective tax on the subsidiary is measured as a weighted average of the tax rate on dividends and that on retained earnings, determined by the dividend remittance ratio α where $0 \leq a \leq 1$. In our case the effective rate of tax on foreign source income, t^E, would be a weighted average of the Canadian CIT (on retained earnings) and either of two rates on dividends depending on whether Canada has a surplus or deficit of foreign tax credits:

$$t^E = (1 - \alpha) t_C + \alpha t_U \qquad \text{deficit of tax credits} \qquad \textbf{(1a)}$$

$$t^E = t_C + \alpha w_D (1 - t_C) \qquad \text{surplus of tax credits} \qquad \textbf{(1b)}$$

If $\alpha = 0$ (complete deferral), $t^E = t_C$ so that foreign-controlled capital income is taxed at the host rate (ensuring capital import neutrality). This corresponds to cases (B)(1)(a) and (C)(1)(a) where the U.S. exempts foreign-source income from taxation so that Canadian taxation causes deadweight losses that rise with the tax rate. If $\alpha = 1$ (no deferral, the branch case), $t^E = t_U$ in the deficit of credits case so all U.S. capital wherever invested is taxed at the home rate (and capital export neutrality prevails). This corresponds to our earlier branch cases (B)(2)(a) and (C)(2)(a) where the optimal Canadian tax should be set at the creditable U.S. rate and Canadian welfare is increased by the tax. In the intermediate cases t^E lies somewhere between capital export and import neutrality, with part of the Canadian tax creditable in the U.S. so that Canadian welfare could either rise or fall. The economic rationale for the standard view can be explained as follows.

Due to the U.S. tax treatment of subsidiaries, American MNEs have an incentive to defer repatriation of profits from their subsidiaries in order to avoid the extra tax payable upon remittance. This incentive exists in both the surplus and deficit of foreign tax credit cases as long as the host country levies a withholding tax on dividend repatriations. As a result, deferral may induce larger U.S.-controlled capital inflows into Canada compared to the branch case. In Figure 9.1, exemption of foreign-source income from U.S. taxation generates an initial equilibrium in the Canadian capital market at point d (the net return to capital under exemption is r_u^1) with U.S. investment equal to the distance cd. Full U.S. taxation and crediting moves the Canadian equilibrium to point b (the net return is r_u^0) with FDI equal to the distance ab. If $O < \alpha < 1$, the net return lies between these two extremes at a point like m with an intermediate amount of foreign investment. The policy implication from this is that a Canadian CIT that lowers the net return to investments in Canada below $\alpha \, r_u$ may generate fewer capital inflows, a fall in total investment and welfare losses. However, taxes that are creditable in the U.S. may not affect total investment, but raise welfare via capital inflows.

The alternative view gaining recognition among economists is that tax deferral is equivalent to tax exemption by the U.S.; i.e., the additional withholding taxes and/or U.S. taxes due upon repatriation can be ignored so that the effective tax on foreign-source income is the host tax rate. Thus the allocation of capital flows between the home and host countries depends only on a comparison between their domestic CIT rates. Two quite different arguments have been put forward, both supporting this new view of deferral. The first argument is an old one, best put by Carl Shoup (1969): "Since a delayed tax is a reduced tax . . . if the delay lasts for, say, fifty years or more, the present value of the tax is reduced close to zero at usual rates of discount" (pp. 636–7). That is, if dividends are deferred long enough, tax deferral by the home country is equivalent to exempting foreign-source income from tax since the net present value (NPV) of the extra tax is zero.

The second argument is the exact reverse of Shoup's point but has the same policy conclusion (see Hartman, 1985; also Warren, 1986). Hartman argues that mature subsidiaries that finance their growth with retained earnings decide whether to reinvest or repatriate their profits by comparing the net return to local reinvestment vis-à-vis the net return from remitting the profits to the home country for reinvestment at home. As long as foreign-source earnings are eventually remitted to the parent company, the MNE cannot avoid the extra tax due upon repatriation. And, if the funds are reinvested in the host country and grow at the average after-tax host rate of return, the NPV of the extra tax payment due on repatriation is unchanged (see Warren). Because all foreign earnings must at some time bear the extra tax, it can be treated as a fixed cost and ignored; the timing of the extra tax payment is irrelevant. The only question for the MNE is which location produces the highest return net of the local CITs, t_C and t_U. Thus in the new view of deferral, the effective tax on foreign-source income is the host CIT, whether the NPV of the deferred tax is zero (as in Shoup) or constant (as in Hartman/Warren).[8] The policy implication is that deferral is equivalent to tax exemption; i.e., cases (B)(1)(a) and (C)(1)(a) apply so the Canadian CIT, whether it is above or below the U.S. level, generates a welfare loss.

A PARTIAL-EQUILIBRIUM ANALYSIS OF INTRAFIRM TRADE AND CAPITAL FLOWS

In this section we develop a simple model of a two-firm manufacturing MNE consisting of a U.S. parent and a Canadian subsidiary engaged in horizontal intrafirm trade. This model is used to predict how MNE capital, intrafirm trade and financial flows react to changes in CIT and tariff rates.

A Model of MNE Capital, Intrafirm Trade and Financial Flows

Each firm produces output, Q_I, for sale in the local market, Y_I, or for export, X, where $I = U, C$. We assume, in accordance with the data, that the Canadian subsidiary is the importer, and that a tariff at rate τ is levied on imports. Intrafirm imports are priced at a transfer price p for a total trade value of pX. The parent therefore sells $Y_U = Q_U - X$ for a total revenue of R_U; while the subsidiary sells $Y_C = Q_C + X$ for sales revenue of R_C. Each firm incurs only capital costs; we ignore labour costs.

Each firm owns $P_{KI}K_I$ in capital which depreciates at a uniform rate d.[9] The opportunity cost of capital is its real return plus the depreciation rate. The real return is assumed given to the firm and equals r_U, the U.S. real return to capital, with arbitrage between countries ensuring $r = r_C = r_U$. Note that although real returns are equal, nominal returns may differ ($i_U \gtrless i_C$) as well as inflation rates ($\Phi_U \gtrless \Phi_C$). Thus the cost of capital is $(r + d) P_{KI}K_I$ to each firm in the absence of taxation. Corporate income taxes complicate matters in three ways. First, interest costs are tax-deductible so that the true opportunity cost is reduced by the CIT rate times the leverage ratio, L_I (the ratio of long-term liabilities to long-term liabilities plus equity); i.e., the new opportunity cost is $(r + d - t_I L_I i_I) P_{KI}K_I$.[10] Second, both countries currently offer an investment tax credit so that some fraction, β_I, of investment expenditures is creditable against the CIT. This reduces the opportunity cost of capital to $(r + d - t_I L_I i_I)(1 - \beta_I) P_{KI}K_I$. Lastly, both countries offer capital cost allowances that provide accelerated depreciation over and above economic depreciation rates as a tax deduction. If the net present value of these allowances is Z_l the true opportunity cost is reduced by the CIT times Z_l. Since U.S. tax law employs a half-year convention that treats all purchases within a year as if they occurred at midyear (see Fazzari, 1987), the final opportunity cost of capital to the U.S. parent is:

$$C_{KU} = (r + d - t_u L_u i_u)(1 - \beta_u - t_u Z_u (1 - .5\,\beta_u)) P_{KU} K_u \qquad \textbf{(2a)}$$

In Canada, the investment tax credit must be deducted from the capital base used to calculate the capital consumption allowance, so the effective cost of capital to the Canadian subsidiary is:

$$C_{KC} = (r + d - t_c L_c I_c)(1 - \beta_c)(1 - t_c Z_c) P_{KC} K_c \qquad \textbf{(2b)}$$

We assume the exchange rate between the two countries is e and that all variables are measured in the home currency. The net profit function of each firm is calculated by determining taxable income; i.e., economic profit minus tax-deductible expenses. Taxable income times the CIT rate yields the initial tax, from which tax credits are subtracted to determine the total tax payable. Economic profit minus actual taxes yields the net profit of the firm, π_l. The net profit function for the Canadian subsidiary is:

$$\pi_C = [\,(1 - t_c)\{R_C - (1/e)(1 + c)\,pX - H\} - C_{KC} = W_H H - (1 + W_D)\,D]\ \textbf{(3)}$$

assuming the subsidiary is charged for head office services and these charges, H, are tax deductible in the host country. The subsidiary remits H, after paying a withholding tax at rate w_H, plus dividends, D, net of a withholding tax at rate w_D, to the parent company.

The after-tax profit function of the U.S. parent is calculated as the CIT times taxable income, minus tax credits. Taxable income equals domestic economic profits plus remittances from the subsidiary (after grossing up the dividends by the host CIT) minus other tax-deductible expenses. The foreign CIT and withholding tax are creditable up to the level of the home CIT. The profit function of the U.S. parent can therefore be written as:

$$\pi_U = (1 - t_u)(R_u + pX) - C_{KU} + e\,[1 - (t_u - w_H)]\,H$$
$$+\ e\,[1 - \{(t_u - (t_c + W_D(1 - t_c)))/(1 - t_c)\}]\,D \qquad \textbf{(4)}$$

where the term in $\{\cdot\}$ brackets must be either zero (if the subsidiary has a surplus of foreign tax credits) or positive (in the deficit of credits case).

Let us rewrite the $\{\cdot\}$ term as $f = 0$ for the surplus case and $f > 0$ for the deficit case. In the surplus case π_U therefore equals:

$$\pi_u = (1 - t_u)(R_u + pX) - C_{Ku} + e[1 - (t_u - W_H)]H + eD \tag{4a}$$

since $f = 0$; and in the deficit case,

$$\pi_u = (1 - t_u)(R_u + pX) - C_{Ku} + e[1 - (t_u - W_H)]H$$
$$+ e[1 - f/(1 - t_c)]D \tag{4b}$$

The objective function of the MNE is to maximize global net profits:

Max $\pi = (\pi_C + \pi_u)$ subject to the constraints that:
$\Sigma Q_I = \Sigma Y_I$ (all output is sold)
$r_C = r_u = r$ (capital arbitrage assumption) (5)

where the decision variables for the MNE are K_C, K_U and X and the financial variables are H, D and p. We assume D is affected by H and p since dividends are a residual item.[11] Substituting (2a, 2b, 3, 4a or 4b) into (5), we differentiate (5) with respect to K_C, K_U and X.

The first order condition for an optimal allocation of K_C is;

$$e(1 - t_c)MRP_{KC} - e(r + d - t_cL_ci_c)(1 - \beta_c)(1 - t_cZ_c)P_{KC} = 0$$

or, rearranging:

$$MRP_{KC}/P_{KC} = [(r + d - t_cL_ci_c)(1 - \beta_c)(1 - t_cZ_c)]/(1 - t_c) \tag{6}$$

Similarly, the optimal allocation of K_U is determined by:

$$MRP_{KU}/P_{KU} = [(r + d - t_uL_ui_u)(1 - \beta_u - t_uZ_u(1 - .5\beta_u))]/(1 - t_u) \tag{7}$$

Lastly, the optimal allocation of intrafirm trade, X, depends on:

$$e(1 - t_c)MR_c - (1 - t_u)MR_u + [t_c - (t_u + \tau(1 - t_c)]p = 0$$

or, rearranging:

$$(1 - t_c)[eMR_c - (1 + \tau)p] = (1 - t_u)[MR_u - p] \tag{8}$$

Equation (8) is well-known from international trade and horizontally-integrated MNE models (see Eden, 1985; Horst, 1973). The MNE should balance the marginal revenue from intrafirm imports (the left-hand side of (8)) to the marginal cost of exports (the right-hand side of (8)) in order to maximize overall profits. The Canadian marginal revenue from imports equals the marginal revenue from domestic sales, $e\, MR_C$, net of importing costs, $(1 + \tau)\, p$, in after-tax terms. The U.S. marginal cost of exports equals the foregone marginal revenue in domestic sales, MR_U, minus earnings from exports, p, after tax.

The left-hand side of equations (6,7) is the marginal revenue product of capital divided by its price. The right-hand side is the tax-adjusted cost of capital per dollar of investment spending; i.e. the gross cost of capital per dollar of capital expenditures. Note that capital arbitrage ensures that the net return, r, is equalized between countries. Since we have assumed similar types of capital (machinery and equipment) in the two firms, we assume identical depreciation rates so that the net cost of capital, $c_N = r + d$, per dollar of investment spending is the same in both firms. However, the gross costs of capital in (6, 7) are unlikely to be equalized since tax rates, leverage ratios, nominal interest rates, tax deductions and credits generally differ between countries.

Equations (6,7) also show that capital flows are affected by the effective marginal tax rates on capital. We can derive the effective rate as follows. Let c_{GI} be the gross cost of capital, the right-hand side of equation (6) or (7). Then the effective marginal tax rate, t_I^M is

$$t_I^M = (C_{GI} - C_N) / C_{GI}]\qquad(9)$$

For example, in the simplest case, assume $\beta_I = Z_I = L_I = 0$. Then $C_{GI} = (r + d)/(1 - t_I)$ so that $t_I^M = t_I$; the effective marginal tax rate is simply the CIT rate. Since we assume the net costs of capital are equal in the two firms, if the CIT rate in Canada is twice as high as in the U.S., this implies that the gross cost of capital in Canada is also twice as high.

Note also that the effective marginal tax rate, which influences gross fixed capital formation by the subsidiary, is independent of the withholding tax on dividends or the extra CIT tax due in the home country on repatriation. Thus the early view that a weighted average of the rates on dividends and retained earnings determines subsidiary investments is not valid. Hartman (1985) is right: capital flows are affected by effective marginal CIT rates in each country; the extra taxes due upon repatriation are ignored.

The optimal financial decisions for the MNE are found by differentiating (5) with respect to p, D and H, using the envelope theorem to eliminate terms.[12] We assume either or both governments impose constraints on the size of p, H and D so that the optimal variables may have to set at these upper or lower government-imposed limits rather than the profit-maximizing ones. The optimal level of D depends on whether a surplus or deficit of tax credits applies to dividends. In the deficit case,

$f > 0$, the optimal size of dividends is determined by substituting (4a) into (5):

$$d\pi/dD = e \, [\, t_c - t_u \,]/\, (1 - t_c) < 0 \qquad \text{(since } t_u > t_c) \qquad \text{(10a)}$$

In the surplus case, $f = 0$, substituting (4b) into (5):

$$d\pi/dD = -ew_D < 0 \qquad \text{(10b)}$$

Therefore in both deficit and surplus of credits cases, the MNE maximizes profits by setting dividends at their lowest possible level. Note that in this financial decision, the important tax variables are the statutory CIT and dividend withholding tax rates. The effective marginal tax rates on capital flows are irrelevant because the MNE is assumed to maximize after-tax global profits with respect to the real variables; dividends are treated as a residual payment out of after-tax subsidiary profits.

The results in (10a, b) imply that Hartman (1985) is mistaken; i.e. the additional taxes do affect remittance decisions. However, if the extra taxes are unavoidable through financial manoeuvers, they become a fixed cost for the MNE, one that must be paid in any case. This also applies to head office charges. The optimal amount of head office charges is determined by:

$$d\pi/dH = e \, (t_c - t_u) + (\delta\pi/\delta D) \, (\delta D/\delta H) \gtrless 0$$

Since $D = \alpha \, \pi_c$, it follows that $\delta D/\delta H = \alpha \, \delta\pi_c/\delta H$. Substituting this into $\delta\pi/\delta H$:

$$d\pi/dH = e \, (t_c - t_u) + (\delta\pi/\delta D) \, [\, e \, \alpha \, \{ -(1 - t_c) - W_H \} \,] \qquad \text{(11)}$$

Equation (11) shows that H has two effects on MNE profits. First, if t_c exceeds (is less than) t_u, head office charges should be raised (lowered) since they are tax-deductible in Canada and taxable income in the U.S.[13] Second, higher charges reduce after-tax subsidiary profits and thus indirectly reduce dividends. Since $\delta\pi/\delta D < 0$ and the term in $\{\cdot\}$ is negative, the impact of higher charges, via dividends, on MNE profits is positive. (This point is also made by Mutti, 1981.) Thus the dividend effect tends to raise the optimal H if $t_c > t_u$; and to reduce it if t_u is higher. Note, of course, that if $\alpha = 0$ (no dividends are remitted), this second effect disappears.

The optimal transfer price on intrafirm trade is determined by:

$$d\pi/dp = [\, t_c - (t_u + \tau \, (1 - t_c) \,] \, X + (\delta\pi/\delta D)(\delta D/\delta p) \gtrless 0$$

which, following the same procedure as in (11) yields:

$$d\pi/dp = [\, t_C - (t_U + \tau\,(1 - t_C)\,)\,]\, X + (\delta\pi/\delta D)\, [\, \alpha\, \{\, - (1 - t_C)\,(1 + \tau)\, X\, \}] \quad (12)$$

Again, since $\delta\pi/\delta D < 0$ and the term in $\{\cdot\}$ is negative, the impact of the transfer price, via dividends, on global profits is positive. The first term in (12), however, may be either positive or negative, depending on the tax and tariff costs; e.g. higher CITs in the host country tend to encourage overinvoicing whereas tariffs encourage underinvoicing.

Implications for Current U.S. and Canadian Tax and Tariff Rules

The three first order conditions (6,7,8) show the profit-maximizing levels of capital and trade flows within a manufacturing MNE. They show that capital flows depend on effective marginal CIT rates in each country and are independent of the extra taxes due upon dividend re-patriation. A higher statutory CIT rate raises the gross cost of capital in that country, lowering the optimal gross fixed capital formation by the firm.[14] This has second-round impacts on output, sales, and trade flows by the two firms. In general, we expect a higher tax rate to discourage output and exports (encourage imports).

Intrafirm trade flows depend on CIT and tariff rates and the transfer pricing policy of the MNE. In our model the MNE maximizes global economic profits net of tax so that statutory tax and tariff rates affect trade flows. With a statutory CIT rate of 46 pecent in the U.S. and 40 percent in Canada; and a average tariff rate of 5 percent, the MNE should set a low transfer price to shift profits to the Canadian subsidiary, according to (12).[15] Thus, in (8) the subsidiary shows a marginal profit on intrafirm trade ($MR_C > (1 + \tau)\, p$), while the parent records a equal marginal loss ($MR_U > p$). Raising t_C lowers the marginal profit of the subsidiary, generating an overall marginal loss on X to the MNE. The MNE, as a result, contracts trade. This has second-round impacts on output, sales, and capital flows. A rise in t_U or τ has the opposite effects.

However, managers of large MNEs do not measure economic profits; their balance sheets record book profits, before and after tax. Therefore managers may be affected by the effective tax rates on book profits, not economic profits. If managers try to maximize book profits net of taxes, the appropriate tax rate for decision purposes is the effective average CIT rate on book profits; i.e., total taxes paid by the firm divided by book profits of the firm. These tax rates are available from each country's income tax statistics. In the next section we calculate effective marginal and average tax rates on U.S. manufacturing parents and their Canadian subsidiaries.

CALCULATING EFFECTIVE MARGINAL AND AVERAGE CORPORATE INCOME TAX RATES

As we saw in the third section, international capital flows within the MNE depend on effective marginal tax rates on capital; whereas financial and trade flows depend on effective average tax rates on book profits. In this section we calculate effective marginal and average rates on U.S. parents and their Canadian affiliates in the manufacturing sector. The rates are calculated for the prereform period, with U.S. reform only, Canadian reform only and joint tax reform. These rates are then used to predict changes in intrafirm capital, trade, and financial flows within the manufacturing sector.

Calculating Effective Marginal Corporate Income Tax Rates

Pre-Reform. Table 9.1 shows the initial values of the variables used to calculate the effective marginal and average CIT taxes in the prereform period. How these variables were obtained is explained in the Data Appendix to this paper.

The gross cost of capital, before reform, in Canada is based on (6), reproduced in a slightly different fashion below:

$$C_{GC} = [\,(1 - \beta_c)\,(1 - t_c Z_c)\,/\,(1 - t_c)\,]\,[\,r + d - t L_c i_c] \qquad (13)$$

The first square-bracketed term in (13) is the gross-up factor; the second is the effective opportunity cost of capital. In the simplest case where $\beta_c = Z_c = 0$, the gross-up factor is $1/(1 - t_c) = 1.7203$. Since the second term equals .1825, $C_{GC} = .3139$ in this case. Using (9) to find the effective marginal CIT rates yields $t_C^M = .3816$, since $C_N = r + d = .1941$. Thus, in the absence of the investment tax credit and the capital consumption allowance, the effective marginal rate on Canadian gross fixed capital formation (GFCF) is 38.16 percent. To calculate the effective marginal rate on new investment or net fixed capital formation (NFCF) we must measure $(r_{GI} - r_N)\,/\,r_{GI}$, or alternatively, measure:

$$T_I^M = (\,C_{GI} - C_{NI})\,/\,(C_{GI} - d\,) \qquad (14)$$

where T_I^M is the effective marginal rate on new investments only. Thus $T_C^M = .5908$ when $\beta_c = Z_c = 0$. The impact of tax deductions and tax credits is to reduce the effective marginal rate on net and replacement investment. Given the actual 1981 values of β_c and Z_c we find the effective marginal CIT rate on GFCF by U.S.-controlled manufacturing

Table 9.1
Effective Corporate Tax Rates on U.S. Manufacturing MNE Parents and Their Canadian Subsidiaries

Variable	Pre-Reform	U.S. Reform r_u fixed	U.S. Reform r_u varies	Canadian Reform	Canadian/U.S. Reform
$r_u = r_c$	.0830	.0830	.0719	.0830	.0719
d	.1111	.1111	.1111	.1111	.1111
$c_{NU} = c_{NC}$	.1941	.1941	.1830	.1941	.1830
Φ_u	.0395	.0395	.0346	.0395	.0346
Φ_c	.0440	.0440	.0440	.0440	.0440
i_u	.1225	.1225	.1066	.1225	.1066
i_c	.1313	.1313	.1187	.1313	.1187
L_u	.3588	.3588	.3588	.3588	.3588
L_c	.2899	.2899	.2899	.2899	.2899
β_u	.0889	0	0	.0889	0
β_c	.0635	.0635	.0635	0	0
Z_u	.8538	.8513	.8673	.8538	.8673
Z_c	.9221	.9221	.9289	.6248	.6378
c_{Gu}	.1731	.1936	.1823	.1731	.1823
c_{Gc}	.1805	.1805	.1687	.2223	.2075
r_{Gu}	.0620	.0825	.0711	.0620	.0711
r_{Gc}	.0694	.0694	.0576	.1112	.0964
t_u	.4946	.3823	.3823	.4946	.3823
t_c	.4187	.4187	.4187	.3487	.3487

subsidiaries in the prereform period was $t_{CM} = -.0756$; while on NFCF the effective rate was $T_C^M = -.1966$ (i.e., Canadaian-subsidized investment in the manufacturing sector).

In the United States, the gross cost of capital is, based on (7):

$$C_{Gu} = [(1 - \beta_u - t_u Z_u (1 - .5 \beta_u)) / (1 - t_u)] [r + d - t_u L_u i_u] \qquad (15)$$

where the first square bracket is the gross-up factor and the second, the opportunity cost of capital. Assuming $\beta_u = Z_u = 0$ leaves a simple

Table 9.1 *(Continued)*

Variable	Pre-Reform	U.S. Reform r_U fixed	U.S. Reform r_U varies	Canadian Reform	Canadian/U.S. Reform
$t_U{}^M$	$-.1213$	$-.0025$	$-.0043$	$-.1213$	$-.0043$
$t_C{}^M$	$-.0756$	$-.0756$	$-.0847$	$+.1269$	$+.1180$
$T_U{}^M$	$-.3386$	$-.0059$	$-.0111$	$-.3386$	$-.0111$
$T_C{}^M$	$-.1966$	$-.1966$	$-.2480$	$+.2537$	$+.2540$
$t_U{}^A$	$.4172$	$.3550$	$.3757$	$.4172$	$.3757$
$t_C{}^A$	$.2772$	$.2772$	$.2989$	$.3223$	$.3335$
$t_C{}^D$	$.3495$	$.3495$	$.3690$	$.3901$	$.4002$

Source: Data Appendix and author's calculations (note: all numbers calculated to seven digits and rounded to four digits in the table)

Key to Variables:

r = real rate of interest

d = economic rate of depreciation

c_N = net cost of capital; equals $r + d$

Φ = inflation rate

i = nominal rate of interest; $i_U = r + \Phi$ in U.S., see Data Appendix for Canada

L = leverage ratio; equals long-term debt to long-term debt plus equity

β = investment tax credit

Z = net present value of one dollar's worth of capital consumption allowance

c_G = gross cost of capital

r_G = gross rate of return

t = statutory corporate income tax rate

t^M = effective marginal rate of corporate income tax on gross capital formation

T^M = effective marginal rate of CIT on net fixed capital formation

t^A = effective average CIT rate on book profits

t^D = effective average Canadian tax rate on remitted dividends gross-up factor of $1/(1 - t_U) = 1.9786$. Since the opportunity cost equals .1724 the gross cost of capital, in the absence of the capital cost allowance and the investment tax credit, is .3411. Given a net cost of capital of .1941, this implies an effective tax rate of .4308 on GFCF in manufacturing. In terms of new investment only, we can use (14) to find $T_U^M = .6390$. The impact of tax deductions and credits is to turn these tax rates into subsidies. With the prereform values for β_U and Z_U, we find $t_U^M = -.1213$ and $T_U^M = -.3386$. Since the respective Canadian rates are $t_C^M = -.0756$ and $T_C^M = -.1966$. The U.S. rates are more generous, even though the statutory U.S. CIT rate is substantially higher (.4946 compared to .4187). This is due to the higher U.S. investment tax credit and lower opportunity cost of capital, which is partly offset by the higher Canadian capital cost allowance.

(B) *Tax Reform in the United States.* The U.S. Congress (1986) made the following changes to the CIT: (1) the statutory federal CIT rate was cut to 34 percent; (2) the investment tax credit was repealed and (3) and the capital cost allowance was changed from a 150 percent to a 200 percent declining balance on basically-unchanged asset lives. Following Fazzari (1987), we assume initially that real and nominal interest rates are unaffected by the tax law changes. The impact of U.S. reform is to slightly lower Z_U from .8538 to .8513, eliminate B_U and reduce t_U to .3823 (combined federal/state). As a result C_{GU} rises from .1731 to .1936; causing the effective marginal tax rate on all investment to rise from $t_U^M = -.1213$ to $-.0025$ (i.e., the subsidy becomes smaller). The effective tax cost of NFCF rises from $T_U^M = -.3386$ to $-.0059$. We can translate these tax changes into predicted changes in gross fixed capital formation, GFCF, using the formula:

$$\% \text{ change in GFCF}_I = 100 \left[(C_{GI}^0 / C_{GI}^N)^S - 1 \right] \tag{16}$$

where zero refers to the original gross cost of capital, N refers to the new cost and S is the elasticity of substitution. Following Fazzari, we assume S equals either 1 (Cobb-Douglas) or .55. The formula for the predicted change in net fixed capital formation, NFCF, is similarly defined as:

$$\% \text{ change in NFCF}_I = 100 \left[(r_{GI}^O / r_{GI}^N)^S - 1 \right] \tag{17}$$

These predicted investment changes are shown in Table 9.2. U.S. tax reform, assuming interest rates are unaffected, causes GFCF_U to fall by 10.59 percent and NFCF_U by 24.85 percent in the Cobb-Douglas case. With a lower elasticity of substitution, these changes are reduced.

U.S. tax reform, however, is expected to cause real and nominal interest rates to fall. Using the percentage point changes outlined in Faz-

Table 9.2
Predicted Percentage Changes in Gross and Net Fixed Capital Formation in Manufacturing Due to Tax Reform

% Change in Capital Formation,	Pre-Reform	U.S. Reform r fixed	U.S. Reform r varies	Canadian Reform	Canadian/U.S. Reform
	(assuming elasticity of substitution S = 1)				
GFCF$_u$	0 %	-10.59 %	-5.02 %	0 %	-5.02 %
NFCF$_u$	0	-24.85	-12.85	0	-12.85
GFCF$_c$	0	0	+6.95	-18.83	-13.04
NFCF$_c$	0	0	+20.34	-37.63	-28.07
	(assuming elasticity of substitution S = .55)				
GFCF$_u$	0	-5.97	-2.79	0	-2.79
NFCF$_u$	0	-14.54	-7.29	0	-7.29
GFCF$_c$	0	0	+3.76	-10.84	-7.40
NFCF$_c$	0	0	+10.72	-22.87	-16.57

<u>Source</u>: Data Appendix and author's calculations based on Table .1 results

zari, we find r drops to .0719, implying i_u = .1066 and i_c = .1187. As a result, Z_u rises, reducing the gross and net costs of capital. The new effective marginal tax rates are t_u^M = −.0043 and T_u^M = −.0111, and the decline in the U.S. capital stock is smaller (see Tables 9.1 and 9.2). In Canada, the lower real interest rate reduces the opportunity cost of capital, raises Z_c from .9221 to .9289 and lowers the gross cost of capital to .1687. As a result, the effective marginal subsidy to capital rises, inducing a total capital expansion in Canada of between 3.76 and 6.95 percent, depending on the elasticity of substitution. The change in NFCF$_c$ is even larger: 10.72 to 20.34 percent. Thus U.S. tax reform, instead of causing an exodus of capital from Canada to the United States as predicted in the newspapers, should cause a substantial investment boom! This confusion results from relying on changes in statutory tax rates rather than changes in effective marginal CIT rates to predict capital flows.

Tax Reform in Canada. On June 18, 1987, the Canadian government announced major changes to the corporate income tax structure to be phased in over the 1988–91 period. The federal statutory rate falls from 46 to 38 percent, with the CIT on the manufacturing sector falling from 40 to 33 percent. The investment tax credit is phased out, while capital consumption allowances become less generous since the two-year write-off for machinery and equipment is reduced to a 25 percent declining balance rate, both subject to the half-year rule (see Canada, 1987).

The impact of these tax changes is shown in Table 9.1. In the absence of U.S. reform, Canadian reform eliminates β_c, substantially reduces Z_c from .9221 to .6248 while reducing the statutory rate to .3487 (assuming provincial rates do not change). The net impact is to raise the gross cost of capital from .1805 to .2223. This causes the effective marginal tax rate on all Canadian capital to shift from a *subsidy* of 7.56 percent to a *tax* of 12.69 percent; a major increase. The change in the marginal rate on new investment is even larger ($-.1966$ to $+.2537$). As a result, the desired total capital stock falls between 10.84 and 18.83 percent, depending on the size of S, with the decline in NFCF even more pronounced. Thus, while U.S. tax reform is widely perceived to have increased effective tax rates on capital income, it is Canadian tax reform that has the most punitive effects. Note, however, that U.S. tax reform has already occurred, whereas the Canadian package is not yet law—and perhaps is unlikely to be, given its probable impacts on investment.

Canadian and U.S. Tax Reform. When we examine the combined effects of Canadian and U.S. tax reform, we see that the drop in U.S. interest rates moderates the negative impact of Canadian reform on Canadian manufacturing investment. The net impact is an effective marginal tax of 11.80 percent in Canada and a subsidy of 0.43 percent in the U.S. on GFCF; and a tax of 25.40 percent in Canada and subsidy of 8.03 percent in the U.S. on NFCF. The gap between effective marginal rates has therefore widened compared to pre-reform levels and we expect manufacturing MNEs to shift investments from Canada to the U.S. as a result. Based on our analysis in sections II and III we therefore predict a minor drop in domestic investment in the U.S., largely offset by an inflow of capital from Canada. The decline in FDI in Canada could be substantial.

Calculating Effective Average Corporate Income Tax Rates

Pre-Reform. While marginal tax rates affect long-run investment flows; short-run financial decisions and intrafirm trade flows depend on average tax rates and customs duties. If managers consider maximizing book profits net of taxes paid as their objective, it is the effective CIT rate on book profits that influences their decisions. In this section, we develop a new method that calculates effective average tax rates on book profits. This method is simple and omits most of the minor tax deductions and credits in actual tax legislation, concentrating solely on the capital consumption allowance and the investment tax credit. Let us define taxes paid in the following manner:

$$\text{TAXES} = t_I [\, \Gamma - (\text{CCA} - \text{DEP})\,] - \beta_I P_{KI} K_I [\, (1 - L_I t_I)\, i_I - \Phi_I + d\,] \quad (18)$$

where Γ is book profit, CCA is the capital consumption allowance and DEP is book depreciation. The effective average tax rate on book profits, t_I^A, is therefore $t_I^A = \text{TAXES} / \Gamma$ or:

$$t_I^A = t_I [\, 1 - (\text{CCA} - \text{DEP}) / \Gamma\,] - \beta_I [\, P_{KI} K_I \{(1 - L_I t_I)\, i_I - \Phi_I + d\} / \Gamma\,] \quad (19)$$

The data for calculating (19) are given in the Data Appendix. Since t_U = .4946, β_U = .0889, (CCA − DEP) / Γ = .0127 and capital expenditures relative to book profits (the second square-bracketed term) equal .7996; we find t_U^A = .4172 in the pre-reform period. For Canada, t_C = .4187, β_C = .0635, (CCA − DEP) / Γ = .2205 and the second square bracket = .7742. This implies an effective CIT rate on book profits of t_C^A = .2772 in the pre-reform period.

Since the U.S. average tax rate is substantially higher than the Canadian average rate due to the larger tax deductions available in Canada, MNEs in the manufacturing sector have an incentive to underinvoice their exports to Canada to avoid the extra U.S. tax on book profits. The Canadian tariff tends to reinforce this result (see (12)). MNEs also have an incentive to minimize head office charges (see (11)). On the other hand, dividend repatriation decisions are affected by the extra tax due upon repatriation. Given W_D = .10, the effective Canadian tax on dividends, t_{CD}, is:

$$t_C^D = t_C^A + W_D (1 - t_C^A) = .2772 + .1 (1 - .2772) = .3495 \quad (20)$$

compared to a U.S. average rate on domestic book profits of .4172. The Canadian subsidiary therefore has a deficit of tax credits and its parent would have to pay extra taxes on remitted profits.[16] The MNE would therefore have a reason to defer repatriating dividends (subject to the Hartman/Warren proviso that fixed costs cannot be avoided by postponing the remittance).

Tax Reform in Canada and the United States. Tax reform has four effects on the calculation of the effective average CIT rate: the statutory tax rate changes, capital consumption allowances change, the investment tax credit disappears and, in the case of U.S. tax reform, the real and nominal interest rates change. Taking each of these effects into account generates the average tax rates shown in Table 9.1. U.S. reform, holding r_U constant initially, lowers the average tax rate from 41.72 percent to 35.50 percent. With the drop in r_U, the effective rate rises slightly to 37.57 percent because the value of the CCA and the interest rate deduction decrease as the nominal interest rate declines. (Note that the Canadian average CIT rate also rises for this reason.)

Canadian tax reform raises the effective average tax rate on book profits in manufacturing from 27.72 to 32.23 percent. Combined with U.S. reform, t_C^A rises to 33.35 percent. Effective Canadian and U.S. rates post-reform would be quite close: 33.35 percent in Canada and 37.57 percent in the U.S., although U.S. rates are still higher. The narrowing of the spread in tax rates should lessen the incentive to minimize charges and underinvoice imports. Also, the fall in tariff rates should have the same impact on transfer pricing. The net impact may be larger outflows on the current account of Canada's balance of payments, both in the goods and services accounts. Coupled with a 10 percent withholding tax, the effective Canadian tax rate on dividends increases to 40.02 percent, giving the Canadian subsidiary a surplus of tax credits! Thus no extra U.S. taxes would be due on repatriated dividends; the binding rate in (10) becomes the withholding tax. The interesting conclusion is that, in the absence of Canadian tax reform, this redirection of incentives would not have occurred; i.e., the Canadian average rate on dividends would have remained below the U.S. rate (36.90 percent), leaving a continuing deficit of tax credits.

CONCLUSIONS

The purpose of this chapter was to explore the probable impacts of tax and tariff reform on U.S.-controlled foreign direct investment in the Canadian manufacturing sector. We outlined a simple model of international capital flows and showed how tax changes could affect capital movements and the welfare level in the host country. We developed a model to predict the impact of tax and tariff changes on a horizontally-integrated manufacturing MNE. These models predicted that effective marginal CIT rates determine capital flows within the MNE, while effective average rates on book profits affect financial and intrafirm trade flows. We estimated effective marginal and average CIT rates for U.S. manufacturing MNEs and their Canadian subsidiaries in the pre-reform period, and then reestimated these rates based on the U.S. tax reform, Canadian reform, and joint reform programs.

Our results showed that, in the pre-reform period, both Canada and the United States were subsidizing investments in machinery and equipment in the manufacturing sector, with the U.S. effective marginal subsidy being larger than the Canadian. The impact of U.S. tax reform was to substantially reduce the U.S. subsidy, causing a decline in the optimal U.S. capital stock in manufacturing. The subsequent fall in U.S. interest rates moderated this effect, but increased the effective Canadian subsidy, encouraging an investment boom in Canada. The impact of Canadian tax reform, however, was to offset this positive external effect, with the marginal effective CIT rate turning from a subsidy to a tax. This could generate substantial long-run capital outflows.

The situation with respect to the effective average tax rate on manufacturing book profits was different. In the pre-reform period, the U.S. rate was much higher than the Canadian one, discouraging remittances to U.S. parents and encouraging underinvoicing of imports from the U.S. The impact of U.S. tax reform was to marginally lessen the U.S. average tax rate with probable minimal effects on financial and trade flows within manufacturing MNEs. However, the Canadian reform proposals would substantially raise the Canadian effective average tax rate on book profits, leaving it slightly below the U.S. level. The incentive to underinvoice and to avoid remittances would be therefore somewhat reduced. When the withholding tax on dividends was added, Canada moved from a deficit of foreign tax credits to a surplus. Coupled with the U.S. tax change from an overall to a per-country limitation on foreign tax credits, the Canadian proposals could significantly affect financial and intrafirm trade flows within manufacturing MNEs.

Given the importance of the manufacturing sector to the Canadian economy, and the vital role of U.S.-controlled subsidiaries in that sector, the effects of tax and tariff reform outlined above imply major changes in Canadian capital, financial, and trade flows over the next few years. With the predicted strong, negative impact on investment of the Canadian tax proposals, it is likely that the reforms may undergo major revisions before becoming law. Even if the Canadian proposals do not become law, the effects of U.S. tax reform will be substantial. Coupled with falling tariff rates, a possible Canada-U.S. free trade deal and/or increasing U.S. protectionism, the Canadian manufacturing sector must be as flexible as possible in order to successfully weather the government-induced changes ahead.

Lastly, note that since Canadian tax rates in the manufacturing are substantially below those in other sectors, Canadian tax reform could push the Canadian average CIT rate well above the U.S. rate in these sectors. The incentives that we have shown exist for U.S.-controlled manufacturing subsidiaries in Canada to shift profits, financial flows, and trade flows to the U.S. could therefore be much stronger in other sectors of the Canadian economy.

NOTES

Helpful comments were received from Carl S. Shoup, Michael Daly, Jack Jung, Barry Mersereau, and participants at a University of Waterloo economics department seminar, where an early version of this chapter was presented.

1. The data are from Canada, *Foreign-owned Subsidiaries* (1984), Tables 2a and 2b (excluding other non-manufacturing); Canada, *Domestic and Foreign Control* (1985), Table 4; and Canada, *Canadian Imports* (1981), Table 2.

2. See U.S. Congress (1986) for details. Analyses of U.S. tax reform can be found in Auerbach (1987), Fazzari (1987), and Warren (1987). All three expect the effective tax on capital income to rise, reducing the long-run capital stock.

3. *The Wall Street Journal* (Aug. 19, 1986), for example, concluded that for many MNEs, U.S. tax reform could create a tax shelter at home because it would be cheaper to manufacture products in the U.S. than in many other developed countries. The *Journal* predicted that tax reform would create jobs in U.S. manufacturing and that some high-tax countries, such as Canada, would be forced to bring their taxes in line with the new U.S. tax system.

4. In later work, we intend to extend this analysis to other sectors, such as mining and services, and to examine the 20 manufacturing industries individually.

5. Asuming Canada is a price taker in the international capital market implies that 100 percent of the burden of foreign (and domestic) taxation falls on Canada. If Canada has monopoly/monopsony power in either international capital or product markets, the optimal Canadian tax may not only be positive, but possibly lie above U.S. levels. See Burgess (1985a), Eden (1988, 1987).

6. See Thirsk (1986) for an estimate of the welfare impact of raising Canadian taxes on capital income. In certain cases, he shows that raising the tax rate increases welfare. See also the analysis in Mintz (1987).

7. The earliest writers on deferral were Richman (1963) and Shoup (1969). For good "traditional" analyses of deferral and its impacts, see Arnold (1986), Brean (1984), and Horst (1977). For the new approach to deferral, see Hartman (1985). Both approaches are discussed in Eden (1988).

8. In fact, there is no conflict in these positions. The net present value of a constant dollar amount, A, does approach zero as the time period, n, rises: i.e., NPV $= A / [1 + (1 - t) i]^N \to 0$ as $N \to$ infinity. However, if A rises yearly by the net return to investments, $(1 - t) i$, the NPV of A is constant.

9. The cost of capital formula derived in this section and used in section IV is outlined in Daly and Jung (1987) and Fazzari (1987). The gross cost varies across industries, types of capital (e.g. machinery, buildings, inventories) and funding of capital (e.g. equity, debt).

10. Setting $L_i = 0$ implies that all capital is equity capital; if $L_i = 1$, all capital is debt funded.

11. For example, higher head office charges reduce dividends by $\alpha (1 - t_c)$ times the change in H. A higher transfer price, for a given X, reduces profits by the change in p times $\alpha (1 - t_c) X$.

12. For example, differentiating (5) with respect to p yields:

$d\pi/dp = \Sigma\ (\delta\pi/\delta K_i)\ (\delta K_i/\delta p) + (\delta\pi/\delta X)/(\delta X/\delta p) + (\delta\pi/\delta D)(\delta D/\delta p) + \delta\pi/\delta p$

However, since the MNE simultaneously optimises over K_1 and X, $\delta\pi/\delta K_1 = \delta\pi/\delta X = 0$, leaving only the impact of p on dividends (we assume $\delta\pi/\delta D = 0$) and $\delta\pi/\delta p$. A similar procedure holds for H and D.

13. Note that the withholding tax, w_H, has no effect on the optimal amount of H. This is because w_H is so low relative to t_U that the tax is always fully deductible in the U.S. The net cost of H to the Canadian subsidiary is $e\ (1 - t_C + w_H)\ H$ and the U.S. parent is $e\ (-1 + t_U - w_H)\ H$ for a total net cost of $e\ (t_U - t_C)\ H$ to the MNE. Note that in the Canadian case with $t_C = .4$ and $w_h = .15$, the Canadian government bears 25 percent of the burden of H in foregone taxes. The U.S. government, on the other hand, receives $t_U - w_H = .46 - .15$, or 31 percent of the return from H to the U.S. parent.

14. By totally differentiating (6, 7, 8) with respect to the various government policy and financial variables, t_I, τ, α, β_I, Z_I, and using Cramer's Rule, we could find the comparative static effects of these variables on K_I and X. Since this has been largely done elsewhere (Eden, 1985) and would substantially lengthen the paper, we omit this analysis. Simple inspection of the effects of a change in each variable on (6, 7, 8) yields much the same results. For example, a rise in t_C raises the numerator and lowers the denominator in (6), raising the gross cost of capital to the subsidiary and causing a fall in the optimal stock of K_C and an outflow of foreign investment.

15. The effective return to the MNE of a high transfer price is $t_C = .4$ while the effective cost is $t_U + \tau\ (1 - t_C) = .46 + .05\ (.6) = .503$. Since the cost exceeds the return, the MNE sets a low price, both to avoid the tariff and the higher U.S. CIT. This is dampened by the positive effect of p on π via D.

16. This may have had little effect in the last few years, because U.S. MNEs could elect either the overall or per-country limitation on the foreign tax credit. A deficit of tax credits could be applied against a surplus elsewhere under the overall limitation, thus offsetting the negative impact on the Canadian subsidiary of the credit deficit. The new U.S. tax law, however, forces MNEs to use the per-country limitation. This increases the extra tax payable by the parent, because pooling of credits is eliminated. See Batten and Ott (1985, p. 12) for an example.

APPENDIX

We make the following assumptions concerning the data:

1. The capital stock in both firms consists wholly of machinery and equipment with an economic life of 18 years (Daly and Jung, 1987). The economic depreciation rate is $d + (2/N)\ (K_T + K_{T-1})/2$, where N is the service life of the asset and K_T is the capital stock in period T; i.e., the depreciation rate is $2/N$ times the average capital stock. (See Statistics Canada, *Fixed Capital Flows and Stocks 1936–83*.) Assuming $N + 18$ implies $d + .11111$.

2. International capital mobility ensures $r_U = r_c = r = .083$ in the pre-reform period. The expected inflation rate in Canada is .044 and in the U.S. is .0395. Thus the nominal interest rate is .1225 in the U.S. After U.S. tax reform, the U.S. real rate falls to .0719 and the inflation rate to .0346 (based on data in Fazzari, 1987) so the nominal U.S. rate becomes .1066. Using Daly and Jung's

fixed-r^* assumption and their equations (6,7) implies a nominal Canadian interest rate of .1313 initially, and a rate after U.S. reform of .1187.

2a. The 1985 statutory CIT, federal plus provincial, on manufacturing profits is .4187 in Canada; i.e. the federal rate is .40 minus an abatement of .10 for the provinces plus a provincial-average rate of .1187. The investment tax credit in Canada is .0635 (Daly and Jung). We assume the provincial tax rate is constant.

The following statistics were calculated from several sources. In all cases the Canadian data are of foreign-controlled manufacturing subsidiaries in Canada with assets of at least $10 million Canadian. The U.S. data are for U.S. manufacturing firms with assets of $250 million U.S. or more. (Since these U.S. firms receive approximately 95 percent of all foreign tax credits, this sample includes almost all U.S. MNEs. See U.S. *Statistics of Income, 1977–81*.)

3. The leverage ratio for Canadian subsidiaries was based on the 1978–81 average ratio of long-term liabilities to long-term liabilities plus equity, calculated from *CALURA (Part I - Corporations*, 1979 and 1981). The leverage ratio for the U.S. parents was similarly calculated as the 1978–81 average, from *1977–81 Statistics of Income*. The ratios are L_c = .2899 and L_u + .3588. We assume, in both cases, that L is constant throughout the analysis, although we would expect tax reform to alter debt-equity ratios.

4. We model the combined effect of U.S. federal and state CITs, because capital flows are affected by both income taxes. The U.S. statutory CIT rate equals the federal CIT rate plus an average state CIT, net of the federal rate, because state taxes are deductible against the federal CIT. The pre-reform 1985 federal rate is .46. The average statutory state CIT rate was calculated by the following method. Total 1979 state income taxes were 13.94 percent of total federal income taxes paid by all manufacturing firms (from *U.S. Quarterly Financial Report*, 1979). Since both taxes were calculated on the same base and the federal rate was .46, the state rate was .0641, implying a net state rate of .0346. $(1 - .46) = .0346$. Thus the statutory combined federal/state pre-reform CIT rate is .4946. We assume the state rate remains constant at .0641.

5. The U.S. investment tax credit is calculated as .0889, based on the 1978–81 average of the ratios of investment tax credits to cost of property used for the tax credit (see *Statistics of Income*). The simple 10 percent rate was not used since the U.S. income tax regulations place limits on the amount of investment tax credits that can be claimed by different firms.

6. The net present value of capital consumption allowances, Z, was calculated using the formula for N years of service life (see Fazzari, 1987):

$$Z_I = \Sigma \; (CCA_I \, / \, (1 + (1 - t_I)i_I)^N) \tag{A.1}$$

In the pre-reform case, Canada allowed machinery to be written off on a two-year straight line method, subject to the half-year rule (see *Income Tax Reform*, 1987). Given the initial values for t_c and i_c above, Z_c = .9221. The pre-reform Z_u was calculated assuming a 150 percent declining balance method with a five-year tax service life, where the corporation could switch to straight-line depreciation to maximize the deduction. Substituting values for t_u and i_u, we find Z_u = .8538.

7. A four-year average, 1978–81, of capital consumption allowances to before-tax book profits for Canadian manufacturing (.5450) was calculated from *Cor-*

porate Taxation Statistics 1979, 1981. This publication was also used to calculate the average ratios of CCA minus book depreciation to book profits (.2205), and recorded capital expenditures to book profits (.7742).

8. U.S. domestic book profits are not explicitly recorded in *Statistics of Income.* They were inferred for manufacturing firms with $250 million or more in assets in the following manner. The U.S. levies a 15 percent additional tax on tax preferences (such as CCA in excess of book depreciation) over $10,000. Tax preferences were estimated as the additional tax divided by .15 plus $10,000. Constructive taxable income from foreign corporations was subtracted from net income (less deficit) and then the tax preferences were added to estimate book domestic profits before CIT. Ratios similar to those in item 7 were then calculated for U.S. MNEs: .0127 for (CCA - DEP) divided by book profits; .5606 for CCA to book profits and .7996 for capital expenditures to book profits.

REFERENCES

Arnold, Brian J. *The Taxation of Controlled Foreign Corporations: An International Comparison.* Toronto: Canadian Tax Foundation, 1986.

Auerbach, Alan J. "The Tax Reform Act of 1986 and the Cost of Capital." *Economic Perspectives I.1*, Summer, 1987.

Batten, Dallas S. and Ott, Mack. "The President's Proposed Corporate Tax Reforms: A Move Toward Tax Neutrality." *The Federal Reserve Bank of St. Louis Review* 67.3, Aug/Sept. 1985.

Brean, Donald J. S. *International Issues in Taxation: The Canadian Perspective.* Toronto: Canadian Tax Foundation, 1984.

Burgess, David F. "On the Relevance of Export Demand Conditions for Capital Income Taxation in Open Economies." Ottawa: Economic Council of Canada Discussion Paper, 1985a.

————. "The Impact of Trade Liberalization on Foreign Direct Investment Flows." In *Canada-U.S. Free Trade*, Whalley, John, research coordinator, Toronto: University of Toronto Press, 1985b.

Canada, Department of Regional Economic Expansion. *Foreign-Owned Subsidiaries in Canada 1973–1979, 1979–1981.* Ottawa: Government of Canada, 1983, 1984.

————. Department of Finance. *Income Tax Reform, June 18, 1987.* Ottawa: Supply and Services Canada, 1987.

————. Statistics Canada. *Canadian Imports by Domestic and Foreign-Controlled Enterprises 1978.* Ottawa: Supply and Services Canada, 1981.

————. *Corporate Taxation Statistics 1979, 1981.* Ottawa: Government of Canada, 1983.

————. *Corporations and Labour Unions Returns Act: Part I Corporations 1978–81,* Ottawa: Supply and Services Canada, 1983.

————. *Domestic and Foreign Control of Manufacturing, Mining and Logging Establishments in Canada 1981.* Ottawa: Supply and Services Canada, 1985.

Daly, Michael J. and Jung, Jack. "The Taxation of Corporate Investment Income in Canada: an Analysis of Marginal Effective Tax Rates." *The Canadian Journal of Economics* XX.3, Aug. 1987.

Eden, Lorraine. "Equity and Neutrality in the International Taxation of Capital." *Osgoode Hall Law Journal* 26(2), forthcoming 1988.

———. "Pitfalls in the Taxation of Foreign Capital." Presented at the Canadian Economic Theory Meetings, University of Montreal, May, 1987.

———. "The Microeconomics of Transfer Pricing". In *Multinationals and Transfer Pricing*, Rugman, Alan, and Eden, Lorraine, editors, London: Croom Helm and St. Martins Press, 1985.

Fazzari, Steven M. "Tax Reform and Investment: How Big an Impact?." *Federal Reserve Bank of St. Louis Review 69.1*, Jan. 1987.

"For Business, Tax Bill Offsets Rate Cut with Loss of Deductions." *The Wall Street Journal*, Aug. 19, 1986.

Hartman, David. "Tax Policy and Foreign Direct Investment." *Journal of Public Economics* 26, 1985, 107–21.

Horst, Thomas. "American Taxation of Multinational Firms." *American Economic Review* 67.3, 1977, 376–89.

———. "The Simple Analytics of Multinational Firm Behaviour." In *International Trade and Money*, Connolly, Michael B., and Swoboda, Alexander K., editors, London: George Allen and Unwin, 1973.

Little, Bruce. "U.S. Tax Reforms Create Problems for Wilson." *The Globe and Mail*, Nov. 11, 1986.

Lush, Patricia. "Going, Going, Gone." *Report on Business Magazine.* Toronto: Globe and Mail Publishers, January 1987.

Mintz, Jack M. *Corporate Tax Design in an International Setting*. Ottawa: Department of Finance, forthcoming, 1987.

Mutti, John. "Tax Incentives and the Repatriation Decisions of U.S. Multinational Corporations." *National Tax Journal* XXXIV, 1981, 241–8.

Richman, P. B. *Taxation of Foreign Investment Income*. Baltimore: Johns Hopkins Press, 1963.

Rugman, Alan M. *Trade Liberalization and International Investment*. Ottawa: Economic Council of Canada, forthcoming 1987.

Shoup, Carl S. *Public Finance*. Chicago: Aldine Publishing Company, 1969.

Thirsk, Wayne R. "The Marginal Welfare Cost of Corporate Taxation in Canada." *Public Finance / Finances Publiques* XXXXI.1, 1986.

U.S. Congress, Staff of the Joint Committee on Taxation. *Tax Reform Act of 1986*. Washington: U.S. Government Printing Office, 1986.

U.S. Federal Trade Commission. *Quarterly Financial Report for Manufacturing, Mining and Trade Corporations 1978–79*. Washington: U.S. Government Printing Office, 1979.

U.S. Internal Revenue Service. *Statistics of Income: 1977–81 Corporation Income Tax Returns*. Washington: U.S. Government Printing Office, 1977–81.

Warren, Alvin C., Jr. "Taxing Corporate Income in the U.S. Twenty Years after the Carter Commission Report: Integration or Disintegration?". In *The Royal Commission on Taxation: Twenty Years Later*, Osgoode Hall Law School Annual Lecture Series, Brooks, Neil, editor, Toronto, forthcoming, 1987a.

———. "The Timing of Taxes." *National Tax Journal* XXXIX.4, 1986.

10
The Development of an Integrated North American Venture Capital Market
David J. Brophy

INTRODUCTION

Like many of the world's nations, Canada aspires to achieve increased international industrial competitiveness in part, at least, by commercial exploitation of technological innovation, partially through technological entrepreneurship [see Rugman, 1985, 1986]. Realization of this aspiration depends upon the joint productivity of an array of interactive public policy and private market factors, not the least of which is the provision of an effective venture capital market system [see Eisenhardt and Forbes, 1984]. Venture capital may be defined as financing extended to an emerging growth company, in the form of equity or complex long-term equity-based debt securities, at stages in the firm's life when access to funding from banks, other financial institutions, and the public equity and debt markets is not yet available.

Most countries consider the United States' venture capital market system worthy of emulation, insofar as domestically feasible. For Canada, with its constant and close contact with the U.S. system, the issue is not only emulation, but also integration to some appropriate extent. In this chapter we illustrate the points of conflict which kept the two markets developing separately in earlier years and show how certain recent elemental changes in law, regulation, and professional investment practices have led to increased Canadian emulation of the U.S. venture capital system and have produced integrative (i.e., cooperative) steps which appear to be generating net benefits for both countries. We argue that efforts to expedite this integration will produce increased mutual benefits and, therefore, should be encouraged.

VENTURE CAPITAL AS A FACTOR INFLUENCING RATES OF TECHNOLOGICAL ENTREPRENEURSHIP

Venture capital plays a key role in the economic growth process now facing the United States, Canada, and other free-market countries. The venture capital market system marshals and focuses resources to attain productivity-enhancing benefits through the financing of innovation. Because it interacts with other factors of production, venture capital should be thought of as "necessary but not sufficient" for generating the types of benefits indicated. However, it is unlikely that a country or region can be internationally competitive in commercial exploitation of innovative processes, products, and service *without* a strong local venture capital market system.

In a study which addresses this issue, Eisenhardt and Forbes [EF, 1984] argue that differences among nations in the rate of technological entrepreneurship may be explained by the degree to which a certain set of associated factors is present in each of the countries studied. The factors they cite are as follows:

- financial factors, such as availability of venture capital, the savings rate, existence of a wealthy elite, and access to a stock market;
- government factors, such as tax incentives, loan programs, and procurement policies;
- infrastructure factors, such as major universities, scientific labor pool, and incubator companies;
- factors which contribute to volatility, such as immigration, industrial diversity, and technological change;
- cultural factors, such as attitudes toward risk and status, and entrepreneurial role models.

Apply this set of factors to the United States, Great Britain, India, and Japan, EF categorized the nations as shown in Table 10.1.

Based upon their observations regarding the incidence of these characteristics, the authors conclude as follows: "A regenerative venture capital cycle stimulated by a favorable tax structure and an active OTC market, appropriate incubator companies, technical and social volatility, and entrepreneurial role models all promote high rates of technical entrepreneurship."[EF, p. 32]

These authors clearly argue that a regenerative venture capital system is the major factor in explaining interregional and international differences in the incidence and rate of technological entrepreneurship. They also conclude that the U.S. venture capital market system is larger than that of any other country and is the principal cause of U.S. preeminence in the successful development of entrepreneurially driven, technology-

Table 10.1
Major Factors Related to Rates of Technological Entrepreneurship

	U.S.	U.K.	India	Japan
Rate of Technological Entrepreneurship	High	Moderate	Low	Low
Tax Structure	Favorable	Becoming Favorable	Mixed	Not Favorable
Venture Capital Pool	Large	Small Growing	Small	Small
OTC Stock Market	High	Moderate Growing	Low	Low
Incubators	High	Moderate to Low	Unknown	Probably Low
Social Volatility	High	Moderate to Low	Low	Low
Entrepreneurial Culture	Yes	Yes/No Changing	No	No

Source: Eisenhardt, K. and Forbes, "Technical Entrepreneurship: An International Perspective," Columbia Journal of World Business, Winter 1984, page 32.

based firms. Support for the position they espouse may be found in Libecap (1986) and others.

We should not be surprised, then, to find countries, including Canada, attempting to learn from the venture capital experience of the United States and perhaps attempting to emulate the U.S. in establishing and forming its own domestic venture capital market system. We should expect such emulation to be bounded, however, due to fundamental differences in culture, institutions, laws, regulations, and a variety of other factors that may exist between the particular country and the U.S. Altering these may require modifications in law, regulations, and institutional arrangements. Differences in cultural and professional practices may be more difficult to diminish, and may only be subject to change through interaction between markets, that is, a certain amount of market integration between the country in question and the U.S.

In such circumstances, it may be difficult not only to emulate the U.S.

. approach in the other country but also to integrate the venture capital investment market activities of the two nations. With respect to integration, it must be realized that while venture capital does flow geographically, investments tend to be made close to the home base of the venture capital investment firm. Aside from occasional investments, the principal way that venture capital funds flow geographically is through coinvestment among professional venture capitalists, that is, syndication. Venture capital investment funds flow more easily, in greater volume, at more favorable terms to those areas in which local professional venture capital firms (i.e., potential syndicate members) exist and are active participants in large and resilient markets. A necessary condition for international flows of venture capital is the existence of institutional, regulatory, and legal symbiosis between the involved countries to reduce the inherent "country" risks involved.

In the case of Canada and the U.S., market expansion through integration has been difficult in the past. Because of changes in factors discussed below, the outlook for increased integration is improved, offering increased market access and market efficiency to all participants. It should be pointed out that other countries such as Germany, France, Australia, and Israel have moved in the same direction. In fact, the extent to which technological entrepreneurship exists in both India and Japan, the countries which appear to be so different from the U.S. in Table 10.1, has dramatically increased since the EF study.

Because integration may have great potential benefits for both countries, both in terms of increasing the productivity of resources and lowering the social costs of innovation by expanding the market for end products and services, emulation of and integration with the U.S. venture capital market system appears to constitute a "game worth the candle" to a country such as Canada. Because the U.S. and Canada share a unique geographically overlapping market for technologically innovative goods and services, both countries continuously transfer technology-based goods and services across their common border along with related people, ideas, training, methodology, and tools. Familiarity of each party with the practices of the other is inevitable, and may serve as the root of emulation. The spontaneous exchange, formal and informal, and technology transfer, along with the fundamental strength of each market, may be affected by issues of the type being considered in the current free-trade negotiations. Among the fundamentally important issues in the Canada-United States free trade negotiations are greater freedom in the flow of capital, increased trade in financial (and other) services, and protection of intellectual property rights. The venture capital market embodies all three of these and has strategic importance for international competitiveness through technological innovation for both countries. It has moved toward "free trade" status so quickly as to suggest the possibility of a fully integrated North American venture capital industry within the near future. We demonstrate below that emulation of the U.S. venture capital market system has been occurring in Canada, and that integration of the Canadian and U.S. venture capital market systems is taking place. We argue that the encouragement of these processes will enhance the ability of Canada and the U.S. to improve their international industrial competitiveness through enhanced levels and rates of technological innovation.

THE U.S. VENTURE CAPITAL MARKET SYSTEM

The U.S. venture capital market system, viewed by many as the development model for countries attempting to stimulate entrepreneurial activity and technological innovation, is a large system, well established, with an impressive track record of accomplishment. The U.S. market for venture capital finance and investment has expanded and deepened since 1950, developing from a fragmented and informal market to one with identifiable components and processes and with an enviable track record of performance. The market, which was in the past highly concentrated with respect to geography (several states), sources of funds (wealthy individuals and families), and distribution of funds (technology-based firms) is in a continuous process of deconcentration and decentralization, expanding regionally and internationally, employing funds from a widening array of sources, and servicing investment demand in an ever-increasing variety of outlets, all innovative and entrepreneurially-driven, and still mostly technology-based.

The visible supply of funds committed explicitly to venture capital investment at any moment is reflected in the "funds under management" by venture capital investment firms. These firms are generally established as limited partnerships, corporations, Business Development Corporations (BDC) or as Federal Government (i.e., Small Business Administration) licensed Small Business Investment Companies (SBIC). The amount outstanding at year-end and the annual change for the period 1969–86 is presented in Table 10.2. Several points are worthy of note. First, the absolute amount of funds under management is very small in relation to other U.S. marcoeconomic statistics (the $24 billion of industry total assets approximates the size in total assets of the twentieth-largest commercial bank in the U.S.). Second, the rapid expansion of total capital in the 1978–86 period followed a period of decline and recovery from 1969 through 1977. Third, the "net cash flow" (capital pool plus additions minus distributions to investee firms) was negative in each of the years 1969–1982 (except 1978), suggesting a steady pressure on the liquid resources of the venture capital investment community over this period. This measure has turned consistently positive since

Table 10.2
Flow of Investment Funds in the U.S. Venture Capital Industry

Year	Capital Pool, Start of Year ($millions)	Invested In VC Funds ($millions)	Disbursed To Investees ($millions)	Net Cash Flow ($millions)
1969	3,000	171	450	(279)
1970	2,900	97	350	(253)
1971	2,800	95	410	(315)
1972	2,800	62	425	(363)
1973	2,700	56	450	(394)
1974	2,700	57	350	(293)
1975	2,800	10	250	(240)
1976	2,900	50	300	(250)
1977	3,000	39	400	(361)
1978	3,500	570	550	20
1979	3,800	319	1,000	(681)
1980	4,500	700	1,100	(200)
1981	5,800	1,300	1,400	(100)
1982	7,600	1,800	1,800	(100)
1983	12,100	4,500	2,800	1,300
1984	16,300	4,200	3,000	1,200
1985	19,600	3,300	2,600	700
1986	24,100	4,500	2,900	1,600
Total		9,526	12,035	991

Source: Venture Capital Journal, Wellesley Hills, MA (Venture Economics, Inc., various issues). The capital pool estimates for the years 1969–1977 were provided by David Arscott, Managing Partner, Arscott and Norton L.P., San Francisco, CA.

1983, indicating an increasingly solid capital base for the industry as well as a tendency toward a willingness to sustain a more patient, less-than-fully-invested position on the part of fund managers.

The time pattern reflected in Table 10.2 may be explained in terms of investment opportunities and tax-related incentives. Following a strong public market demand for equities of emerging technology-based firms in the late 1960s, investors lost interest in this type of investment in the early 1970s. This was due in large measure to the reduction in Federal government funding support for technological R&D and the cutback in the space and military spending programs, both major sources of product demand from technology-based firms. To these problems were added the debilitating effects of the generally poor economic conditions of the early- to mid-1970s, during which time young innovative firms were especially hard hit by rising rates of inflation, recession, and cost of funds. With respect to technology, a major contribution of this early 1970s period was the introduction of the semiconductor to consumer and industrial applications (e.g., handheld calculators, mini- and early microcomputers). This dramatically influenced the orientation of emerging technologically innovative firms away from full dependency on government funding and purchasing policy to a strong market base increasingly extended to include very strong private sector consumer and industrial demand. This development positioned such firms to move ahead rapidly across a broad front characterized by a strong trend to technological innovation.

In 1978, the capital gains tax differential—removed by the Tax Reform Act of 1969—was restored, with capital gains tax reduced to 28 percent. This was subsequently lowered to 20 percent in 1980. At this same time, the Employee Retirement Investment Security Act (ERISA) was clarified to the satisfaction of pension fund investment managers interested in venture capital investments. These changes provided incentives for, on the one hand, taxpaying investors (financial and nonfinancial corporations), and, on the other hand, the nation's major tax-exempt investment pool to seek opportunities for investment with capital appreciation potential.

The results of these developments are reflected both in the aggregate volume of funds invested over time (Table 10.2) and in the distribution of funds by investor source. The sources of funds for private investment firms are shown in Table 10.3, which reflects the increasing importance of pension funds as ultimate investors. The growth of these firms, in dollar volume and in professional human resources, is reflected in Table 10.4. These data show that the change in capital per firm over the 1977–86 period has been greater than has the increase in capital per professional, indicating that investment firms are staying ahead of their capital growth in the addition of professional personnel. What is not shown in this Table 10.4 is the fact that the average tenure in venture capital of the professional base is now between four and five years, with a bimodal distribution between "veterans" (15–20 years) and newcomers to this relatively young industry. The geographic distribution of venture capital

Table 10.3
Venture Capital Commitments, U.S., 1982–1986
(Independent Private Firms Only)

	Total Capital Committed $ (Millions)					Total Capital Committed				
	1982	1983	1984	1985	1986	1982	1983	1984	1985	1986
Pension Funds	474	1070	1085	767	1672	33%	31%	34%	33%	49%
Foreign	188	531	463	274	400	13%	16%	15%	12%	12%
Individuals and Families	290	707	467	303	392	20%	21%	15%	13%	12%
Corporations	175	415	573	548	361	12%	12%	18%	24%	11%
Insurance Companies	200	410	419	254	348	14%	12%	13%	11%	10%
Endowments and Foundations	96	267	178	181	209	7%	8%	6%	8%	6%
Total	1423	3400	3185	2327	3382	100%	100%	100%	100%	100%

Source: <u>Venture Capital Journal</u>, January 1987, page 6, and selected earlier issues.

Table 10.4
Growth of Capital and Professional Resources of Venture Capital Firms,
U.S., 1977–1985

	Average Capital/Firm ($ Millions)		Median Size of Firm ($ Millions)		Average Capital/ Professional	
	1977	1985	1983	1985	1977	1985
Independent– Private	$9.0	$51.7	$18.0	$25.0	$3.8	$12.2
Corporate– Financial	25.4	49.1	14.5	50.5	7.7	10.3
Corporate– Industrial	8.9	27.6	10.0	15.0	4.0	9.4
Other V.C. SBICs	5.9	5.0	2.0	2.5	2.4	2.5
Total Industry	10.6	36.8	10.0	15.0	4.2	10.3

Source: Venture Capital Journal, June 1986, page 9.

investment resources has become proportionally more concentrated in the 1977–86 period, as shown in Table 10.5. While California clearly dominated this pattern, it is important to note that venture capital resources have appeared for the first time in some states and have increased in absolute and proportional importance in an increasing number of states over time.

It is also important to understand the investment pattern of professional venture capital managers with respect to stage of life cycle of investee firms and to see how it has changed over time. Data on venture capital disbursements are presented in Table 10.6. In the 1960s, venture capital investment stressed new business formation rather than ongoing development of firms. During the mid-1970s, expansion financing dominated and start-up financing declined to less than 10 percent of total activity. While the initial investment focus after the increase in available funds in 1978 was toward expansion financing, a strong shift toward start-up financing appeared in 1980. This reflects both the increased number of entrepreneurs attracted to the idea of starting a new business

Table 10.5
Geographic Distribution of Venture Capital Resources by Leading State in the U.S.

	Capital ($Millions)				Firms			
	1977	% of Total	1985	% of Total	1977	% of Total	1985	% of Total
California	524	26%	6,424	33%	44	27%	183	27%
New York	718	36%	3,868	20%	56	34%	102	15%
Massachusetts	334	17%	2,568	13%	28	17%	63	9%
Illinois	255	13%	1,070	5%	14	8%	25	4%
Connecticut	89	4%	1,030	5%	10	6%	25	4%
Texas	83	4%	824	4%	14	8%	52	8%
Other States	____	0%	3,789	19%	___	0%	218	33%
Total	$2,003	100%	$19,573	100%	166	100%	668	100%

Source: Venture Capital Journal, June 1986, page 13.

and competition among venture capitalists to capture the emerging "hot" companies at an early stage when the prospective returns are highest. As shown in Table 10.7, the relation between new and follow-on financing has changed significantly during the 1980s, with the bulk of investments and capital devoted to follow-on financing, presumably of the companies founded and funded earlier in the 1980s.

As professional venture capital managers seek exceptional rates of return for their investors, they exhibit a "preferred habitat" for their investments which has changed only slightly in recent years. This preference is reflected by the concentration of disbursements by geography and industry and its consistency over time. The geographic concentration of venture capital disbursements is shown in Table 10.8. It is evident that the northeast and west coast regions have been the primary recipients of venture capital disbursements. The fact that these are also the regions to which the largest volume of commitments of capital to venture capital funds has flowed indicates that both investment managers and investee firms tend to cluster in the same location and that, on balance, venture capital funds tend to be invested "close to home."

A review of the distribution of investment by industry sharpens the focus of this geographic distribution picture. As shown in Table 10.9, the bulk of venture capital investment is directed toward technology-

Table 10.6
Venture Capital Disbursements in the U.S. by Financing Stage

	Percent of Number of Companies Financed*		Percent of Dollars Amount Invested	
	1982	1985	1982	1985
Seed	5%	6%	2%	2%
Startup	20%	13%	17%	11%
Other Early Stage	18%	17%	17%	12%
Total Early Stage	43%	36%	36%	25%
Second Stage	24%	30%	30%	33%
Later Stage	21%	24%	22%	30%
Total Expansion	45%	54%	52%	63%
LBO/Acquisition	5%	5%	8%	8%
Other	7%	5%	4%	4%
Total Other	12%	10%	12%	12%
Total	100%	100%	100%	100%

*Percent of number of financing rounds rather than number of companies, because a company may receive different stages of financing in the same year.

Source: Venture Capital Journal, May 1984, page 10 and June 1986, page 13.

based industry such as telecommunications, electronics, computers, and biomedical firms. These are industries in which explosive growth has been obtained over the past 20 years. Even the casual observer is aware of the concentrations of technology-based industry in California and Massachusetts. It should come as no surprise to find venture capital activity concentrated in those areas in which technology-based firms are clustered.

"Going public"—the sale through a registered offering of equity securities to the public at large—and selling the securities of the company through a merger or acquisition are both attractive "exit routes" or sources of investment liquidity for the entrepreneur, the venture capitalist and other inside investors. Demand for such shares in the initial public offering (IPO) market has been in the past related in a pro-cyclical

Table 10.7
New and Follow-On Financing in the U.S., 1980–1985

Year	Amount ($Million)	% of Financing		% of Amount Invested	
		New	Follow-On	New	Follow-On
1980	$1.1	59%	41%	58%	42%
1981	1.4	60%	40%	55%	45%
1982	1.8	46%	54%	39%	61%
1983	2.8	45%	55%	34%	66%
1984	3.0	38%	62%	31%	69%
1985	2.6	31%	69%	23%	77%

Source: Venture Capital Journal, May 1986, page 11.

way to broad stock market indexes, while exhibiting, from time to time, "hot market" or "speculative bubble" characteristics. For most of its history the IPO market, and its over-the-counter (OTC) after-market, have been highly unstable as sources of funds and as investment vehicles. For the most part, they have been considered unreliable both by fund-raising companies and by investors.

For much of the 1978-86 period the IPO market experienced a steadily increased volume of new issues. The demand for these shares, though variable, rose on average, lifting secondary market (OTC) prices to attractive premiums over broad market indices. The relationship between the IPO market and its secondary OTC market performance, on the one hand, and the venture capital market, on the other, has at least two important dimensions. The existence of a strong and reasonably stable investment demand for IPO shares encourages earlier stage venture capital investment by promising an early opportunity to realize capital gains on the IPO issue and subsequent public sales of stockholdings. Also, the IPO market provides a vehicle for "price discovery" by those negotiating venture capital financings. In more than a few cases, qualifying young companies chose to "go public" instead of raising funds through the private venture capital route.

In the last part of 1983 and through 1984 the IPO market imposed a much finer "filter" on prospective issues, thus lowering the quantity of issues and the price paid on average for these shares and raising the quality of issues sold. This is reflected in Table 10.10 which shows valuation and volume data for venture capital-backed IPO. Following this

Table 10.8
Geographic Distribution of U.S. Venture Capital Disbursements, 1982–1985

	Percent of Number of Companies Financed		Percent of Dollar Amount Invested	
	1982	1985	1982	1985
California	37%	37%	45%	44%
Massachusetts	14%	15%	13%	13%
Texas	8%	7%	8%	6%
New York	7%	4%	8%	3%
Four State Total	66%	63%	74%	66%
Northeast (CT, DE, ME, MA NH, NJ, NY, RI, PA, VT)	28%	27%	26%	24%
Southeast (AL, DC, FL, GA, MD, MS, NC, SC, TN, VA, WV)	7%	9%	5%	7%
Midwest/Plains (IL, IN, IA, KS, KY, MI, MN, MO, NE, ND, OH, SD, WI)	9%	9%	8%	8%
Southwest/Rockies (AZ, AR, CO, ID, LA, MT, NV, NM, OK, TX, UT, WY)	15%	14%	13%	13%
West Coast (CA, OR, WA)	41%	41%	48%	48%
Total	100%	100%	100%	100%

Source: <u>Venture Capital Journal</u>, May 1984, page 10 and June 1986, page 14.

"cooling off," the IPO market regained its momentum and, until the market crash of October 19, 1987, provided a net positive incentive for venture capital investors interested in "cashing out" after reasonably short (3–5 year) holding periods.

The mergers and acquisition (M&A) market has been a very stable, though perhaps less publicized, exit vehicle over this same period of time. Table 10.11 shows the pattern of exit for venture capital-backed companies over the 1980–86 period.

Whereas the IPO market exhibits great variability, the M&A exit route has been remarkably consistent over the period. The maintenance of a freely functioning M&A market therefore seems to be an important factor in developing a strong regenerative venture capital market system.

Table 10.9
Venture Capital Disbursements in the U.S. by Industry Category

	Percent of Number of Companies Financed		Percent of Dollar Amount Invested	
	1982	1985	1982	1985
Computer Hardware and Systems	29%	20%	37%	25%
Software and Services	8%	15%	6%	10%
Telephone and Data Communications	7%	10%	7%	12%
Other Electronics	11%	13%	13%	14%
Total Electronics Related	55%	58%	63%	61%
Medical/Health Care Related	8%	11%	7%	10%
Commercial Communications	3%	4%	3%	4%
Genetic Engineering	3%	3%	3%	5%
Energy Related	6%	2%	6%	1%
Industrial Automation	5%	4%	3%	4%
Industrial Products and Machinery	5%	4%	4%	2%
Consumer Related	6%	8%	5%	7%
Other Products and Services	9%	6%	6%	6%
Total	100%	100%	100%	100%

Source: **Venture Capital Journal, May 1984, page 12 and May 1986, page 12.**

Several important trends in the U.S. venture capital industry have been noted above. They, along with several environmental factors, will affect the immediate future of the industry. The outlook presented here is based upon these trends and factors.

Despite the euphoric excitement surrounding the "discovery of high tech" by most of the investment world since 1978, and the valuation excesses and subsequent disappointments which resulted, the venture capital industry has made substantial net gains since that time. Perhaps most important is the movement, not yet complete, toward a rationalized structure, defined professionalism, and sense of mission in the venture capital industry significantly greater than that of the informal, fragmented, ad hoc business of the 1950s, 1960s, and early 1970s. Venture capital firms are now staffed by people better equipped to build busi-

Table 10.10
Venture Backed Initial Public Offerings in the U.S., 1978–1986

Year of IPO	Number of Companies	Total Amount Offered $(000)	Average Offering Size $(000)	Median Offering Size $(000)	Average Offering Valuation $(000)
1978	10	$91,038	$9,104	$6,885	$32,425
1979	12	104,482	8,707	7,450	34,143
1980	27	420,490	15,574	10,500	97,248
1981	68	770,342	11,329	10,050	53,092
1982	27	548,748	20,324	12,969	87,926
1983	121	3,031,308	25,052	16,150	115,989
1984	53	743,064	14,020	11,209	65,989
1985	47	843,347	17,944	15,188	69,746
1986	96	2,107,833	21,957	16,384	87,310

Source: Venture Capital Journal, February 1987, page 6.

nesses—people with strong backgrounds in technology, operations, and marketing. This is a marked change from the historical model that featured partners trained principally in financial analysis and the law. The increased supply of investment funds is now emanating from investors who are much more sophisticated about technological assessment and market analysis than were their predecessors. The result is that the large volume of funding available to venture capital pools is coming from a better-informed clientele who demand outstanding results in an increasingly competitive market environment.

The application of technology to economically important problems has developed an expansion rate which may already be geometric. Much of the technology being applied today is based on "old" science and the competition driven by the ability to form and fund new, technology-based firms is accelerating technology transfer through this vehicle. It appears unwise, therefore, even in the face of the positive cash-flow data presented above, to adopt the view that there is a situation of "too much money and too few deals," except in the most parochial and limited sense.

For these and other reasons it is highly likely that 1988 will see a level of new venture capital funding of $3 to $4 billion, mostly in the form of extensions of existing funds. Disbursements will likely be higher than

Table 10.11
Number of Venture Capital Backed Acquisitions and Initial Public Offerings in the U.S., 1980–1986

Year	Acquisitions Public & Private	Initial Public Offerings
1980	28	27
1981	32	68
1982	40	27
1983	49	121
1984	86	53
1985	101	47
1986	120	97

Source: <u>Venture Capital Yearbook</u>, Wellesley, MA (Venture Economics, Ltd., 1987), page 54.

in recent years, partly due to a more selective IPO market posture. The venture capital investment process will become more fully accepted by a broader range of financial institutions, and the range and volume of private placement capital and services available to emerging growth companies will continue to increase. This will push the economy in the direction in which it began to move ten years ago—from the large-firm model of industrial activity to the innovative, entrepreneurial risk-taking, inherently less stable smaller-firm model which will increasingly influence the U.S. economy in the years ahead. The provision of venture capital to form and fund such firms is critically important to this type of industrial development.

THE CANADIAN VENTURE CAPITAL MARKET SYSTEM

While there has been a venture capital market system in Canada for about as long as there has been one in the U.S., the Canadian system developed more slowly, in a significantly different fashion, and to a disproportionately smaller absolute level, at least up until 1985. Since that year, and due to several identifiable factors, Canada's venture capital industry has grown rapidly and has positioned itself to more closely resemble the U.S. system and to become selectively integrated with it.

The venture capital market in Canada has grown in total resources from an estimated U.S. $150 million in 1974 to U.S. $1.5 billion at the end of 1986. While the Canadian volume does not yet meet the "10 to 1" ratio simplistically used to express expected U.S/Canadian proportions, certain recent developments in the nature, character, and rate of growth of the Canadian market system suggest that the market is becoming increasingly similar to, and interactive with, that of the U.S. and that such interaction will likely enhance the market growth in both countries. In order to properly appreciate these developments, it is useful to review the development of the Canadian market over time.

The earliest identifiable venture capital investment firm in Canada was Charterhouse Canada, Ltd. (a foreign subsidiary of a combined English-French parent company) which established operations in 1952. Alone in the marketplace until 1962, Charterhouse was joined in that year by Canadian Enterprise Development Corporation (CED) which was modeled after the successful American Research and Development, Inc. of Boston. In the late 1960s and early 1970s several distinctly Canadian venture capital firms (TD Capital Group, Roymark, Cavendish, VenturesWest, and Helix) entered the business.

According to Fells [1984], the early venture capital firms in Canada shared distinctive characteristics:

- They were essentially minority equity investors, typically 20 percent to 49 percent owners.
- Their investments were long term, with no returns anticipated for at least five years and frequently as long as ten.
- Little emphasis was placed upon liquidity, instead the attitude was "if it's a good investment there will always be a way out."
- They were primarily passive investors, with "boardroom" rather than "hands-on" management participation.

This approach was similar to that of many U.S. venture capital firms and worked reasonably well, particularly since the public stock markets and large, acquisition-minded firms had an appetite for emerging, technology-based growth companies.

Following the downturn in U.S. and Canadian equity markets in the early 1970s and the fall from investor favor of technology-based growth companies on both markets, the earlier strategy proved untenable. Both U.S. and Canadian venture capital investors faced diminished sources of liquidity for their portfolio firms because of the declining stock market interest. Canadian venture firms were especially hard hit because of the Foreign Investment Review Act (FIRA), which effectively blocked Canadian access to the U.S. mergers and acquisition market as well as to the U.S. equity markets in general. As a result, Canadian venture capitalists shifted from the investment parameters indicated above to increased use of complex securities designed to return their investment through sinking funds and to realize profits through dividends and interest, rather than relying entirely upon equity appreciation and an exit through sale of the firm or a public stock issue. They became much more control-oriented, both in terms of ongoing management influence and with respect to the percentage of ownership required in financings.

As the decade of the 1970s advanced, the Canadian venture capital market assumed the same low profile as its U.S. counterpart. High and rising interest rates combined with high tax rates and the low prospects of profitable exit caused most of this discouragement. While there were several new entrants in the Canadian market (SB Capital, Inco Ventures, Canada Development Corproation) several corporate venture capital investors dropped out (Northern Telecom, McMillan Bloedel).

In the late 1970s a renewed interest in stimulating new and small business formation and growth developed in Canada, as in the U.S. and other countries. This might be considered the beginning of the modern reign of the entrepreneur! Government involvement at the provincial level—most notably the Small Business Development Corporations program in Ontario—contributed importantly to this resurgence. While other provinces established incentive-based programs (Nova Scotia, Prince Edward Island, Alberta) little was done in this vein at the Federal level.

In the private sector, the venture capital business was changing in fundamental ways. In 1980, Inco (having enjoyed success in its U.S. venture capital activity) joined with SB Capital to become general partner of North American Ventures Fund (NAVF), the first application of the limited partnership vehicle to a major venture capital pool in Canada. This introduced to the Canadian market a fund vehicle—long used in the U.S.—which used fund managers' "carried interest" incentives, and which pooled capital from taxable and nontaxable institutional investors into a single fund. This opened up the institutional market as a source of venture capital funds by providing a vehicle for indirect investment by institutions, which may have wanted to invest but felt uncomfortable investing directly and managing the portfolios themselves.

While these advances were important, Canada seemed destined in the early 1980s to see its venture capital market develop as a closed system, a niche market without outside participation. FIRA was a debilitating factor in attracting U.S. venture capital investors into Canadian investments, both with respect to bringing the initial funds into Canada and with respect to the liquidity problem discussed above. Also, the National Energy Policy of Canada struck uncertainty if not fear into the hearts of outside investors, who were alarmed by the treatment of U.S. investors in the Canadian oil business. Along the same lines, those U.S. banks which responded to the opportunity to establish limited banking charters in Canada experienced unanticipated restrictions after the fact, thus cooling their enthusiasm for venture capital investment opportunities in Canada. One of the distressing results of this set of conflicts was the growing incidence of Canadian venture capital companies involved in U.S. investment opportunities, and of Canadian institutional and corporate investors involved in placing funds with U.S. venture capital pools for investment in U.S. deals.

Among the policy programs introduced since 1984, several have been of direct benefit to the venture capital market. The Federal tax reform program, similar in ways to that of the U.S., has shifted investor interest from primarily tax-driven deals to "economic" deals. Deregulation in financial services and other industries has had a great leavening effect and has stimulated investment interest from sources hitherto uninvolved. Perhaps most significantly, the removal of FIRA and NEP as barriers to foreign investment offers the prospect of a Canadian market open to inflows of capital and related services from the U.S. and other countries. For the venture capital market, this means that Canadian-based venture capital investment companies are able to attract investors from the U.S. and other countries, that their portfolio companies can go public in the U.S. or other countries, or can merge with or be acquired by companies from the U.S. or other countries. Instead of having to look to the U.S. for investment opportunities, Canadian venture capital investment firms—employing the capital of foreigners as well as their own—can invest in Canadian firms with confidence that the regulatory impediments to timely and profitable exit have been greatly reduced.

Largely due to these changes, but also due to increased familiarity and lagged emulation of the U.S. venture capital market system, the Canadian venture capital market system has come, since 1984, increasingly to resemble the U.S. model with respect to structure, philosophy, and methods of operation. While some differences remain, these seem to be eroding over time and will approach some bedrock level in the near future. The information presented below reflects this pattern and some of the major differences.

In Table 10.12, for example, it is clear that the structural developments discussed above are reflected in the current distribution of types of venture capital investment companies in the Canadian and U.S. systems. While the overwhelming (75 percent) share of 1986 funds (total U.S. $24 billion) is managed by private, independent funds, the bulk of total funds under management in Canada is in corporate or government funds. The shift in private, independent content between 1985 (36 percent) and 1986 (41 percent) points out the movement toward the U.S. structural model.

Several important basic factors help explain the structural changes shown in these data. Because of clarification of the regulations regarding Canadian pension fund investment in limited partnerships (i.e., such

Table 10.12
Venture Capital Industry Resources by Investor Type, United States and Canada, 1985 and 1986

	1985			1986	
	U.S.	Canada		U.S.	Canada
Private	73%	36%		75%	41%
Corporate	17	36		16	36
Government (1)	10	28		9	23
Total	100%	100%		100%	100%
Amount ($billions)	$19.6	$1.3		$24.1	$1.5

(1) Crown corporations in Canada, Federally chartered Small Business Investment Companies in U.S.

Source: "The Changing Face of the Canadian Venture Capital Industry," Canadian Venture Capital, Toronto, (Venture Economics Canada Ltd, May 1987), page 17.

investment is no longer counted as part of the allowable foreign investment for pension funds), several new venture funds—in limited partnership form—have been created with capital provided largely by Canadian pension funds. Because of the reduction in barriers to foreign investment referred to above (e.g., FIRA and NEP) and the increased awareness of the U.S. system by Canadian venture capitalists, U.S. institutions have been included as investors in these new funds—another step toward integration of the two systems and the expansion of the market of each. At the same time the IDEA Corporation, a Crown related venture capital firm, was wound up, thus cutting down the representation of Government companies in the Canadian market. Corporate activity increased sufficiently to maintain its relative rank in the market.

These same pressures toward change and emulation are evident in data presented in Table 10.13, which show the sources of funding for Canadian and U.S. venture capital in 1985 and 1986.

These data show the distribution of the funds flowing into venture

Table 10.13
Sources of Venture Capital Industry Capital, Canada and the United States, 1985 and 1986

Sources of Capital	Percentage of Annual Flow			
	1985		1986	
	Canada	United States	Canada	United States
Pension Funds	37%	33%	67%	49%
Corporations	20	12	21	12
Individuals & Families	13	13	3	12
Insurance Companies	11	11	9	10
Government	19	0	0	0
Foreign	5	23	0	11
Endowments & Foundations	0	8	0	6
Total	100.0	100.0	100.0	100.0
Dollar Amount	$53 M	$3.3 Billion	$161 M	$4.6 Billion

Source: "The Changing Face of the Canadian Venture Capital Industry,"
Canadian Venture Capital, Toronto (Venture Economics Canada, Ltd., May
1987), page 18.

capital pools in 1985 and 1986 by capital source. The differences in the Canadian industry between the two years are dramatic. They reflect the increased importance of pension funds, as noted above, as well as the decline in the role of Government as a source of funds for venture capital activity. Other sources, which continued to be active investors, are down significantly in a relative sense because of the increased role of pension funds. These incremental percentage changes will cause the Canadian configuration to more closely resemble that of the U.S. The comparable changes in the U.S. were not so great in the 1985–86 period because the

Table 10.14
**Venture Capital Financial and Human Resources by Type of Firm, Canada
    and U.S., 1985**

	Average Capital Per Firm		Median Size Per Firm		Average Capital Per Professional	
	Canada	U.S.	Canada	U.S.	Canada	U.S.
Private Independent	$21.4	$51.7	$19.2	$25.0	$5.1	$12.2
Corporate Financial	59.5	49.1	N.M.	20.5	11.3	10.3
Corporate Nonfinancial	20.0	27.6	15.0	15.0	8.4	9.4
Crown/SBIC	91.8	5.0	52.5	2.5	11.4	2.5
Total Industry	30.2	36.8	20.0	15.0	6.7	10.3

* Capital is stated in millions of Canadian and U.S. dollars respectively

N.M. -- not meaningful due to small number of firms.

Source: "Venture Capital Industry Sources", Canadian Venture Capital,"
Toronto (Venture Economics Canada, Ltd., August 1986), page 15.

radical, pension-driven change in the U.S. distribution had occurred in
the 1983–84 period. As shown here, the flow of funds to U.S. venture
capital funds from foreign investors is still very large compared to its
Canadian counterpart. With the increased integration of these two markets, the Canadian percentage will undoubtedly rise in the near term.

Another dimension across which to compare Canadian and U.S. venture capital is in terms of capital per firm and per professional in each
firm. Data showing such a comparison as of year-end 1985 are presented
in Table 10.14.

The fact that these data are presented in Canadian (roughly U.S. $0.72
at the time) and U.S. currency, respectively, makes direct comparison
of these numbers difficult. Nevertheless it is clear that in 1985, corporate
financial- and Crown-sponsored venture capital funds were dominant
in Canada while private independent- and corporate-sponsored funds
were dominant in the U.S.. Given the shifts noted earlier, the Canadian
distribution is likely to change in the direction of the U.S. pattern. The
size-of-firm discrepancies, as well as the differences in capital invested
per professional, will also pull closer together as increased volumes of
funds are invested in a Canadian industry structure, which increasingly
resembles that of the U.S.

Canada's venture capital industry differs somewhat from the U.S.

Table 10.15
Venture Capital Disbursements by Industry, U.S. and Canada, 1985 and 1986

Industry	United States		Canada	
	1985	1986	1985	1986
Computer	22%	19%	17%	14%
Consumer	7	9	14	15
Industrial Products	3	2	8	9
Biotechnology	4	4	10	9
Medical/Health	9	12	2	8
Communications	18	19	7	6
Energy	1	2	6	6
Industrial Automation	4	2	1	2
Software	22	19	NEC	NEC
Investment Groups	NEC	NEC	13	6
Other	8	11	13	19
Total	100%	100%	100%	100%

Source: "The Changing Face of the Canadian Venture Capital Industry,"
Canadian Venture Capital, Toronto (Venture Economics Canada, Ltd., May
1987), page 20.

system in the distribution of its investment pattern by industry. Information presented in Table 10.15 provides insight on these differences.

These data show that U.S. venture capital investments are more heavily concentrated in technology-based industry groups than are Canadian venture capital portfolios. This reflects in part the relatively small size of Canada's high technology industry [see Hay 1984] as well as the fact that Canadian venture capital firms have faced little competition from other financing sources in serving emerging growth companies in service, retail, and other low-technology types of industry. The distribution is also affected by the fact that Canadian venture funds place a significant part of their portfolios in investments in other (principally U.S.) venture capital funds, i.e., "Investment Groups" in Table 10.15. It is interesting that U.S. venture capital funds seem to be gradually seeking to expand their interest to industries other than high technology-intensive ones,

Table 10.16
Venture Capital Disbursements by Stage of Investment Cycle, Canada and the U.S., 1985 and 1986

	Canada		United States	
	1985	1986	1985	1986
Seed/Startup	22%	19%	12%	18%
Other Early	3	7	12	17
Expansion	41	40	60	44
LBO, Other	34	34	16	21
Total	100%	100%	100%	100%

Source: "The Changing Face of the Canadian Venture Capital Industry,"
Canadian Venture Capital, Toronto (Venture Economics Canada, Ltd., May
1987), p. 21.

and are hampered somewhat in this respect due to the large and attractive opportunities open to them in U.S. high technology companies.

Despite the differences cited above, the two market systems are quite similar with respect to the distribution of their capital disbursements by life cycle stage of investee companies. The comparison between the two is presented in Table 10.16.

The life cycle investment patterns reflected by this data suggest greater similarities than differences. The larger portion of Canadian portfolios invested in "LBO and other" reflects the impact of the increased pension fund infusion of capital and the regulatory-driven investment preferences that accompany it. Further, the volume of LBO and mezzanine financing demand in Canada has increased dramatically, thus attracting the interest of the venture capital community. Increased integration of the two markets could serve to drive the two life cycle patterns closer together through increased cross-border competition for investment deals and increased syndication among U.S. and Canadian venture capital firms.

In the U.S., venture capital disbursement activity is geographically concentrated, as discussed in an earlier section of this chapter. In Canada, a similar concentration exists, but for somewhat different reasons. Information comparing the geographic concentration in the two countries is shown in Table 10.17.

The fact that Ontario leads all provinces in disbursements reflects its position as the industrial heartland and financial center of Canada. It is

Table 10.17
Venture Capital Disbursements by Region, U.S. and Canada, 1986

United States		Canada	
West Coast	41%	Ontario	31%
Northeast	31	Alberta	25
Southwest/Rockies	10	Quebec	17
Southeast	7	Foreign	14
Midwest/Plains	7	B.C.	7
Mid-Atlantic	4	Prairies	4
Foreign	0	Canada N.E.C.	2
Total	100%		100%

Source: "The Changing Face of the Canadian Venture Capital Industry," Canadian Venture Capital, Toronto (Venture Economics, Canada, Ltd., May 1987), page 20.

followed closely by Alberta, a province which, while dominated by the energy industry, has nonetheless developed a strong base of entrepreneurially-driven companies in recent years along with a set of local venture capital investment firms. Quebec is in third place, reflecting the fact that provincial legislation in 1985 established tax incentives for the purchase of initial public share offerings of Quebec-based companies. The major difference between the two countries is the large percentage of disbursements by Canadian venture capital funds to foreign investees, principally U.S. companies. As mentioned earlier, Canada is only now beginning to attract foreign institutional investment to its venture capital industry, and yet has been "exporting" its dollars (or "importing" investment deals) for some time. The U.S., in contrast, has been a net "importer" of capital (i.e., "exporter" of deals). With increased integration, a greater balance in flows between the two countries would result.

CONCLUSIONS

The evidence presented in this chapter documents the development to date of the venture capital industry in the United States and Canada, demonstrating similarities and differences in the nature and rate of development of each system. The Canadian system developed more slowly and to a lower scale of operations relative to the U.S. system throughout the 1960s and 1970s, but was influenced by the same set of macroeconomic influences (i.e., inflation, high and rising interest rates, and sharply declining equity values). Whereas the U.S. system enjoyed a boom period in the early 1980s, the Canadian system was impeded by several legal and regulatory factors, principally ones which limited access to the U.S. market for public stock issues, merger and acquisition partners, and institutional investment. Until legislative and regulatory changes were made in the mid-1980s, Canada's venture capital system was essentially engaged in exporting a portion of domestically generated funds to finance investment opportunities in the U.S. and other foreign countries, while being unable to attract foreign funds to Canada due to legal restrictions imposed by the Foreign Investment Review Act and the National Energy Policy. With the removal of those barriers, tax code revisions, and liberalization of pension fund investment regulations, the Canadian venture capital industry has enjoyed a surge of development and growth since 1985.

Given the thrust of the current free-trade negotiations, the evidence presented here should be viewed as a strong recommendation for diminishing conflict between the systems and improving cooperation. Emulation of operating practice will occur spontaneously on both sides of the border so long as the legislative and regulatory symbiosis mentioned earlier is maintained. Integration of the two systems will follow from this process, and a natural fit between components of the two systems will result. While the size differential alone suggests that Canada stands to benefit more from integration than the U.S., the comparisons made in this paper indicate that the benefits are likely to be mutual and proportional over time. The venture capital market system is at least one aspect of Canadian-United States economic relations where the letter and spirit of free trade has proven valuable to both nations and appears to be a sound foundation upon which to build a future based in part upon a North American market strategy.

REFERENCES

Brophy, David J., "Venture Capital Research," *The Art and Science of Entrepreneurship*, D. L. Sexton and R. W. Similor (eds), Cambridge, MA (Ballinger Publishing Company, 1986, pp. 119–149.

"The Changing Face of the Canadian Venture Capital Industry," *Canadian Venture Capital* (Venture Economics Canada Limited, May 1987), pp. 17–24.

Eisenhardt, Kathleen M. and N. Forbes, "Technical Entrepreneurship: An International Perspective," *Colombia Journal of World Business*, Winter 1984, pp. 31–38.

Fells, George, "Venture Capital in Canada—A Ten Year Review," *Business Quarterly*, Spring 1984, pp. 70–77.

Hambrecht, William R. "Venture Capital and the Growth of Silicon Valley," *California Management Review*, Vol. XXVI, No. 2, Winter 1984, pp. 74–82.

Hardy, Kenneth G., "Key Success Factors for Small/Medium Sized Canadian Manufacturers Doing Business in the United States," *Business Quarterly*, March 1987, pp. 67–73.

Hay, Keith A. J., "Can Canada Sustain a High-Tech Industry?" *Business Quarterly*, Fall 1984, pp. 52–59.

Libecap, Gary (ed.) *Advances in the Study of Entrepreneurship, Innovation, and Economic Growth*, Greenwich, CT (Jai Press, Inc, Vol. 1, 1986), 213 pp.

"Liquidity of Canadian Venture Capital Investments: 1986 IPO and M&A Marketplaces," *Canadian Venture Capital* (Venture Economics Canada Limited, August 1987), pp. 14–19.

Litvak, Isaiah A., "Freer Trade With Canada: The Conflicting Views of U.S. Business," *Business Quarterly*, November 1986.

MacDonald, Stuart, "High Technology Policy and the Silicon Valley Model: An Australian Perspective," *Prometheus*, St. Lucie, University of Queensland, Vol. 1, No. 2, December 1983, pp. 330–348.

Rugman, Alan M., "A Canadian Strategy for International Competitiveness," *Business Quarterly*, Fall, 1985, pp. 18–21.

Rugman, Alan M., "Canada's Agenda for Bilateral Trade Negotiations," *Business Quarterly*, Spring 1986, pp. 37–41.

Thompson, Donald N., "Canada Has Ignored Intellectual Property Rights: Our Researchers Pay the Price," *Business Quarterly*, Winter 1984, pp. 30–33.

"Venture Capital in Canada: 1985," *Canadian Venture Capital*, Toronto (Venture Economics Canada Limited, May 1986), pp. 13–20.

Viard, Alan D., "Taxation and Venture Capital," *Tax Notes*, August 19, 1985, pp. 915–919.

11
The Patterns of Bilateral Foreign Direct Investment
Alan M. Rugman

This chapter examines the extent of bilateral (U.S.-Canadian) direct investment. There are three sections. The first section considers the performance of U.S. subsidiaries in Canada. A major finding is that, on average, the U.S. subsidiaries export about one-quarter of their output—a fact often neglected by persons who view foreign-owned subsidiaries in Canada as being in import-competing sectors. The second section of the chapter reports new data on the performance of Canadian-owned affiliates in the United States. It is found that these Canadian multinationals purchase, on average, five times as much from their parent firms in Canada as they "export" back to Canada. The third section examines the balance of trade to Canada due to the intra-firm trade by these two sets of multinationals and the benefits to Canada of such activity.

The presentation of this empirical material emphasizes the conceptual linkages between examination of the performance of U.S. subsidiaries in Canada and Canadian affiliates in the United States. There has been an unfortunate tendency by Canadian policy makers and negotiators to concentrate on the former and neglect the latter. Only when both elements of direct investment are considered can the impact of bilateral trade liberalization be predicted. A useful analysis of the balance of bilateral intra-firm trade requires that the basic data on the two-way flows and stocks of direct investment be properly understood; that is the objective of this chapter. This is an extension of work by Rugman (1980) on U.S. subsidiaries in Canada and Rugman and McIlveen (1985) on Canadian multinationals.

BILATERAL TRADE PERFORMANCE OF U.S.-OWNED SUBSIDIARIES IN CANADA

There is still a common perception in Canada that foreign-owned firms, which were often set up originally to bypass the Canadian tariff, are still branch plants selling entirely within the Canadian market. This perception is inaccurate. The foreign-owned subsidiaries are in practice involved in as much international trade activity as domestically-owned corporations. For example, in 1981, the largest 300 foreign-owned companies in Canada exported nearly one-quarter of their output.

The data source for this section is the annual survey on *Foreign-Owned Subsidiaries in Canada*. This survey was started over 20 years ago to help the Government of Canada monitor the economic performance of foreign-owned companies, in accordance with the so-called "Winters" guidelines of 31 March 1966. Winter was the Minister of Industry, Trade and Commerce (I T & C) at that time, and his department became responsible for the collection of data based on an annual questionnaire. I T & C's work was reinforced by the "Gillespie" guidelines of 1975, which followed the passage of Phase II of the Foreign Investment Review Act.

The questionnaire was sent to the entire set of the largest nonfinancial foreign-owned subsidiaries in Canada, defined as those with sales of $5 million or greater and foreign-ownership of 50 percent or more. There are usually about 300 such respondents, by which the survey covers the activities of about 1,000 separate companies (since some firms consolidate returns for a number of affiliate companies). In the last year for which data were collected, a total of 274 companies responded on behalf of a "stable total of between 970 to 1,000 respondents." The last report, produced by the Department of Regional Industrial Expansion (DRIE) which contains part of the now-defunct I T & C, was published in September 1984 and contains information up to 1981.

Data for subsequent years were collected by Statistics Canada but are still in raw form, and have not been published nor made available to independent researchers. Beginning with the 1983 and 1984 questionnaires, the data began to be integrated into CALURA data. Unfortunately, because of the new regulatory changes in 1985 governing the collection of data from corporations, the collection and presentation of these data at the firm level has been virtually eliminated. Further, these data are increasingly integrated with tax data, which are now used by Statistics Canada to supply the same information. Tax data, of course, are confidential and not available to independent researchers.

THE BALANCE OF TRADE FOR U.S. SUBSIDIARIES IN CANADA

Table 11.1 reports data on intra-industry trade. This term is used to define trade between foreign-owned affiliates and all their trading part-

Table 11.1
Intraindustry Trade by U.S. Subsidiaries in Canada
(C $ M)

Year	Foreign Sales by U.S. Subsidiaries in Canada (X)	Foreign Purchases by U.S. Subsidiaries in Canada (M)	Canadian Balance
1981	20,305	22,389	(2,084)
1980	19,417	20,193	(776)
1979	18,844	20,624	(1,780)
1978	18,013	18,076	(63)
1977	15,261	15,614	(353)
1976	13,173	13,815	(642)
1975	11,459	11,736	(277)
1974	9,846	10,628	(782)
1973	8,177	8,017	160
1972	7,193	6,456	737
1971	6,575	5,760	815
1970	5,688	4,864	824
1969	5,568	5,066	502
1968	4,920	4,422	498
1967	4,025	3,591	434
1966	3,388	2,968	420
1965	2,486	2,445	41
1964	2,278	1,898	380

Sources: Canada, Department of Regional Industrial Expansion, Foreign-Owned Subsidiaries in Canada: 1979 - 1981 (Ottawa: Surveys and Analysis, Statistical and Data Base Services, DRIE, September, 1984): Table 13.

Canada, Department of Industry, Trade and Commerce, Foreign-Owned Subsidiaries in Canada, [various years] (Ottawa: Statistical and Data Base Services, IT & C (DRIE), April 1983, May 1975, 1974, August 1972 and 1970): Table 13, Appendix VII and Summary Table 27.

ners. The term is distinguished from intra-firm trade (used later in other tables), which is defined as internal trade between the subsidiary and its parent. Table 11.2 reports data on the balance of trade on foreign sales (X) and purchases (M) for all reporting U.S. subsidiary corporations in Canada covered by the I T & C and DRIE survey. Between 1964 and 1973 the balance of intra-industry trade was favorable to Canada, but since 1974, foreign purchases by the U.S. subsidiaries have remained larger than foreign sales. Over the five-year period, from 1977 to 1981, foreign sales have averaged Cdn. $18.4 billion, while foreign purchases have averaged Cdn. $19.4 billion, for an average deficit of Cdn. $1.0 billion. (The total deficit is Cdn. $5 billion for these five years).

The merchandise imports and exports are those made directly by the respondents, and hence, goods sold by them in Canada and subsequently exported are not included in their export figures and imported

Table 11.2
Foreign Sales and Purchases by U.S. Subsidiaries in Canada

Year	Sales Ratio (X/TX) %)	Purchases Ratio (M/TM) (%)
1981	24.84	27.39
1980	24.23	25.19
1979	24.89	27.24
1978	27.39	27.48
1977	26.35	26.96
1976	25.64	26.89
1975	24.80	25.40
1974	24.73	26.70
1973	25.51	25.01
1972	26.28	23.59
1971	26.86	23.53
1970	26.78	22.90
1969	26.27	23.90
1968	25.01	20.86
1967	22.48	20.06
1966	N/A	N/A
1965	N/A	N/A
1964	17.86	14.89

Notes: N/A - Not Available.

Sources: Canada, Department of Regional Industrial Expansion, Foreign - Owned Subsidiaries in Canada: 1979 - 1981 (Ottawa: Surveys and Analysis, Statistical and Data Base Services, DRIE, September, 1984):   Tables 12 and 13.

Canada, Department of Industry, Trade and Commerce, Foreign - Owned Subsidiaries in Canada, various years (Ottawa: Statistical and Data Base Services, IT & C (DRIE), April 1983, May 1975, 1974, August 1972 and 1970).   Tables 1, Summary Table 2 and Summary Table 27.

goods purchased from Canadian suppliers are excluded from their imports. Import figures include duties, sales taxes, and the cost of transportation in Canada, in most cases. The decline in growth in foreign sales was particularly responsible for the larger-than-normal deficits in 1979 and 1981. Foreign sales growth between 1979 and 1981 averaged 4 percent, while for the earlier period 1974 to 1978, it averaged 17 percent (an average growth of 12 percent over the entire 1974–81 period). For purchases over the same periods; from 1979 to 1981 they averaged 8 percent, and 18 percent for 1974 to 1978 (an average growth of 14 percent for the entire 1974–81 period).

Over the 1964–81 period, the growth of foreign sales and purchases by the U.S. subsidiaries in Canada has remained relatively stable; averaging 14 percent for sales and 16 percent for purchases. The growth in foreign purchases has, however, been more susceptible to decline than exports, though this phenomenon appears to have been confined to the early 1970s. Purchases declined four percent in 1970, and there was also a small decline in 1980 of two percent.

The most important interpretation to be drawn from Table 11.1 is the approximate balance between imports and exports by foreign-owned subsidiaries in Canada. These U.S. affiliates are not purely branch plants, importing components and knowledge from their parents and selling their entire output in the Canadian host market. Instead they export nearly as much as they import. This is a remarkable performance if the classic theoretical reason for foreign direct investment in Canada (the tariff) is correct. [For a review of this literature, see Rugman (1980).] It is argued that high Canadian tariffs, first imposed to protect domestic industry, caused a switch to foreign direct investment in Canada, from exporting, as foreign firms (mainly American) sought to jump the tariff wall. The result was (allegedly) branch plants that were miniature replicas of their parents. Obviously these foreign-owned subsidiaries were supposed to be in import-competing sectors. Yet, for the last 20 years, these U.S. subsidiaries have exported as much as they imported—hardly confirmation of the branch plant hypothesis. Rather, these subsidiaries embody characteristics of modern multinationals, in which two-way flows of direct investment (Intra-industry trade) are common, see Rugman (1981). This evidence for such intra-industry trade and investment is explored further below.

The relative stability in the growth of foreign sales and purchases by the U.S. subsidiaries in Canada can also be seen in Table 11.2. This table shows the ratio of foreign sales and purchases to all (both foreign and Canadian) sales (TX) and purchases (TM) of the U.S. subsidiaries in Canada. Over the ten years, from 1972 to 1981, these percentages have remained remarkably stable, averaging 25.47 percent for foreign to total sales (exports) and 26.19 percent for foreign to total purchases (imports). These ratios are 25.54 percent and 26.85 percent, respectively, for the five years between 1977 and 1981.

The import and export ratios in Table 11.2, for the period between 1964 and 1972, confirm the earlier indication that U.S. subsidiaries in Canada, rather than being in branch plant operations (which only service the Canadian markets), have consistently sold (exported) approximately 25 percent of their production. Most of these exports go to the United States, in particular back to their parent groups in the United States, as is shown in the data in Tables 11.3 and 11.4.

Table 11.3 presents data on the intra-firm trade by the affiliates of U.S. multinationals operating in Canada, which consist of sales by U.S. subsidiaries in Canada to their parent groups (X_p) and purchases by the

Table 11.3
Intrafirm Trade by U.S. Subsidiaries in Canada
(C $ M)

Year	Sales by U.S. Subsidiaries in Canada to their Parent Groups (X_p)	Purchases by U.S. Subsidiaries in Canada from their Parent Groups (M_p)	Canadian Balance
1981	14,647	15,718	(1,071)
1980	13,347	14,353	(1,006)
1979	13,715	15,639	(1,924)
1978	13,793	13,342	451
1977	11,667	11,357	310
1976	9,953	9,944	9
1975	8,097	8,014	83
1974	7,036	7,253	(217)
1973	6,190	5,891	299
1972	5,389	4,948	441
1971	4,848	4,192	656
1970	4,188	3,352	836
1969	4,216	3,553	663
1968	3,413	3,072	341
1967	2,707	2,310	397
1966	2,006	1,938	68
1965	1,195	1,546	(351)
1964	1,025	1,173	(148)

Sources: Canada, Department of Regional Industrial Expansion,
           Foreign - Owned Subsidiaries in Canada: 1979 - 1981
           (Ottawa: Surveys and Analysis, Statistical and Data
           Base Services, DRIE, September, 1984):   Tables 1, 8 and
           14.

           Canada, Department of Industry, Trade and Commerce,
           Foreign - Owned Subsidiaries in Canada   [various years]
           (Ottawa: Statistical and Data Base Services, IT & C
           (DRIE), April 1983, May 1975 and 1974):   Tables 1, 3,
           8, 14, and Appendix VIII.

U.S. subsidiaries from their parent groups (M_p). The balance of intra-firm trade is very similar in size to that reported for the intra-industry trade balance in Table 11.1. From 1977 to 1981, U.S. parent-subsidiary trade resulted in an average deficit for Canada of Cdn. $828 million, versus the average deficit of Cdn. $1.0 billion for all U.S. subsidiary trade, as was indicated when discussing Table 11.1. In the period from 1977 to 1981, the growth rates for intra-firm (U.S. parent–subsidiary) trade were virtually identical at 9.46 and 10.04 percent for sales and purchases, respectively. However, over the period from 1964 to 1981, exports, from the U.S. subsidiaries to their parent groups or affiliates

Table 11.4
Intrafirm Trade Ratios for U.S. Subsidiaries in Canada

Year	Sales by the U.S. Subsidiaries to the Parent Groups (X_p) as a Percentage of all Foreign Sales (X) (X_p/X) %	Purchases by the U.S. Subsidiaries from the Parent Groups (Mp) as a Percentage of all Foreign Purchases (M) (M_p/M) %
1981	72.13	70.20
1980	68.74	71.08
1979	72.78	75.83
1978	76.57	73.81
1977	76.45	72.74
1976	75.56	71.98
1975	70.66	68.29
1974	71.46	68.24
1973	75.70	73.48
1972	74.92	76.64
1971	73.73	72.78
1970	73.63	68.91
1969	75.72	70.13
1968	69.37	69.47
1967	67.25	64.33
1966	59.21	65.30
1965	48.07	63.23
1964	45.00	61.87

Sources: Canada, Department of Regional Industrial Expansion, Foreign - Owned Subsidiaries in Canada: 1979 - 1981 (Ottawa: Surveys and Analysis, Statistical and Data Base Services, DRIE, September, 1984): Tables 1, 8, 13 and 14.

Canada, Department of Industry, Trade and Commerce, Foreign - Owned Subsidiaries in Canada [various years] (Ottawa: Statistical and Data Base Services, IT & C (DRIE), April 1983, May 1975, 1974, August 1972 and 1970):   Tables 1, 8, 3, 13, 14, Summary Table 27, Appendix VII and Appendix VIII.

grew by 18 percent while imports grew at 17 percent. The initially faster growth in intra-firm export trade (1964–1969) was compensated for by the relatively faster import (foreign purchases) growth rate in the 1972 to 1981 period (15 percent for purchases and 13 percent for sales), which reduced the benefit to Canada's balance of trade.

The great degree of intra-firm (U.S. parent–subsidiary) trade relative to intra-industry trade can be seen in Table 11.4. This table reports the ratio of sales (M_p) and purchases (X_p) by the U.S. parent groups, to all foreign purchases (M) and sales (X) by the U.S.-owned affiliates in Canada. The vast majority of trade is intra-firm. From 1964 to 1981, the U.S.

affiliates imported 70 percent and exported 69 percent, on average, of all their foreign purchases and sales to and from their parent corporations in the United States. The trend with sales appears to have increased. Since 1969, sales to the parent groups accounted for 73 percent of all foreign sales by the U.S. subsidiaries. The relative importance of purchases from the U.S. parents appears to have increased; from the mid-1960s percent range of total foreign purchases in the late 1960s and early 1970s, to an average of 72 percent since 1969. This would confirm the observations, from Table 11.3, that sales to the U.S. parent groups from the Canadian subsidiaries (exports) grew slower than did purchases (imports) by U.S. subsidiaries from their parent groups.

The extremely high degree of intra-firm trade, reflected in both sales and purchases, is due to the high degree of integration between U.S. subsidiary corporations and their parent groups. This indicates that the U.S. parent groups are viewing the United States–Canada market as an integrated market area; they plan their subsidiary production within this larger framework. These data undermine the notion that U.S. subsidiaries in Canada are purely branch plants. The "tariff factory" theory of production argues that U.S. subsidiaries in Canada were set up to avoid the higher Canadian tariff. Yet, in many cases these tariffs have been lowered or removed over the last fifteen years, in accordance with the seven rounds of GATT trade liberalization. Today, however, there are nontariff barriers to trade, but their impact on the decisions of where to locate affiliates is more complex than the branch plant argument.

To summarize, these data confirm the two key observations made with reference to Tables 11.2 and 11.3. First, U.S. subsidiaries in Canada tend to import as much as they export, therefore, trade is relatively balanced. Second, the deficit in trade (from Canada's point of view), is not due primarily to non-parent or affiliate to subsidiary trade, but is also due to other two-way trade between Canada and the United States and other countries. The five year accumulated "deficit" from Table 11.1 is Cdn. $5,056 million for foreign sales and purchases of all U.S. subsidiaries, foreign sales and purchases, but it is only Cdn. $3,550 million for their intra-firm trade as indicated by Table 11.3. Overall, the data in Tables 11.1 to 11.4 provide strong confirmation for the conclusion that U.S. subsidiaries in Canada do more than just produce for the Canadian market; they also contribute in a major way to Canadian exports.

BILATERAL TRADE PERFORMANCE OF CANADIAN-OWNED AFFILIATES

In this section attention is directed toward the trade performance of Canada's multinationals operating in the United States. The analysis is based on the data gathered in the annual surveys by the U.S. Department of Commerce of all foreign affiliates in the United States. In 1984 there were 1,395 Canadian-owned affiliates in the United States identified by the Commerce data. Therefore, this section reviews the extent of intra-firm trade for *all* of the Canadian subsidiaries in the United States, not just the largest 21 studied by Rugman and McIlveen (1985) and Rugman (1987). The objective of this section is to investigate the nature of intra-industry and intra-firm trade by Canadian-owned multinationals: Canada enjoys a large trade surplus in such trade with its U.S. affiliates.

Table 11.5 presents data on the sales and trade performance of Canada's affiliates in the United States from 1977 to 1984. Column one shows the amount of sales, column two their foreign sales, while column three shows the amount of foreign purchases by Canada's subsidiaries in the United States. There is a data break between 1980 and 1981, due to a change in methodology involved in a Commerce Department benchmark survey. This means that the data for the 1981 and following years are not directly comparable for 1980 and previous years. In 1984, the total sales by Canadian affiliates in the United States were U.S. $82.5 billion, but their foreign sales were only U.S. $4.5 billion. The vast majority of sales by Canada's multinationals are made within the U.S. market itself; only about six percent of production and sales by Canada's affiliates is not made within the United States.

Over the most recent period of data availability (1982 to 1984) the foreign sales by Canada's U.S. affiliates grew by five percent per annum. This was only half as fast as the growth of total sales (which includes the small amount of foreign sales) of these affiliates over the same period, which was 11 percent per annum. Foreign sales of the Canadian affiliates slowed down in the 1982 and 1983 periods, from U.S. $4.5 billion in 1981, to U.S. $4.2 billion in 1982, before climbing back in 1983 to nearly the same level as in 1981. Foreign purchases declined by 16 percent from 1981 to 1982 and fell a further 1 percent in the 1982–83 period before rebounding by 20 percent in 1984, to U.S. $7.2 billion. These temporary reductions in the trade deficits of Canada's U.S. affiliates, over the 1981 to 1984 period, were probably due to the differential impact of the recession. The United States was less affected by the recession than Canada; total sales of Canadian affiliates grew faster (at over 10 percent per annum) from 1981–84, but purchases from their Canadian parents grew slower (at under 1 percent).

It is apparent from the data in Table 11.5 that Canada's affiliates have consistently purchased more outside the United States ("imported") than they have "exported" from the United States. From the perspective of the U.S. Commerce Department, the data in Table 11.5 indicate a negative balance for the United States on the trade of the Canadian affiliates, a form of intra-industry trade. In 1984 they imported U.S. $2.7 billion more than they exported. This has been a consistent pattern since

Table 11.5
Sales, Foreign Sales, and Purchases by Canadian Affiliates in the United States
(U.S. $M)

Year	(1) Sales by Canadian Affiliates in the United States	(2) Foreign Sales by Canadian Affiliates in the United States	(3) Foreign Purchases by Canadian Affiliates in the United States	(4) U.S. Balance of Intra-Industry Trade
1984	82,483	4,506	7,213	(2,709)
1983	72,037	4,290	5,995	(1,705)
1982	64,909	4,162	6,071	(1,909)
1981	60,927	4,528	8,223	(3,195)
1980	35,456	1,792	5,553	(3,761)
1979	29,067	1,763	5,194	(3,431)
1978	24,555	1,325	4,664	(3,339)
1977	19,733	854	3,853	(2,999)

Sources: U.S. Department of Commerce, Bureau of Economic Analysis, Foreign Direct Investment in the United States: Operations of U.S. Affiliates 1977-80 (Washington, D.C.: 1985): Data for 1977 - 1980.

U.S. Department of Commerce, Bureau of Economic Analysis, Foreign Direct Investment in the United States: Annual Survey Results: 1981 Estimates, Revised 1982 Estimates, Revised 1983 Estimates and Preliminary 1984 Estimates (Washington, D.C.: December 1984, December 1985, October 1986): Data for 1981 through 1984, Table G.4).

Table 11.6
Foreign Sales and Purchases by Canadian Affiliates in the United States,
1977–1984

Year	(1) Sales Ratio %	(2) Purchases Ratio %
1984	5.46	8.74
1983	5.96	8.32
1982	6.41	9.35
1981	7.43	13.50
1980	5.05	15.66
1979	6.07	17.87
1978	5.40	18.99
1977	4.33	19.53

Sources: U.S. Department of Commerce, Bureau of Economic
            Analysis, Foreign Direct Investment in the United
            States: Operations of U.S. Affiliates, 1977 – 80
            (Washington, D.C.: 1985): Data for 1977 – 1980.

            U.S. Department of Commerce, Bureau of Economic
            Analysis, Foreign Direct Investment in the United
            States: Annual Survey Results: Revised 1981
            Estimates, Revised 1982 Estimates, Revised 1983
            Estimates and Preliminary 1984 Estimates (Washington,
            D.C.: December 1984, December 1985, October 1986):
            Data for 1981 and 1982 (From Table G.4).

1977. As will be demonstrated later, most of the imports of Canadian affiliates are from their Canadian parents. This means that, from a Canadian perspective, there is a balance of intra-industry trade surplus with Canada's affiliates in the United States.

Table 11.6 indicates the degree of international involvement of Canada's affiliates in the United States. The foreign sales of Canada's U.S. affiliates are given as a percentage of total sales by these affiliates in Column one. In 1984, Canadian affiliates had sales of U.S. $82.5 billion and export sales of $4.5 billion, for a foreign-sales–to–total-sales ratio of 5.46 percent. For Canadian multinationals the vast majority of sales are made basically in the U.S. market. Since 1981, this ratio has been declining, showing that Canada's subsidiaries in the United States are now selling even greater shares of their output in the United States than in other countries. But while the relative amount of foreign sales to total sales is falling, it was already documented in Table 11.5, that in absolute terms, the foreign sales of these subsidiaries are still increasing.

Column two of Table 11.6 reports the ratio of foreign purchases for Canadian affiliates in the United States. From 1977 to 1984, foreign purchases compared to sales of Canada's U.S. subsidiaries have fallen from 19.53 percent in 1977 to 8.74 percent in 1984. This indicates that, in relative terms, foreign purchases have been declining in importance as sources of inputs to Canada's subsidiaries in the United States. Once again, in absolute terms, it is important to keep in mind that the subsidiaries' foreign purchases are still increasing, as was shown in Table 11.5. However, for 1984 the export ratio of 5.46 percent and the import ratio of 8.74 percent reflect the nearly U.S. $3 billion deficit in trade for the United States by Canada's multinationals. Conversely, since most of the "imports" are sourced from Canada itself, there is a surplus in Canada's trade with its U.S. affiliates, as confirmed by more precise measures of intra-firm trade (to which we now turn).

Table 11.7 presents data on the sales and purchases between Canada's subsidiaries in the United States and their parent groups in Canada; these are measures of intra-firm trade. Column 1 shows sales by the Canadian affiliates in the United States to their parent groups (X_p), while Column 2 shows purchases by the Canadian affiliates from their parent groups in Canada (M_p).

As the first two columns of Table 11.7 demonstrate, sales by Canadian affiliates to their parents have been growing at approximately 9 percent since 1982, while purchases have been growing at approximately 7 percent over the same period. Just as the recession appeared to have slowed down *total* purchases by the Canadian subsidiaries in the 1982 and 1983 period (Table 11.5), similarly, sales to their affiliates by the parent groups declined from a peak in 1981, of U.S. $5.5 billion, to U.S. $4.2 billion in 1982.

The difference between the intra-firm sales and purchases, is the bilateral balance of intra-firm trade due to activities of Canadian multinationals operating in the United States. Column 3 of Table 11.7 reveals that Canada enjoys about a U.S. $4 billion surplus in such intra-firm trade. Canadian affiliates in the United States purchase about U.S. $4 billion more from their Canadian parents than they sell back to them from their U.S. production and distribution facilities. This trade surplus, from a Canadian perspective, generates jobs and wealth in Canada, due to the market access achieved by the presence of these Canadian multinationals in the United States.

Column 3 of Table 11.7 confirms the absolute size of Canada's trade

Table 11.7
Intrafirm Trade by Canadian Affiliates in the United States

Year	(1) Sales by Canadian Affiliates in the Unites States to their Parent Groups (X_p)	(2) Purchases by Canadian Affiliates in the United States from their Parent Groups (M_p)	(3) Canadian Balance
1984	881	4,847	3,966
1983	811	4,357	3,546
1982	740	4,218	3,478
1981	928	5,462	4,534
1980	953	4,559	3,606
1979	964	4,367	3,403
1978	715	3,903	3,188
1977	454	3,300	2,846

Sources: U.S. Department of Commerce, Bureau of Economic
Analysis, Foreign Direct Investment in the United
States: Operations of U.S. Affiliates, 1977 - 80
(Washington, D.C.: 1985): Data for 1977 - 1980.

U.S. Department of Commerce, Bureau of Economic
Analysis, Foreign Direct Investment in the United
States: Annual Survey Results: Revised 1981
Estimates, Revised 1982 Estimates, Revised 1983
Estimates and Preliminary 1984 Estimates (Washington,
D.C.: December 1984, December 1985, October 1986):
Data for 1981 and 1982 (From Table G.4).

surplus with its U.S. affiliates, i.e., the balance of purchases by the
Canadian affiliates in the United States compared to sales to the parent
groups in Canada. From 1981, purchases from the parent groups in
Canada have been approximately five times the level of sales by the
Canadian affiliates back to their parent groups, averaging a U.S. $4
billion deficit from the U.S. perspective. This is explained by our theoretical knowledge that the Canadian-owned affiliates operating in the
United States are often relatively new companies that need supplies,
components, and know-how from their parents. It also reflects the key
reason why these subsidiaries were set up in the first place— to secure
access to the United States market. The vast majority of the sales of

Table 11.8
Intrafirm Trade Ratios for Canadian Affiliates in the United States

Year	Sales by the Canadian Affiliates to the Parent Group (X_p) as a Percentage of all Foreign Sales (X)	Purchases by the Canadian Affiliates from the Parent Groups (M_p) as a Percentage of all Foreign Purchases (M)
	(X_p/X) %	(M_p/M) %
1984	19.55	67.20
1983	18.90	72.68
1982	17.78	66.48
1981	20.49	69.42
1980	53.18	82.10
1979	54.68	84.08
1978	53.96	83.68
1977	53.16	85.65

Sources: U.S. Department of Commerce, Bureau of Economic
            Analysis, Foreign Direct Investment in the United
            States: Operations of U.S. Affiliates, 1977 - 80
            (Washington, D.C.: 1985): Data for 1977 - 1980.

            U.S. Department of Commerce, Bureau of Economic
            Analysis, Foreign Direct Investment in the United
            States: Annual Survey Results: Revised 1981
            Estimates, Revised 1982 Estimates, Revised 1983
            Estimates and Preliminary 1984 Estimates (Washington,
            D.C.: December 1984, December 1985, October 1986):
            Data for 1981 and 1982 (From Table G.4).

these affiliates are in the United States itself; only a small proportion is exported (under 6 percent in 1984 as discussed previously in Table 11.6).

The relative degree of importance of the Canadian parent affiliates in the United States, as a percentage of total foreign sales and purchases is shown in Table 11.8. The ratio of sales by the Canadian affiliates to the parent groups (X_p) as a percentage of all foreign sales (X), is shown in Column 1. This ratio in 1984 stood at 19.55 percent and since 1981 has averaged 19.18 percent. Column 2 shows the ratio of purchases by the Canadian affiliates from their parents' groups (M_p) as a percentage of all foreign purchases (M). In 1984 this ratio stood at 67.20 percent, down from 72.68 percent the year before. Since 1981, the ratio has averaged 68.95 percent. The breaks in the ratio in 1981 are mainly explained by methodological changes in the Department of Commerce benchmark survey.

The data in Table 11.8 are further evidence of the high degree of intra-firm sales and purchases between Canadian parent multinationals and their U.S. affiliates. With some 70 percent of their purchases coming from their Canadian parents, but only about 20 percent of their foreign sales going to their parents, it is apparent that Canada enjoys a surplus on this type of intra-firm trade. The U.S. affiliates are closely tied to their parents, being dependent upon them for knowledge and other imports. However, most of their sales are in the United States itself, and most of their foreign sales are to countries other than Canada. This indicates that the U.S. affiliates of Canadian multinationals are champions for Canadian exchange, selling into foreign markets much more than back to their home country.

SUMMARY

In the first two sections of this chapter it was demonstrated that Canadian multinationals play an important role in maximizing the benefit to Canada of its foreign direct investment in the United States. Over the last ten years they have substantially increased their stake in the United States. This has resulted in a benefit to Canada, because Canada's affiliates purchase five times as much from Canada as they ship back to Canada. While this may gradually change as the firms in the United States mature and become self-reliant, over the forseeable future the trend of the affiliate's reliance on Canadian inputs is likely to continue.

On the other hand it has been shown that the more mature U.S. subsidiaries in Canada for the last 20 years have purchased roughly the same amount from the United States — in most cases from their parent groups—as they sell back to them. This evidence dismisses the belief that all U.S. subsidiaries are still just branch plant factories in the Canadian economy.

An implication of the two findings is that adjustment following bilateral trade liberalization will be more involved than the common perception that U.S. subsidiaries will be closing down their plants and going home. Many of the U.S. operations in Canada form part of a larger, strategically-integrated network of companies. These companies, in many cases, have large sums of capital tied up in production facilities, human capital, marketing, and distribution networks. While some part of these capital investments may be explained by tariffs or even nontariff barriers, a large number of them are determined by competitive market conditions.

THE BENEFITS TO CANADA OF MULTINATIONAL ENTERPRISES

This section combines the data introduced in the previous two to evaluate the benefits and costs to Canada of foreign direct investment. The bilateral balance of trade, due to intra-firm trade, is found. This involves finding the deficit incurred by Canada on the net purchases of U.S.-owned subsidiaries in Canada and comparing it with the net surplus on purchases from Canada by Canadian-owned affiliates in the United States. These data are adjusted into Canadian dollars. It is found that there is a net surplus to Canada on the intra-firm trade of these two types of multinationals. The high degree of integration of the United States and Canadian economies, as demonstrated by the data on intra-firm trade suggest that Canada benefits from the jobs secured by multinational enterprises (mainly from the manner in which Canadian-owned multinationals generate jobs by their sales in the United States) and that trade liberalization will probably enhance such benefits.

To determine the net balance of trade for Canada from the activity of multinational enterprises requires that the net trade performance of U.S. subsidiaries in Canada be compared with that of Canadian-owned affiliates in the United States. As demonstrated earlier, there is a net deficit on the trade of the former and a net surplus (from Canada's perspective) on the latter. Table 11.9 reports the data on Canada's balance of trade for multinational enterprises. Actual data for Column 1 on the balance of trade for U.S. subsidiaries in Canada are available only until 1981. The data for 1982–84 are projections, based on extrapolated averages of the sales and purchases of these subsidiaries over previous periods, as explained in Appendix 4A of Rugman (1987).

Building on Table 11.3, for 1981, the last year for observable data, Canada's trade deficit was just over Cdn. $1 billion, as shown in Column 1 of Table 11.9. This is due to the foreign purchases of U.S. subsidiaries in Canada being greater than their sales. However, as Column 2 reveals, in 1981 there was a larger trade surplus of over Cdn. $5.3 billion, due to the purchases of Canadian-owned affiliates in the United States from their parent groups as being much greater than the sales back to their parents. Therefore, Canada's net balance of trade surplus on multinational enterprise activity, for 1981 was Cdn. $4.3 billion.

In more recent years, Canada's projected trade balance has also been positive, due to the continued surplus generated by Canadian-owned subsidiaries, as shown by the actual data in Column 2. Even if the projected data for 1982–84 on U.S. subsidiaries in Canada are subject to error, it is highly unlikely that the pattern of the persistent trade surplus indicated in Column 3 would be reversed. The conclusion is inescapable: Canada enjoys a large and stable trade surplus due to the presence of

Table 11.9
The Balance of Intrafirm Trade
(CDN. $M)

Year	(1) Foreign Sales Less Purchases by U.S Subsidiaries in Canada	(2) Purchases Less Sales by Canadian Affiliates in the United States to their Parent Groups (a)	(3) Canada's Net Balance
1984	(2,210) (b)	5,241	3,031
1983	(1,596) (b)	4,413	2,817
1982	(1,197) (b)	4,276	3,079
1981	(1,071)	5,377	4,306
1980	(1,006)	4,308	3,302
1979	(1,924)	3,975	2,051
1978	(451)	3,781	4,232
1977	310	3,115	3,425
1976	9	2,789 (c)	2,798
1975	83	2,724 (c)	2,807

Notes: (a) Column (2) is derived from Commerce data in U.S. $ multiplied by the year end exchange rate to convert the data to Cdn.$. For example the 1981 exchange rate was 1.1859.

(b) Data for 1982, 1983 and 1984 are the extrapolated averages for sales and for purchases, based on the mean of the averages of their immediate past 5 and 16 years growth.

(c) Data for 1976 and 1975 are extrapolated from averages for sales and for purchases, based on the mean of the average sales from 1981 to 1984.

multinational enterprises in its economy. The development of Canadian-owned multinationals has led to growing trade surpluses as their U.S. affiliates purchase much more from Canada than they sell to Canada. These huge surpluses offset the relatively small trade deficits incurred by U.S.-owned subsidiaries in Canada.

From Table 11.9 the average trade surplus for Canada over the 1981–

84 period was Cdn. $3.3 billion, while for the 1975–80 period it was Cdn. $ 3.1 billion. A word of caution on this figure is necessary, however, due to the Department of Commerce data break between 1980 and 1981. Because of this data break the $ 3.1 billion surplus should be regarded as indicative of the pattern of trade but not the average absolute figure for the balance of trade.

The implications of this finding are only just beginning to be appreciated. They include recognition of the economic benefits of multinational activity, including beneficial employment effects. The net trade surplus also suggests that adjustment problems due to trade liberalization could be resolved to Canada's benefit, given the key role played by Canadian-owned multinationals in generating the bilateral intra-industry trade surplus.

REFERENCES

Rugman, Alan M. *Multinationals in Canada: Theory, Performance and Economic Impact*. Boston: Martinus Nijhoff, 1980.
————. *Inside the Multinationals: The Economics of Internal Markets*. New York: Columbia University Press, 1981.
————. *Trade Liberalization and International Investment*. Ottawa: Economic Council of Canada Discussion Paper, September, 1987.
Rugman, Alan M., and John McIlveen. *Megafirms: Strategies for Canada's Multinationals*. Toronto: Methuen, 1985.

PART V
CONCLUSION

12
Canada–U.S. Trade: A Business Perspective
Stephen N. Bowen

To the average American, or at least the viewers of the CBS Evening News on September 24th, 1987 the subject of the break-off of the free trade talks between Cananda and the United States was evidently less important than a feature on the fall colors in Colorado. That story made the news; the trade talks with Canada didn't. It is a sad fact of life that Americans take Canada for granted, don't know much about it, and care even less. The world's longest underfended border has bred affable indifference, and a deep-seated ignorance regarding our neighbor to the north.

As an American citizen living and working in Canada for a Canadian-owned company, Northern Telecom Limited, I have acquired what you might call a binational perspective. It has also sensitized me to the reality that most Americans think of Canada as that blank spot at the top of the TV weather map, where cold fronts always come from. Most Americans think, for example, that our principal trading partner is Japan. Not true. More trade flows between Canada and the United States than between any other pair of countries: well over $150 billion-worth of goods and services in 1986. Last year, three-quarters of Canada's exports by value, equivalent to about one-fifth of its GNP, went south of the border. And in turn, Canada was the biggest customer for U.S. goods: it took 21 percent of America's exports.

Canada has a population of about 26 million people, mostly living in a southern strip within 100 miles of the U.S. border. The rest are scattered over a vast land mass that makes Canada the largest country in the Western Hemisphere and the second-largest in the world. It is more than Sergeant Preston of the Yukon and Rose Marie country; Canada is one of the world's leading trading nations. In 1985, it was the seventh-largest exporter, with export trade valued at U.S. $88 billion, which accounts for 4.6 percent of the U.S. dollar value of world exports. In that same year, it was also the world's eighth largest importer, accounting for 3.8 percent of global imports.

Canada is also one of the world's leading industrial countries, a major world exporter of agricultural products, and in terms of value, the world's leading fish and seafood exporter. The main Canadian exports in 1985 were motor vehicles and parts, crude petroleum, newsprint paper, softwood lumber, natural gas, wheat, and wood pulp. Canada is the world's largest producer of nickel, asbestos, potash, uranium, and gypsum.

I admit that gypsum is pretty dull stuff, but what all this really means is that the Pontiac or Buick you drive[1] was quite possibly made in a Canadian plant under the Canada-U.S. auto pact. In fact, during the 1970s, during the oil crisis, the U.S. plants making GM's big car models switched to making small cars. When U.S. consumers wanted big cars again, the only GM plant left making them was in Quebec.

There are many other examples. The aluminum foil wrapping the kids' sandwiches may have come from Alcan—the Aluminum Company of Canada. The newspaper you read this morning might have been owned by the Canadian-owned-and-operated Thomson chain, and was very likely printed on Canadian newsprint, probably from Abitibi-Price, which is part of the Toronto-based Reichmann family empire. The house you live in might well have been made of Canadian softwood lumber, and that glass of good Canadian rye, or even the French brandy you sipped after dinner, was a brand probably owned by Seagram's, another Canadian-owned-and-operated company.

The preceding is offered only to illustrate that the vast majority of U.S. citizens, or at least those who do not reside near the border of the two nations, are woefully ignorant of the real impact Canada, her political system, her industries, and her people have on the U.S. standard of living and way of life.

Under existing agreements between the two countries, about 70 percent of Canadian exports entering the U.S. are duty-free, as are approximately 72 percent of U.S. exports to Canada.

It's the residuals that really matter because that's where protectionism—on both sides of the border—becomes the big issue. To protect two small, reportedly obsolescent potash mines in New Mexico, the U.S. Department of Commerce instituted preliminary tariffs on Canadian potash as high as 82.5 percent. Now, U.S. farmers rely heavily on potash to fertilize their crops, and Canada is the largest exporter of potash in

[1]Bowen was addressing a U.S. audience.

the world. More than 60 percent of Saskatchewan's potash goes to the U.S., where it supplies more than 80 percent of American farmers' needs. In 1986, this translated into U.S. $340 million in Canadian exports.

The New Mexico Mining Companies alleged that Canadian producers were selling potash in the U.S. at less than the cost of production. It is quite possibly true that more efficient, more modern Canadian mines, which have lower transportation and production costs, and a higher grade of ore, *can* sell potash for less than do the New Mexico mines, which, it is estimated, will be exhausted within five to thirteen years.

Needless to say, there are two sides to every trade issue. The other side of this coin is that the brunt of these protectionist duties must be borne by U.S. producers of wheat, corn, alfalfa, cotton, and soybean. In response to Washington's tariffs, the Potash Corporation of Saskatchewan, Canada's major potash producer, with more than 40 percent of the province's capacity, has hiked its prices by 60 percent, to $93 a ton.

The American Farm Bureau Federation, the world's largest farm organization, with 3.5 million members, estimates the potash duties could add $300 million to U.S. farmers' fertilizer costs. A representative of the South Dakota Farmers' Union says that they have taken a position against the tariff because, according to their own state commerce department, it's going to mean an increase in the cost of corn of six cents a bushel, and for soybeans of eight cents a bushel. This represents a big impact. The representative added that the U.S. mines can't be permanently protected by a tariff, but in the meantime, it does cost U.S. farmers extra money they can ill afford. It is ironic that, at a crucial economic time for American farmers, U.S. trade intervention moves in the opposite direction by in this case raising farm costs, reducing income, and leading to calls for more government assistance and increased consumer prices.

Protectionism cuts both ways. You can protect one special interest group, but usually, at everyone else's expense. It's an economic rule of thumb that you can't make an uncompetitive business competitive by shutting out the competition. That just raises the price for everyone, and does nothing to solve the real problem of why that business was uncompetitive in the first place.

Potash isn't an isolated case. We did the same thing last year with softwood lumber. To protect some West Coast lumber interests, we forced the Canadian government to slap a 15 percent export tax on the softwood lumber it ships to U.S. homebuilders. It was still cheaper, largely thanks to a cheap Canadian dollar, to buy the Canadian softwood lumber; but it made every American home built with it cost at least 15 percent more. And, in the meantime, Canada imposed a countervailing duty against U.S. corn.

Since the beginning of this year, U.S. imports of live hogs from Canada have dropped sharply as the result of U.S. countervailing duties to protect U.S. pork producers. Imports were down 12 percent from a year earlier. A duty of Cdn. $4.39 was levied on every 100 pounds of hogs entering the U.S. from Canada.

Not everything boils down to the price of bacon. In the high-tech world of telecommunications, major U.S. suppliers have argued that the Canadian market is closed, or at least, less open than the U.S. market. In reality, there are no "Buy Canada" laws for telecommunications equipment purchases like the very specific "Buy American" statute (41 U.S.C. 10a-d), which has been carried forward in various forms and incorporated into the laws of 38 states. What does apply are contracts for the Government of Canada's own use—whose total purchases of telecommunications equipment amount to less than five percent of the Canadian market.

But even as the Government of Canada, when purchasing for its own use, does support Canadian economic objectives by favoring Canadian-based suppliers, provided sufficient competition exists and Canada's international commitments are respected, it should also be noted that foreign-owned Canadian-based suppliers get the same treatment as Canadian-owned, domestic suppliers in this regard.

In fact, in some ways, the Canadian market is more open than the U.S. Indeed, it should be noted that Canada permits Canadian telephone companies to be foreign-owned. For example, GTE and its subsidiaries have controlling interest in Quebec Telephone and British Columbia Telephone Company. AT&T also owns a small international carrier, Eastern Telephone and Telegraph Company. By contrast, the U.S. Federal Communications Act of 1934 limits foreign ownership of domestic telephone companies (47 U.S.C. S310).

The free-trade agreement will presumably address all of these issues. It will have to satisfy U.S. concerns about Canadian subsidies, and it will have to calm Canadian fears that political interests will create new U.S. trade barriers with no neutral means of adjudicating disputes. So far, the issue has assumed far larger dimensions in Canada, due to the disproportionately greater importance of the U.S. as a customer.

The threat of U.S. protectionism, as embodied in these isolated cases, as well as in the all-encompassing 1,000-page Omnibus Trade Bill about to be debated in Congress, created the principal motive, from the Canadian point of view, for the Canada–U.S. free-trade talks, which began in 1986.

Canada's position was that it would only accept a deal that included:

- Rules applying to fair and unfair trade such as dumping, countervailing duties, and subsidies, spelled out in extremely clear terms and subject, in the event of disagreement, to "impartial, binational, and definitive resolution."

- Clear general rules interpreted in an objective fashion with all elements of the agreement subject to speedy dispute settlement procedures.

- Balanced widening of access for each country's agricultural and food products in the other's market.

- Changes to automotive trade rules only if they hold the potential for more trade, production, and employment in both countries.

- And finally, a 10-year period during which virtually all tariff and nontariff barriers to almost all trade would be removed with no new barriers introduced.

One of the key stumbling blocks was Canada's demand for a binational panel to settle trade disputes with binding force. While prepared to consider such a mechanism, the United States wanted to retain its current trade law. In effect, the U.S. government did not want to accept any proposal that prevented it from using its laws to offset subsidized, dumped, or other unfairly traded products. Reasonable though this position might seem, it contains hidden landmines. Which subsidies are relevant in trade matters, and what weight should they carry? When are products traded unfairly? What criteria are used in making the decision?

The difficulty, from Canada's point of view, is not in the use of U.S. laws to enforce fair trade practices, but in the misuse or abuse of the laws for the purpose of eliminating import competition. This point requires emphasis. The claim is sometimes made that Canada wants a bilateral trade commission that would have the power to override the laws pased by the U.S. Congress. But it is not the U.S. law that is at issue; it is the application of the U.S. trade remedy law that Canada sees as being arbitrary, unpredictable, and unfair.

There are other difficult, if not insurmountable, issues, such as regional development policies, cultural interests, and investment policy. Besides these concerns, it should also be noted that not everyone in Canada favors free trade. There has been very real public and political opposition in Canada to a free trade agreement. There are fears, for example, about the loss of Canada's cultural identity if Canadian books, magazines, publishers, record companies, television production, filmmakers, and the like are overwhelmed by American imports and takeovers.

On the other side of that coin, few Americans appreciate just how far Hollywood North and the cheap Canadian dollar have gone in luring American film and television productions across the border. It has become something of a media inside joke how Canadian locations are given American signage and substituted for the real thing, so to speak.

Rambo I was shot in British Columbia. The notorious TV miniseries, *Amerika* was shot in Canada. So were movies as disparate as *Meatballs*, *The Fly, Agnes of God*, even the made-for-TV movie, *An American Scrooge* with Henry Winkler. Two of last summer's biggest comedy hits, *Stake-out* and Steve Martin's *Roxanne* were made in Canada, as were *Mrs. Soffel* with Diane Keaton, *Police Academy IV*, and the just-released *Big Town*, with Matt Dillon. And there are Canadian TV series like "Night Heat" and "Adderley," which cleverly "pass" for American.

There are also fears in Canada about the loss of Canadian jobs, which were expressed in the recent election in the largest and most prosperous Canadian province, Ontario, which reelected a government that has loudly questioned the benefits of a free-trade agreement. That government was formed by the Liberal Party. It campaigned on a platform that advocated wariness and caution, even as the relatively socialist New Democratic Party (NDP) stood with the labor unions as being opposed to free trade.

The Canadian federal government is in the hands of the Progressive Conservative party, led by Prime Minister Brian Mulroney, who has championed free trade. Currently, however, his party is well behind in the polls, trailing the federal Liberal Party and the federal NDP Party, both of which outright oppose free trade, or urge caution in any deal with the U.S.

But, of course, as of the moment, Canada and the United States have a trade deal, thus avoiding adding another footnote to the none-too-exciting history of Canada-U.S. trade. To be exact, this was the third attempt in this century. And, like in the game of baseball—with three opportunities to swing at the ball—both countries connected after two strikes.

What next? It is clear that the deal has a long, bumpy road ahead before it becomes truly effective, if, indeed, it ever does. First, there is the matter of the next 90 days during which time the Reagan administration shapes the deal with leaders of Congress and a host of others who will want a voice in the process. This brings us to January 3, 1988, when the agreement goes before the U.S. Congress for 60 days of action or inaction, without amendment. In the interim, the omnibus trade bill will have been debated for better or worse. Second, while there is no similar process in Canada, Prime Minister Mulroney faces the task of getting the country's provincial premiers on board and in full support. This is not as simple a task as it might appear. Unlike governors of states in the U.S., Canadian provincial premiers play a far stronger and more important political role in trade matters. Without their endorsement and support, the deal will fall through. It would be a pity for this agreement to fall apart on either side, because there is so much to be gained for all.

13
Some General Policy Reflections
David L. McKee

The preparation of the work that went into this volume straddled the completion of the trade talks between Canada and the United States in early October of 1987. That circumstance necessitated some fine tuning on the part of individual contributors in cases where their work was impacted by the negotiated agreement. Thus, the overall thrust of the volume reflects the economic situation between the two countries after the agreement was signed.

Because the ratification process has not been completed at this writing, it is important to point out that various economic issues between the two nations will not be resolved by simple penstrokes. Just as a prenuptial agreement is no assurance of a harmonious future, since it cannot change the basic nature of the partners, so the present economic agreement cannot be expected to resolve basic differences if the causes of those differences are in the nature of the societies that spawned them.

Of course, prenuptial agreements are designed to protect the property rights of marriage partners, should the marriage go astray. Even poetic license does not permit the implication that the cohabitation of a continent is a marriage. Unlike a marriage, the potential cohabitation must continue whether or not the individual tenants are in accord and whether or not formal agreements have been signed.

The joint history of the two nations shows more affinity than discord. In this century they have become friends and allies, and beyond that, they have become each other's best customer. All of these associations will undoubtedly continue in spite of the occasional stridencies reported in the media. It would appear to be in the policy interests of both nations

to insure that the stridencies are not over-emphasized in the formal
aspects of the agreement.

There are those who have taken the position that both nations will
gain if the agreement is made operational. Perhaps the most obvious
gain from the Canadian point of view would be a continuing unimpaired
access to large markets in the United States. Such an access might go a
long way toward dispelling the critical-mass problems that have always
seemed to plague the Canadian economy. Despite the fact that markets
in the United States are already providing substantial economic opportunities in Canada, a detailed agreement by being explicit in its pro-
nouncements might dramatically alter the perceived risks for Canadians
in planning their facilities with the larger potential of the United States
market in mind.

Access to Canadian markets is a much less spectacular benefit to the
business community in the United States, because of the size differential
between the two economies. Nonetheless, certain areas of the United
States, notably those with easy access to Canadian population centers,
may stand to gain through such an agreement. Once again, such potential benefits can hardly be expected to yield spectacular results immediately. In nations which are already each other's largest customer,
a deepening of market-related intercourse may eventually emerge from
the climate of greater confidence elicited from the explicit provisions of
the agreement and their implementation.

Despite these seemingly positive results from a trade agreement, there
are no assurances at this writing that the one which has just been negotiated will be implemented. A perusal of the discussions in the present
volume suggests very real concerns. Certainly size and economic power
enter into any trade agreement. That being the case, Canada, as the
smaller economic partner, has been in the weaker bargaining position
throughout the course of the current negotiations. Reactions to the agreement north of the border suggest a wariness on the part of Canadians,
particularly in areas that they perceive may effect their sovereignty.

If Canadians are uneasy about the agreement, a certain skepticism
may be evident in the United States as well. At this writing, business
and economic interests in the larger nation have every reason to be
concerned about their country's performance in the international economy. Faced as they are with very large adverse trade balances, problems
with their industrial base, and a situation where the United States has
become a large debtor nation, they may not find the times propitious
for a comprehensive bilateral trade agreement such as the one that has
been negotiated with Canada.

At this writing, the major issue facing the two countries may not be
the ratification of the current agreement. Beyond that, the issue is not
the real or imagined problems which the agreement itself may trigger.

The real issue at the moment is the need for the two partners, who are heavily involved economically, to have the facility and perhaps the maturity to deliver on the day-to-day needs of their relationship. From a Canadian point of view, John Weir put the issue succinctly back in 1971: "Canada cannot hope to be economically independent of the United States, nor can she hope to be the economic equal of that country."[1] Despite occasionally strident political rhetoric, most Canadians are as realistic as Weir, who went on to suggest that what Canada can "hope for is a situation in which her rights will be generally respected."[2] From the Canadian point of view, the main concern has changed very little since 1971. Issues relating to sovereignty and internal governance appear to have high priority as they relate to the current agreement.

In the United States the timing of the agreement may be unfortunate, not from the point of view of how it is viewed by Congress, but rather from a concern for what that viewing may precipitate. If the actions of Congress are conditioned by upcoming elections (1989) and the concerns of special interest groups, not to mention a desire to send a message, or for that matter to not send a message to other trading partners, then negative externalities may emerge vis-à-vis the relations between the two countries. The avoidance of such externalities may even be more important for bilateral economic relations than the fate of the agreement itself.

Irrespective of the existence of a trade agreement, economic issues are bound to emerge on a continuing basis between Canada and the United States. Prominent among such issues is a whole cadre of concerns, which would be largely beyond the preserve of any trade agreement. Many of those issues relate to environmental matters and to the specifics of resource conservation. Both nations are in trouble because of a declining world demand for their agricultural surpluses. Not only does this throw them into competition for dwindling markets, but there is no reason to expect that the situation can be eased by a bilateral trade agreement.

Writing in 1983, Kenneth M. Curtis and John E. Carroll suggested that "At any given time, the top ten items on the list of irritants on the U.S.–Canadian diplomatic agenda includes a number of transboundary environmental issues."[3] They go on to point out that any such list will also include matters to do with fisheries and water resources, and finish by suggesting that such issues are "invariably perceived as local or regional, and thereby inconsequential, by Americans."[4] In Canada, they point out that the same issues take on national scope.[5] Certainly, such issues have a great potential for abrasiveness and should be dealt with on a continuing basis, in order to insure that the negative perceptions, which they generate, do not spill over into other aspects of the relationship. The ongoing difficulties associated with acid rain do not bode well for bilateral cooperation. Both nations should be concerned on a continuing basis with diffusing such problems. The environmental damage is generally more evident than the subtle incursions that such episodes make on the overall relationship.

Irrespective of formal arrangements, two nations as closely entwined as Canada and the United States should work at diffusing potential problems, particularly if the climate which such problems engender can be further influenced by the media. Both nations have a stake in refraining from the public applications of strictures and penalties, which generate not just bad publicity but responses in kind. Both nations should be sensitive to the traditions and ideology of each. It is probably not an ideal situation when friends become business partners. When they do, business dealings may well be more difficult than might ordinarily have been anticipated. Certainly such dealings must proceed in a climate of mutual respect and understanding. If this can be accomplished between Canada and the United States, there may be less need for formal agreements. Certainly there would be less need for the stridencies that appear in the media, and the two nations could continue the practice of being themselves, complicated business and economic linkages notwithstanding.

NOTES

1. Weir, John A., "U.S. Dollars Make Good Sense for Canada," in John H. Redekop (Ed.), *The Star-Spangled Beaver*, Toronto: Peter Martin Associates Limited, 1971, p. 180.
2. Weir.
3. Curtis, Kenneth M., and John E. Carroll. *Canadian-American Relations: The Promise and the Challenges*. Lexington, Massachusetts: D. C. Health and Company, 1983, p. 27.
4. Curtis and Carroll.
5. Curtis and Carroll.

Selected Bibliography

Arnold, Brian J. *The Taxation of Controlled Foreign Corporations: An International Comparison*. Toronto: Canadian Tax Foundation, 1986.

Atkins, Frank. "Free Trade, Economic Regions and the Foreign Exchange Rate." *Canadian Journal of Regional Science*, Autumn 1986, pp. 377–380.

Averyt, William F. "Canadian Development Priorities and U.S. Trade Policy: Recent Trends and a Changing Future." *The American Review of Canadian Studies*, Volume 16, Spring 1986, pp. 59–73.

Baldwin, John R. *The Role of Scale in Canada-U.S. Productivity Differences in the Manufacturing Sector, 1970–1979*. Toronto: University of Toronto Press, 1986.

Baldwin, J. R., and P. K. Gorecki, *The Relationship Between Plant Scale and Product Diversity in Canadian Manufacturing Industries*. Ottawa: Economic Council of Canada, 1983.

Beigie, Carl, and Alfred O. Hero, Jr. *Natural Resources in U.S.-Canadian Relations*, Vols. 1 and 2. Boulder: Westview Press, 1980.

Bilkey, Warren J. *Industrial Stimulation* Lexington: Health Lexington Books, 1970.

Brean, Donald J. S. *International Issues in Taxation: The Canadian Perspective*. Toronto: Canadian Tax Foundation, 1984.

Brophy, David J. *Finance, Entrepreneurship and Economic Development*, Ann Arbor: Institute of Science and Technology, The University of Michigan, 1975 and 1980.

Carroll, John E. *Acid Rain: An Issue in Canadian-American Relations*. Washington and Toronto: Canadian-American Committee, 1982.

———. *Environmental Diplomacy: An Examination and Prospective of Canadian-U.S. Transboundary Environmental Relations*. Ann Arbor: University of Michigan Press, 1983.

———, and Rod Logan, *The Garrison Diversion Issue: A Case Study on U.S.-Canadian Environmental Relations*. Montreal: Canada-U.S. Future Prospects Series, C. D. Howe Institute, 1980.

————, and Newell B. Mack. "On living Together in North America: Canada, the United States and International Environmental Relations." *Denver Journal of International Law and Policy*, Volume 12, Number 1, Fall 1982, pp. 35–50.

Chambers, Edward J. "Canadian-U.S. Trade: Some Current Options in Developing a Freer Trading Relationship."*Journal of Contemporary Business*, Volume 10, Number 4, 1981, pp. 1–16.

Clarkson, Stephen. *Canada and the Reagan Challenge*. Toronto: James Lorimer & Co., Publishers in association with the Canadian Institute for Economic Policy, 1982.

Cohen, Maxwell. "Canada and the United States: Dispute Settlement and the International Joint Commission—Can This Experience be Applied to Law of the Sea Issues?" *Journal of International Law*, Volume 8, Winter 1976–77.

————. "Canada and the U.S.—New Approaches to Undeadly Quarrels." *International Perspectives*, March/April 1985, pp. 16–22.

Courchene, Thomas J., and James R. Melvin, "Canadian Regional Policy: Lessons from the Past and Prospects for the Future." *Canadian Journal of Regional Science*, Spring 1986, pp. 49–67.

Cox, David, and Richard G. Harris. "A Quantitative Assessment of the Economic Impact on Canada of Sectoral Free Trade with the United States." *Canadian Journal of Economics*, Volume 19, August 1986, pp. 377–394.

Curtis, Kenneth M., and John E. Carroll. *Canadian-American Relations: The Promise and the Challenge*. Lexington: D. C. Health and Company, 1983.

Daly, Donald J. "Economies of Scale and Canadian Manufacturing." in L. Auerback (ed.), *Appropriate Scale for Canadian Manufacturing*. Ottawa: Science Council of Canada, 1978.

————. *Managerial Macroeconomics: A Canadian Perspective*. Homewood: Irwin, 1988.

————. "Micro Economic Performance: Interrelations Between Trade and Industrial Policies." In David V. Conklin and Thomas J. Courchene (eds.), *Canadian Trade at a Crossroads: Options for New International Agreements*. Toronto: Ontario Economic Council, 1985, pp. 156–187.

————. "Mineral Resources in the Canadian Economy—Macroeconomic Implications." In Carl Beigie and Alfred O. Hero, (eds.), *National Resources in U.S.-Canadian Relations, Vol 1*. Boulder: Westview Press 1980, pp. 125–165.

————. "Rationalization and Specialization in Canadian Manufacturing." In Donald D. McFertridge (ed.), *Canadian Industry in Transition*, Ottawa: Supply and Services, 1986, pp. 177–209.

————, and D. C. MacCharles, *Canadian Manufactured Exports: Constraints, and Opportunities*. Montreal: IRPP Studies in International Economics, June 1986.

————, and Dorothy Walters, "Factors in Canada-United States Real Income Differences." *International Review of Income and Wealth*. December 1967, pp. 285–309.

Dickey, John Sloan. *Canada and the American Presence: The United States Interest in an Independent Canada*. New York: New York University Press, 1975.

Doran, Charles F. *Forgotten Partnership: U.S.-Canada Relations Today*. Baltimore: Johns Hopkins University Press, 1984.

Dugan, Peter. *The Macroeconomic Impacts of Free Trade with the United States: Lessons from the FOCUS-PRISM Models*. Toronto: University of Toronto Press, 1985.

Eastman, H. C., and S. Stykott, *The Tariff and Competition in Canada*. Toronto: Macmillan of Canada, 1967.

Eden, Lorraine. "Transfer Pricing Policies under Tariff Barriers." *Canadian Journal of Economics*, Volume XVI, November 1983, pp. 669–685.

———. "Vertically-Integrated Multinationals—A Microeconomic Analysis." *Canadian Journal of Economics*, Volume XI, August 1978, pp. 534–541.

Fretz, Deborah. *Canada/United States Trade and Investment*. Toronto: Ontario Economic Council, 1985.

Fried, Jonathan T. "Barriers to United States-Canadian Trade: Problems and Solutions, the Canadian Perspective." *The George Washington Journal of International Law and Economics*, Volume 19, Number 2, 1985, pp. 433–442.

Gertler, Meric S. "Regional Dynamics of Manufacturing and Non-Manufacturing Investment in Canada." *Regional Studies*, October 1986, pp. 523–534.

Harris, Richard. *Trade, Industrial Policy and International Competition*. Toronto: University of Toronto Press, 1985.

Hartman, David. "Tax Policy and Foreign Direct Investment." *Journal of Public Economics*, Volume 26, 1985, pp. 107–121.

Helliwell, John F., and Robert N. McRae. "The National Energy Conflict." *Canadian Public Policy*, Volume VII, Number 1, Winter 1981, pp. 15–23.

———. "Resolving the Energy Conflict: From the National Energy Program to the Energy Agreements," *Canadian Public Policy*, Volume VIII, Number 7, Winter 1982, pp. 14–23.

Holmes, John W. *Life With Uncle: the Canadian-American Relationship*. Toronto: University of Toronto Press.

Horst, Thomas. "American Taxation of Multinational Firms," *American Economic Review*, Volume 67, Number 3, 1977, pp. 376–389.

Jenkins, Glenn P., *Costs and Consequences of the New Protectionism: the Case of Canada's Clothing Sector*. Ottawa: North-South Institute, 1982.

Laxer, James. *Leap of Faith: Free Trade and the Future of Canada*. Winnipeg: Hurtig, 1986.

Levitt, Kari. *Silent Surrender: The American Economic Empire in Canada*. New York: Liveright, 1970.

McNiven, James D. "Regional Development Policy in the Next Decade." *Canadian Journal of Regional Science*, Spring 1986, pp. 79–88.

McRae, Robert N. "A Major Shift in Canada's Energy Policy: Impact of the National Energy Program." *Journal of Energy and Development*, Spring 1982, pp. 173–198.

———. "A Survey of Canadian Energy Policy: 1974–83," *The Energy Journal*, Volume 6, Number 4, 1985, pp. 48–64.

———, and Alan R. Webster. "The Robustness of a Translog Model to Describe Regional Energy Demand by Canadian Manufacturing Industries." *Resources and Energy*, Volume 4, Number 1, 1982, pp. 1–25.

Morici, Peter, and Laura L. Megna. *Canada-United States Trade and Economic Interdependence*. Montreal: C. D. Howe Institute, 1978.

Moroz, A. R., and K. J. Back. "Prospects for a Canada-United States Bilateral Free Trade Agreement: The Other Side of the Fence." *International Journal*, Volume 36, Autumn 1981, pp. 827–850.

————, and Gregory J. Meredeth. *Economic Effects of Trade Liberalization with the USA: Evidence and Questions*. Ottawa: Institute for Research on Public Policy, 1985.

Mutti, John. "Tax Incentives and Repatriation Decisions of U.S. Multinational Corporations." *National Tax Journal*, Volume XXXIV, 1987, pp. 241–248.

Norton, R. D. "Industrial Policy and American Renewal." *Journal of Economic Literature*, Volume XXIV, Number 1, March 1986, pp. 1–40.

Papadopoulos, Nicolas. "The Free Trade Zone as a Strategic Element in International Business." *Canadian Business Review*, Volume 12, Spring 1985, pp. 51–55.

Parker, Richard W. "Barriers to United States-Canadian Trade: Problems and Solutions—The United States Perspective." *The George Washington Journal of International Law and Economics*, Volume 19, 1985, pp. 443–449.

Peaceful, Leonard G. "Tidal Power Generation in the Fundy Region." *The Canadian Geographer*, Volume 30, Number 3, pp. 254–260.

Pestieau, Caroline. *The Sector Approach to Trade Negotiations: Canadian and United States Interests*. Montreal: C. D. Howe Institute, 1979.

Reisman, Simon. "Canada-United States Trade at the Crossroads: Options for Growth." *Canadian Business Review*, Volume 12, Autumn 1985, pp. 17–23.

Ridekop, John H. ed. *The Star-Spangled Beaver*. Toronto: Peter Martin Associates, Ltd., 1971.

Rugman, Alan M. *International Diversification and the Multinational Enterprise*. Lexington: D.C. Heath, 1979.

————. *Multinationals in Canada: Theory, Performance and Economic Impact*. Boston: Martinus Nijhoff, 1980 and 1983.

———— ed., *Multinationals and Technology Transfer: The Canadian Experience*. New York: Praeger, 1983.

————, and Lorraine Eden, eds. *Multinationals and Transfer Pricing*, London: Croom Helm, 1985.

————. *Administered Protection in America: Implications for U.S.-Canadian Trade Policy*. Montreal: Institute for Research on Public Policy, 1987.

————, and John McIlveen. "Canadian Multinationals Identification: Performance and Strategic Management." *Management International Review*, Volume 25, Number 3, Fall 1985, pp. 41–56.

————. "The Role of Multinational Enterprises in U.S.-Canadian Economic Relations."*Columbia Journal of World Business*, Volume XXI, Number 2, Summer 1986.

Sarna, A. J. "The Impact of a Canada-U.S. Free-Trade Area." *Journal of Common Market Studies*, Volume 23, June 1985, pp. 299–318.

Savitt, Ronald. "Canada and a North American Common Market." *Journal of Contemporary Business*, Volume 10, 1987, pp. 17–28.

Scott, Bruce, and George C. Lodge, eds. *U.S. Competitiveness in the World Economy*. Boston: Harvard Business School University Press, 1984.

Stanbury, W. T., Fred Thompson, and William Zumeta. "Regulatory Reform:

American Experience and Canadian Prospects." *Journal of Contemporary Business*, Volume 10, 1981, pp. 81–96.

Stone, Frank. *Toward a Canada-United States Trade Agreement: A Canadian Perspective*. Ottawa: Institute for Research on Public Policy, 1986.

Swanson, Roger Frank. *Intergovernmental Perspectives on the Canada-U.S. Relationship*. New York: New York University Press, 1978.

Tremblay, Rodrigue. "The Regional Impact of Free Trade." *Canadian Journal of Regional Science*, Spring 1985, pp. 85–99.

Whalley, J., and Rod Hill. *Canada-U.S. Free Trade: Royal Commission on the Economic Union and Development Prospects for Canada*. Toronto: University of Toronto Press, 1985.

Wilkinson, Bruce W. *Canada in the Changing World Economy*. Montreal: C. D. Howe Institute, 1980.

————. "Foreign Ownership and Canadian Manufacturing." *Western Economic Review*, April 1983, pp. 53–75.

————. "Canada-U.S. Trade Policy Relations." *Canadian Public Policy*, Volume 10, March 1984, pp. 96–103.

Willoughby, William R. *The Joint Organizations of Canada and the United States*. Toronto; University of Toronto Press, 1979.

Wolf, Alan W. "Observations on the Implementation of a U.S.-Canadian Free Trade Agreement: The Politics and Legal Considerations." *Canada-United States Law Journal*, Volume 10, 1985, pp. 235–243.

Wonnacott, R. J. "Canadian-U.S. Trade: Toward Free Trade Between Canada and the United States." *Canadian Business Review*, Volume 12, Autumn 1985, pp. 12–16.

————. "On the Employment Effects of Free Trade with the United States." *Canadian Public Policy*, Volume 12, March 1986, pp. 258–263.

————, and P. Wonnacott. *Free Trade Between the United States and Canada: The Potential Economic Effects*, Cambridge: Harvard University Press, 1967.

————, and P. Wonnacott. "Free Trade Between the United States and Canada: Fifteen Years Later." *Canadian Public Policy*, Volume 8, pp. 412–427.

Index

bankruptcies/plant closures, 78, 80;
and the Bilateral Trade Agreement,
83, 93; and the Canadian balance
of payments, 123–24; and the
Canadian balance of trade, 47, 69–
70; and the Canadian GDP, 77; and
capital stock, 14; and
competitiveness, 75, 77;
conclusions about, 123; and
corporate income taxes, 121–46;
and costs, 77; development of the,
83; domination of American firms
in, 96; and economies of scale, 83;
and employment, 78; foreign
control of, 121; future of, 14; and
the international market, 75; and
intrafirm trade, 121, 122, 123, 124–
37; and investments, 78; and
protectionism, 80, 81, 103, 146; and
regional specialization, 10, 11; and
tariffs, 121–46; and technology, 70,
83, 96; and the U.S. balance of
payments, 74, 75; and the U.S.
balance of trade, 69–70; and the
U.S. GNP, 75; and U.S.
investments in Canada, 121–46
maritime boundaries, 55–56, 59–60
Maritime provinces, 10, 15. *See also*
    name of specific province
market competitiveness, 22–24
market distortion, 26–27
market location/size, 22
markets. *See* international markets
Massachusetts, 163
meat products, 25, 28
mercantilist theory of trade, 111–12,
114
merchandise trade, 67, 68–71, 74,
183–84
mergers and acquisitions market,
165, 169, 178
metal industries, 47, 48, 69
Mexico, 20
Midwestern United States, 25, 32
millwork, 53
mineral security, 50–51
minerals. *See* mining industries

mining industries, 47, 48–51, 60, 69,
70, 74, 75, 104, 122
Model Tax Treaty Convention on
Income and Capital (OECD), 124
model of U.S.–Canada capital flows,
125–32
motor vehicles. *See* automobiles
Mulroney, Brian, 87, 94, 206
multinational corporations: benefits
to Canada of, 196–98; and
Canadian government policies, 96–
97; international taxation of, 124–
32; subsidiaries compared with,
185. *See also* Canadian businesses
in U.S.; U.S. businesses/
investments in Canada

National Energy Board (Canada), 33
National Energy Policy (Canada),
170, 171, 172, 178
national identity, Canadian, 9–10
nationalism: in Canada, 7; in Quebec,
97; in U.S., 95, 97–98
National Oil Policy (Canada), 32
National Policy of 1879 (Canada), 10
natural gas, 32, 33, 34, 36, 37, 38–39,
40, 44–45, 69, 88, 202. *See also*
energy industries
natural resources, 47, 70, 84. *See also*
resource industries; *name of specific
resource*
nested production, 34–36
The Netherlands, 20, 96
New Brunswick, 22, 56
New Democratic Party (Canada), 206
New England, 4–5, 59
Newfoundland, 56
newly-industrialized nations, 84
New Mexico, 95, 202–3
newsprint, 51–52, 53, 54–55, 202
New Zealand, 54
nickel, 51, 60, 202
nonferrous metals, 48
nontariff barriers, 26, 75, 80, 81, 121–
22, 188, 205
North American Ventures Fund
(NAVF), 170

About the Editor and Contributors

WARREN J. BILKEY is professor of business and chairman of the Department of International Business at the University of Wisconsin-Madison. An economist by training, Dr. Bilkey is internationally known for his work on industrial stimulation. A widely travelled consultant and lecturer, his articles have appeared in professional/journals in the United States and abroad.

STEPHEN N. BOWEN is senior vice president, public affairs, Northern Telecom Limited, Mississauga, Ontario. Prior to joining Northern Telecom, he was vice president, communications for NCR Corporation, Dayton, Ohio. He has also held vice presidential responsibilities for TRW. He is an accredited member of the Public Relations Society of America, a member of the board of editors of the *International Marketing Review*, and a frequent university lecturer on corporate communications effectiveness.

DAVID J. BROPHY is associate professor of finance in the Graduate School of Business Administration, of the University of Michigan. Dr. Brophy is also director of the Annual Growth Capital Symposium and director of the University of Michigan Financial Services Executive Program. His book, *Finance, Entrepreneurship and Economic Development*, was published by the University of Michigan.

DONALD J. DALY is professor in the faculty of Administrative Studies of York University. He has had considerable federal government experience and served as senior economist for the Economic Council of

Canada. His recent research has emphasized the competitive position of Canadian manufacturing in world markets, and the scope for both government policy and corporate strategies to achieve improved performance.

LORRAINE EDEN is associate professor of economics at Brock University. Her publications include work on transfer pricing and multinational enterprise, as well as intergovernmental financial relations in Canada. She is currently investigating the efficiency of international intra-corporate income tax differentials.

DAVID L. McKEE is professor of economics at Kent State University. Dr. McKee is a specialist in regional economics and economic development. His research on those subjects has been widely published in professional journals in the United States and abroad.

ROBERT N. McRAE is professor of economics at the University of Calgary. An energy specialist, Dr. McRae's expertise is much in demand among Canadian news media. His professional research has been widely published in Canada and the United States.

FRANK W. MILLERD is associate professor of economics and chairman of the Economics Department at Wilfrid Laurier University. Dr. Millerd is a specialist in natural resource economics. His professional experience includes work with federal and provincial governments in Canada. His research has appeared in professional journals in Canada and the United States.

R. D. NORTON holds the Norman Sarkisian Chair in Business Economics at Bryant College. Dr. Norton is a regional economist with special interest in changes in industrial structure. He has served as a consultant to the Joint Economic Committee of Congress, the President's Commission for a National Agenda for the Eighties, and the White House Conference on Small Business. He is also the editor and originator of *The Survey of Regional Literature*.

GERALD F. ORTMANN is senior lecturer at the University of Natal, South Africa. During 1986 he was visiting professor in the Department of Agricultural Economics and Rural Sociology at Ohio State University. Dr. Ortmann's research interests are centered upon problems relating to the international marketing of agricultural commodities.

NORMAN RASK is professor of agricultural economics at Ohio State University. Dr. Rask holds both research and extension appointments, with primary responsibilities in foreign market development, trade, and energy policy. He has served as a consultant to the Brazilian Ministry of Agriculture, and FAO. USAID missions have taken him to Brazil and Portugal. He has also served as a consultant with World Bank Missions to Syria, Brazil, Thailand, Costa Rica, and Nicaragua.

ALAN M. RUGMAN is professor of international business administration at the University of Toronto. An economist by training, Dr. Rugman has held visiting appointments at the Graduate School of Business, Columbia University, the London Business School, Harvard University, and the University of Hawaii. His numerous books and articles enjoy an international readership.

BRUCE W. WILKINSON is professor of economics at the University of Alberta. Dr. Wilkinson has had a continuing interest in Canada's trade relations and is well known for his work on problems relating to trade between Canada and the United States. His investigations have generated a continuing stream of lectures and publications on those issues.